COMPUTER LITERACY BASICS:

Microsoft Office 2007 Companion

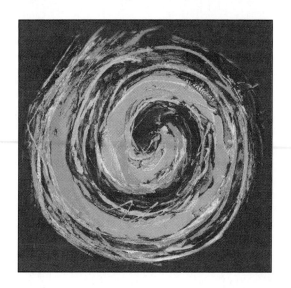

Jennifer T. Campbell

COURSE TECHNOLOGY
CENGAGE Learning

Australia • Brazil • Japan • Korea • Mexico • Singapore • Spain • United Kingdom • United States

COURSE TECHNOLOGY
CENGAGE Learning

Computer Literacy Basics: Microsoft Office 2007 **Companion is published by Cengage Course Technology.**
by Jennifer T. Campbell

Managing Editor: Donna Gridley

Product Manager: Allison O'Meara

Developmental Editor: Barbara Waxer

Editorial Assistant: Amanda Lyons

Content Project Manager: Matt Hutchinson

Marketing Coordinator: Tiffany Hodes

Quality Assurance Testers: Teresa Storch, Serge Palladino, Marianne Snow, Susan Whalen

Manuscript Quality Assurance Lead: Jeff Schwartz

Composition: GEX Publishing Services

Art Director: Kun-Tee Chang

> For product information and technology assistance, contact us at
> **Professional & Career Group Customer Support, 1-800-648-7450**
>
> For permission to use material from this text or product, submit all requests online at **cengage.com/permissions** Further permissions questions can be emailed to **permissionrequest@cengage.com**

Disclaimer:
Cengage Course Technology reserves the right to revise this publication and make changes from time to time in its content without notice.

Some of the product names and company names used in this book have been used for identification purposed only and may be trademarks or registered trademarks of their respective manufacturers and sellers.

Certiport and the IC3 logo are either registered trademarks or trademarks of Certiport Inc. in the United States and/or other countries. Course Technology/Cengage Learning is an independent entity from Certiport Inc. and not affiliated with Certiport Inc. in any manner. This text may be used in assisting students to prepare for the Internet and Computing Core Certification (IC3) program exams. Neither Certiport Inc. nor Course Technology/Cengage Learning warrants that use of this publication will ensure passing the relevant IC3 exam.

Microsoft and the Office logo are either registered trademarks or trademarks of Microsoft Corporation in the United States and/or other countries. Cengage Course Technology is an independent entity from the Microsoft Corporation, and not affiliated with Microsoft in any manner.

ExamView® and ExamView Pro® are registered trademarks of FSCreations, Inc. Windows is a registered trademark of the Microsoft Corporation used herein under license. Macintosh and Power Macintosh are registered trademarks of Apple Computer, Inc. Used herein under license.

© 2007 Cengage Learning. All Rights Reserved. Cengage Learning WebTutor™ is a trademark of Cengage Learning.

Library of Congress Control Number: 2007922480

ISBN-13: 9781423904311

ISBN-10: 1423904311

Course Technology
25 Thomson Place
Boston, MA 02210
USA

Cengage Learning is a leading provider of customized learning solutions with office locations around the globe, including Singapore, the United Kingdom, Australia, Mexico, Brazil and Japan. Locate your local office at:

international.cengage.com/region

Cengage Learning products are represented in Canada by Nelson Education, Ltd.

For your lifelong learning solutions, visit **course.cengage.com**

Purchase any of our products at your local college store or at our preferred online store **www.ichapters.com**

Printed in the United States of America
1 2 3 4 5 6 7 14 13 12 11 10 09 08

Get Back to the Basics...
With these *exciting new products*

Our exciting new series of short, programming, and application suite books will provide everything needed to learn this software. Other books include:

NEW! Digital Video BASICS by Schaefermeyer
20+ hours of instruction for beginning through intermediate features

978-1-4188-6513-9	Textbook, Hard Bound Cover
978-1-4239-0394-9	Instructor Resource Kit
978-1-4239-0440-3	Review Pack (Data CD)

HTML and JavaScript BASICS, 3rd Ed. by Barksdale and Turner
15+ hours of instruction for beginning through intermediate features

978-0-619-26625-7	Textbook, Soft Bound Cover
978-0-619-26628-8	Instructor Resource Kit
978-0-619-26629-5	Review Pack (Data CD)

HTML BASICS, 3rd Ed. by Barksdale and Turner
10+ hours of instruction for beginning features

978-0-619-26626-4	Textbook, Soft Bound Cover
978-0-619-26628-8	Instructor Resource Kit
978-0-619-26629-5	Review Pack (Data CD)

Internet BASICS by Barksdale, Rutter, & Teeter
35+ hours of instruction for beginning through intermediate features

978-0-619-05905-7	Textbook, Soft Spiral Bound Cover
978-0-619-05906-4	Instructor Resource Kit
978-0-619-05907-1	Review Pack (Data CD)

Programming BASICS, Using Microsoft Visual Basic, C++, HTML, and Java
by Knowlton & Barksdale
35+ hours of instruction for beginning through intermediate features

978-0-619-05803-6	Textbook, Hard Bound Cover
978-0-619-05801-2	Textbook, Soft Bound Cover
978-0-619-05802-9	Instructor Resource Kit
978-0-619-05800-5	Activities Workbook
978-0-619-05949-1	Review Pack (Data CD)

How to Use This Book

What makes a good computer instructional text? Sound pedagogy and the most current, complete coverage. In this book, you will find not only an inviting layout, but also many features to enhance learning.

Objectives— Objectives are listed at the beginning of each lesson, along with a suggested time for completion of the lesson. This allows you to look ahead to what you will be learning and to pace your work.

Internet and Computing Core Certification (IC3)— Using Microsoft Office 2007 as a platform, all program skills for the Key Applications module for the Internet and Computing Core Certification program skills are covered. To find a topic, use the map at the beginning of the book, or look for a logo next to the text or step where it occurs.

Step-by-Step Exercises—Preceded by a short topic discussion, these exercises offer hands-on practice. Each lesson is a series of step-by-step

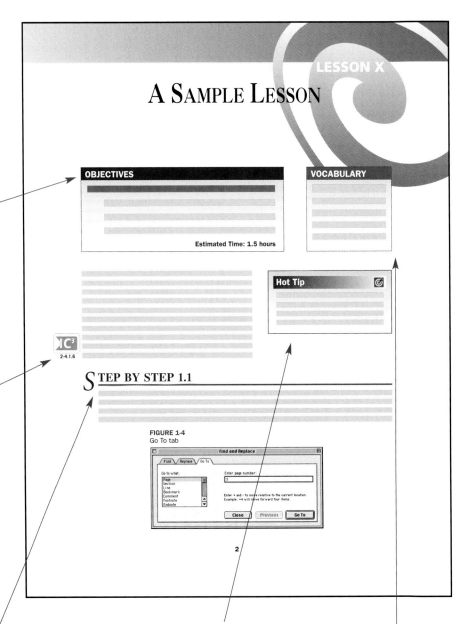

exercises. At the end of each lesson, you will have created one or more complete files, either from scratch or starting with a Data File, that demonstrate the skills for the lesson.

Marginal Elements— Boxes such as *Computer Concepts, Notes, Did You Know?, Technology Timeline, Ethics in Technology,* and *Working in a Connected World* provide additional information of interest to students.

Vocabulary—Terms are identified in bold-face throughout the lesson and listed at the beginning and end of each lesson.

Enhanced Screen Shots—Screen shots come to life on each page with color and depth.

How to Use This Book

Summary—At the end of each lesson is a bulleted list of the skills and concepts you learned in the lesson to prepare you to complete the end-of-lesson activities.

Vocabulary/Review Questions—Review material at the end of the Step-by-Step exercises enables you to prepare for assessment of the content presented.

[New!] Screen Identification – Using a screenshot from the book, you are asked to identify four elements.

[New!] Hands-on Review – a project that covers topics from all of the Step-by-Step exercises in one document or file.

Lesson Projects—End-of-lesson hands-on application of what has been learned in the lesson allow you to actually apply the techniques covered.

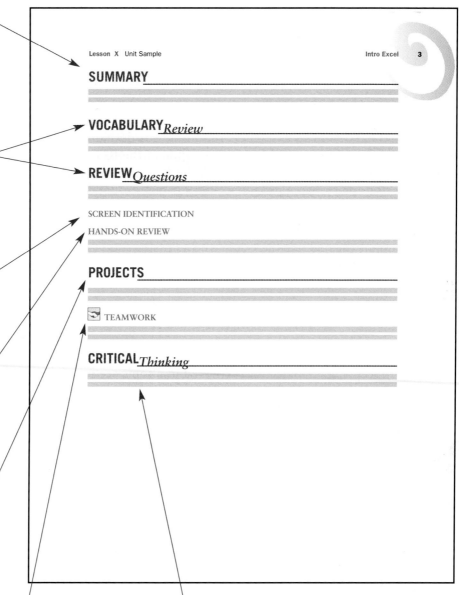

Lesson X   Unit Sample   Intro Excel   **3**

SUMMARY

VOCABULARY*Review*

REVIEW*Questions*

SCREEN IDENTIFICATION

HANDS-ON REVIEW

PROJECTS

 TEAMWORK

CRITICAL*Thinking*

Teamwork—In the business world you will often be asked to work with others on a project. By working as a group to complete a project, quiz each other on topics, or review each other's work, you practice this essential skill.

Critical Thinking Activities—Each lesson gives you an opportunity to apply creative analysis and use various resources to solve problems.

[New!] Final Project—A lesson at the end of the book uses concepts and skills learned in the text to complete projects that integrate information from various applications. Mail merge, importing, exporting, and linking files are covered.

PREFACE

About this Book

Using the IC3 skill set as a guide, this book was developed to not only provide the necessary instruction to pass the Key Applications module of the IC3 certification exam, but also to be an overview of program skills. In addition to the IC3 skills for word processing, spreadsheets, and presentation graphics, we have added two lessons on database skills, and a Final Project that reviews coverage of the lessons and provides additional information on integrating applications.

This book uses Microsoft Office 2007 as a learning platform to practice the skills, but the concepts taught throughout the book will help students use other applications, and to understand how they would use the skills in business, personal, and educational settings.

Organization

Lessons list the objectives up front, followed by an introductory section that discusses the necessary concepts. Each objective is covered in a topic section, followed by a Step-by-Step exercise where students practice the skills. In many lessons, students use or create a single file in order to build a complete project by the end of the lesson.

Throughout the book, vocabulary words are identified and defined where they are covered. Marginal elements provide additional conceptual or skills-based information, such as careers, ethics, or keyboard shortcuts.

The end-of-lesson materials start with a review of the concepts: summary, vocabulary, screen identification, multiple choice, and true/false questions. The Hands-on Review exercise combines all of the objectives for the lesson in one exercise. Lesson Projects, Teamwork, and Critical Thinking activities require students to apply the skills learned in the lesson.

Acknowledgements

Thank you to Donna Gridley, Allison O'Meara, and Amanda Lyons for allowing me the privilege of writing this book, and to Jeff Schwartz and his amazing quality assurance team. Thank you to Barbara Waxer, my editor, for your expertise, patience, and humor. I want to acknowledge my mother, Dianne Thompson, for your help with the database coverage. Last, but not least, this book is dedicated to my loving family: Michael, Emma, and Lucy.

START-UP CHECKLIST

Minimum Hardware Configuration

- PC with Pentium processor
- Hard disk with 400 MB free for typical installation
- CD-ROM drive, or access to network drive for downloading and saving Data and Solution Files
- Monitor set at 1024x768 or higher resolution. If your resolution differs, you will see differences in the Ribbon and task panes, and may have to scroll up or down to view the information on your screen
- Printer
- Internet connection. If you are not connected to the Internet, see your instructor

Software Installation

- A typical installation of Microsoft Office 2007
- Microsoft Windows Vista running with Aero off
- Microsoft Internet Explorer 7 browser

For Windows XP Users

The screenshots in this book show Microsoft Office 2007 running on Windows Vista. If you are using Microsoft Windows XP, use these alternate steps.

Starting a program

1. Click the **Start button** on the taskbar.

2. Point to **All Programs**, point to **Microsoft Office**, then click the application you want to use.

Saving a file for the first time

1. Click the **Office Button**, then click Save As.

2. Type a name for your file in the File Name text box.

3. Click the **Save in list arrow,** then navigate to the drive and folder where you store your Data Files.

4. Click Save.

Opening a file

1. Click the **Office Button**, then click **Open.**

2. Click the **Look in list arrow,** then navigate to the drive and folder where you store your Data Files.

3. Click the file you want to open.

4. Click **Open.**

TEACHING AND LEARNING RESOURCES FOR THIS BOOK

Instructor Resources CD

The *Instructor Resources CD* contains the following teaching resources:

■ The Data and Solution Files for this course.

■ ExamView® tests for each lesson. ExamView is a powerful testing software package that allows instructors to create and administer printed, computer (LAN-based), and Internet exams.

■ Instructor's Manual that includes lecture notes for each lesson, answers to the lesson review questions, references to the solutions for Step-by-Step exercises and end-of-lesson activities.

■ Copies of the figures that appear in the student text.

■ Suggested Syllabus with block, two-quarter, and 18-week schedule.

■ PowerPoint presentations for each lesson.

ExamView®

ExamView is a powerful objective-based test generator that enables you to create paper, LAN, or Web-based tests from test banks designed specifically for your Course Technology text. Utilize the ultra-efficient QuickTest Wizard to create tests in less than five minutes by taking advantage of Course Technology's question banks, or customize your own exams from scratch.

TABLE OF CONTENTS

KEY APPLICATIONS Module

KEY APPLICATIONS

Module

 Estimated Time for Module: 15 hours

KEY APPLICATIONS

Lesson 1
Using Microsoft Office 2007

2-1.1.1	2-1.2.2	2-1.2.9
2-1.1.2	2-1.2.4	2-1.2.10
2-1.1.3	2-1.2.5	2-1.3.1
2-1.1.4	2-1.2.7	2-1.4.2
2-1.2.1	2-1.2.8	2-1.4.3

Lesson 2
Word Processing Basics

2-1.1.1	2-1.3.2	2-2.1.9
2-1.2.4	2-2.1.2	2-2.1.20
2-1.2.6	2-2.1.1	

Lesson 3
Editing and Formatting Documents

2-1.3.1	2-1.4.3	2-2.1.7
2-1.3.3	2-1.4.4	2-2.1.8
2-1.3.4	2-1.4.5	2-2.1.10
2-1.3.5	2-2.1.1	2-2.1.11
2-1.3.6	2-2.1.3	2-2.1.12
2-1.3.7	2-2.1.4	2-2.1.18
2-1.3.8	2-2.1.5	2-2.1.19
2-1.4.1	2-2.1.6	2-2.1.21
2-1.4.2		

Lesson 4
Using Tables

2-2.2.1	2-2.2.3	2-2.2.5
2-2.2.2	2-2.2.4	

Lesson 5
Adding Features to Multipage Documents

2-1.2.6	2-2.1.13	2-2.1.16
2-1.3.9	2-2.1.14	2-2.1.17
2-1.3.10	2-2.1.15	2-2.1.9
2-1.3.11		

Lesson 6
Spreadsheet Basics

2-1.2.1	2-3.1.2	2-3.1.5
2-1.3.4	2-3.1.3	2-3.1.6
2-3.1.1	2-3.1.4	2-3.1.7

Lesson 7
Arranging Worksheet Data

2-1.4.1	2-3.1.3	2-3.1.8
2-1.4.3	2-3.1.4	2-3.2.1
2-1.4.4	2-3.1.7	

Lesson 8
Using Formulas and Creating Charts

2-3.2.2	2-3.2.6	2-3.2.10
2-3.2.3	2-3.2.7	2-3.2.11
2-3.2.4	2-3.2.8	2-3.2.12
2-3.2.5	2-3.2.9	

Lesson 9
Presentation Basics

2-1.2.1	2-1.3.1	2-4.1.4
2-1.2.3	2-4.1.1	2-4.1.6
2-1.2.7	2-4.1.2	2-4.1.10
2-1.2.8	2-4.1.3	2-4.1.11

Lesson 10
Customizing Presentations

2-4.1.3	2-4.1.7	2-4.1.9
2-4.1.5	2-4.1.8	

Lesson 11
Database Essentials

Lesson 12
Modifying and Analyzing Database Information

USING MICROSOFT OFFICE 2007

OBJECTIVES

Upon completion of this lesson, you should be able to:

- Learn about Microsoft Office 2007
- Start an Office program and navigate through the screen
- Customize and change the view of the program window
- Open and save files
- Preview and print files
- Close files and programs
- Get help

Estimated Time: 1.5 hours

VOCABULARY

Application

Closing

Dialog box launcher

Exiting

File extension

Help

Help Desk

Mini Toolbar

Operating system

Quick Access Toolbar

Print

Program window

Ribbon

Save/Save As

ScreenTip

Scroll bars

Status bar

Suite

Zoom

Microsoft Office 2007 is a suite of programs, each with its own function, that are designed to work together to share information and create a variety of files. Table 1-1 describes the programs available in Microsoft Office 2007. Depending on the version of Microsoft Office you have installed, the programs available to you might differ. The programs, or applications, share common screen elements, which makes it easy to learn new programs.

The program that controls the basic operation of your computer is called an operating system. Your steps and screens might differ slightly if you are using an operating system other than Microsoft Windows Vista. Refer to the steps in the frontmatter of this book for any differences.

TABLE 1-1
Microsoft Office 2007 programs

APPLICATION	PROGRAM TYPE	USED TO
Microsoft Office Word 2007	Word processing	Create letters, memos, and long documents
Microsoft Office Excel 2007	Spreadsheet	Analyze data in rows and columns, and display data in charts and graphs
Microsoft Office Access 2007	Database	Store information in fields and records, and create reports
Microsoft Office PowerPoint 2007	Presentation graphics	Create slide shows and handouts using text and graphics to accompany a presentation
Microsoft Office Outlook 2007	Personal information manager	Send and receive e-mail and keep track of appointments
Microsoft Office Publisher 2007	Desktop publishing	Create publications such as flyers, Web sites, and brochures

Starting an Office Program

2-1.1.1

The way you start an Office program is the same for all programs but will differ based on the operating system you are using, as well as any customizations made to your Start menu or desktop. If there is a program icon on your desktop, you can double-click it to open the program. You can also click a button on the taskbar to open a program.

STEP-BY-STEP 1.1

1. Click the **Start** button on the Windows taskbar. The Start menu opens, as shown in Figure 1.1.

2. Click **All Programs** on the Start menu.

3. Click **Microsoft Office**.

Did You Know?

You can create a shortcut to the desktop for any program or file. Right-click the icon for the program or file either in the Documents window or on the Start menu, point to Send To, then click Desktop (create shortcut). You can double-click any icon on the desktop to open the program or the file from within its associated program.

STEP-BY-STEP 1.1 Continued

4. Click the **Microsoft Office Word 2007** program icon.

5. Microsoft Word opens with a new, blank document.

FIGURE 1-1
Start menu

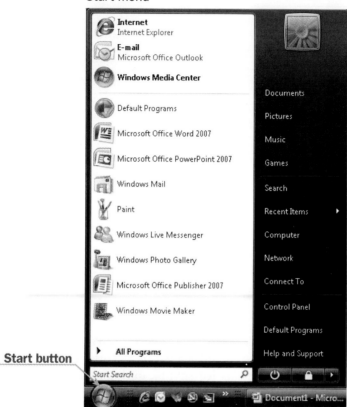

Navigating the Word Program Window

The Microsoft Office Word 2007 program window, shown in Figure 1-2, has many of the same features as other Office programs.

FIGURE 1-2
Microsoft Office Word 2007 program window

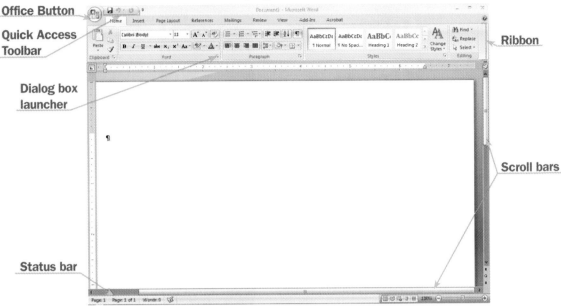

The Office Button is at the top of the screen and includes options for common program tasks such as opening, saving, and printing. It also includes a list of recently opened or edited files. The default Quick Access Toolbar contains buttons for saving, undoing, and redoing tasks. On this toolbar, and on the Ribbon, if a command is not available, it will appear grayed out or dimmed.

The Ribbon is a new feature of Office 2007. The Ribbon has several tabs that group command buttons into related categories. The commands shown will differ depending on which program or task you are using at the time. You can use these tasks to format, set up, review, and more. Buttons on the Ribbon have names or icons that help you know the task each is used for. Some groups have a dialog box launcher, a small arrow in the corner, that provides access to a new window or pane from which you can choose additional options. To learn more about each button, move the mouse over the button to display a ScreenTip. The ScreenTip will give a brief description about the button's function.

2-1.2.1
2-1.3.1

The program window is the main work area where you will enter, format, and edit information. If you have more content in your file than can be viewed at one time on the screen, use the scroll bars to move up and down in the file. When you are working in your document, sometimes a Mini toolbar appears. This task-specific toolbar appears and disappears depending on the task you are performing. The status bar is at the bottom of the program window. It includes options for changing the view or navigating in your file.

Did You Know?

When you have multiple programs and files open, icons appear on the taskbar. You can click a button on the taskbar to view the program or file. When many files and programs are open, Windows will group files or windows into a single button.

S TEP-BY-STEP 1.2

1. Click the **Office Button**. The Office menu appears, as shown in Figure 1-3. Click the title bar to close the menu.

Computer Concepts

The tabs on the Ribbon will vary depending on the program you are using. In addition, some tasks will activate a contextual tab, which gives you access to specific features you need at the time. For example, if you insert or select a shape, the Drawing Tools tab appears on the Ribbon. When you deselect the shape, the tab disappears.

FIGURE 1-3
The Office Button, Quick Access Toolbar, and the Ribbon

2. Move the pointer over each button on the Quick Access Toolbar to view its ScreenTip.

3. Click each **tab** on the Ribbon to see the categories of groups and buttons.

4. Click the **Home** tab. In the Font group, click the **dialog box launcher**.

5. View the options in the Font dialog box, as shown in Figure 1-4, then click **Cancel** to close the dialog box.

FIGURE 1-4
The Font dialog box

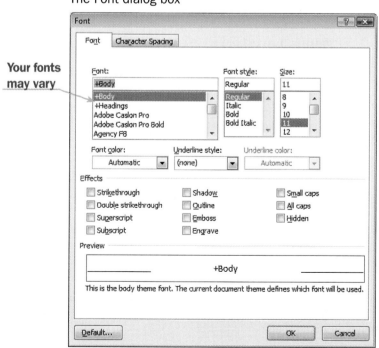

STEP-BY-STEP 1.2 Continued

6. Click the blank document in the program window. Type **Your Name**.

7. Click the left mouse button, then drag it to select your name. The Mini toolbar appears. A sample Mini toolbar is shown in Figure 1-5.

FIGURE 1-5
A sample Mini toolbar

8. Click away from your name to close the Mini toolbar.

9. Drag the **scroll bar** up and down.

10. Leave Word open for the next Step-by-Step.

Customizing the Program Window

Many features of the program window can be changed to reflect your personal tastes and needs. Adding or removing buttons from the Quick Access Toolbar and minimizing the Ribbon are two ways to customize programs. Minimizing the Ribbon increases your work area, and you can easily redisplay it to access the many tools available on the Ribbon.

2-1.2.2

STEP-BY-STEP 1.3

1. Click the **Customize Quick Access Toolbar** button, as shown in Figure 1-6.

FIGURE 1-6
Customizing the Quick Access Toolbar

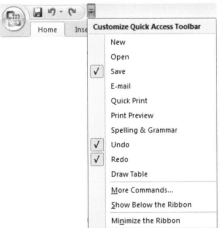

2. Click **More Commands** from the menu.

STEP-BY-STEP 1.3 Continued

3. View the options in the Word Options dialog box, then click **Cancel**.

4. Click the **Customize Quick Access Toolbar** button again.

5. Click one of the options that does not have a check mark next to it. The button now appears on the Quick Access Toolbar.

6. Click the **Customize Quick Access Toolbar** button again, then deselect the button you just added to remove it from the Quick Access Toolbar.

7. Right-click the **Ribbon**, then click **Minimize the Ribbon**. The Ribbon is hidden, but the tabs are still visible.

8. Click the **Insert** tab to redisplay the Ribbon, then click in the program window. The Ribbon is hidden again.

9. Right-click the **tab area**, then click **Minimize the Ribbon**. The Ribbon reappears.

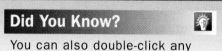

Did You Know?

You can also double-click any tab to maximize the Ribbon when it is hidden.

Changing the View of the Program Window

2-1.2.4
2-1.2.5

There are many different views from within a program window. Some views display how a page will look when printed, some views show only the text, and others can help to create an outline of your work. To change the program window to another view, such as outline or Web Layout, or to change the magnification, or zoom, use the buttons and slider on the status bar.

STEP-BY-STEP 1.4

1. Position the pointer over each **View** button on the status bar to view its ScreenTip, as shown in Figure 1-7.

FIGURE 1-7
Changing the view

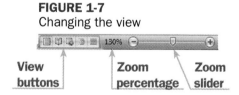

View buttons   Zoom percentage   Zoom slider

2. Click the **Full Screen Reading** button, then click **Close** on the title bar.

3. Click the **Draft** button. The document displays without page breaks or margins.

4. Click the **Print Layout** button.

STEP-BY-STEP 1.4 Continued

5. Note the percentage next to the Zoom slider. Drag the **Zoom** slider left and right to change the view.

6. Click the **Zoom Out** and **Zoom In** buttons as necessary to return to the original zoom percentage.

Opening, Saving, and Printing Files

Y ou can open a previously created file in order to make changes to it. You can save it either with the same filename and in the same location, or save it with a new name in order to retain two copies: an original and one with your edits. Printing files creates a hard copy that you can distribute to others.

Opening a File

2-1.2.7
2-1.2.10
2-1.2.3

Each file has a unique name and saved location. To open a previously created file, you need to know where the file is located and what its name is. You can sometimes open files created in other applications, but many features will be lost. You can usually open a file created in a previous version of the software, although some features may be lost, but often cannot open files created in a later version of software. If you are opening a file you have recently edited within the same program, it may appear in the Recent Documents list on the Office Button menu. You can use the Open dialog box to navigate to and search for files to open. When you have multiple open files, you can use the buttons on the Windows taskbar to switch between them.

> **Did You Know?**
>
> Each program has a unique suffix added to the filename, called a **file extension**. Your Open and Save dialog boxes may or may not show file extensions. The file extension for Word 2007 is .docx, and for Excel 2007 it is .xlsx.

STEP-BY-STEP 1.5

1. Click the **Office Button**, then click **Open**. The Open dialog box opens, as shown in Figure 1-8.

FIGURE 1-8
The Open dialog box

Your path
will differ

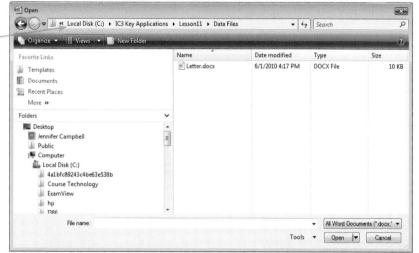

2. In the Open dialog box, use the Folders list to navigate to your Data Files folder for this lesson. *See your instructor if you need directions.*

3. Click the **Letter.docx** file to select it.

4. Click **Open**. The file appears in the Word window.

 Technology Timeline

When viewing an Office 2007 file, what does the "x" stand for? As noted above, the file extension for Word 2007 is .docx. Previous versions of Microsoft Office did not include an "x" at the end of the file extension, which was simply .doc. The "x" refers to XML (Extensible Markup Language), which is what the new file format for Office 2007 files is based on. The new format is called Microsoft Office Open XML and is available for Word, Excel, and PowerPoint. Some of the benefits of using the Office Open XML format are as follows:

- **More compact files:** Files are automatically compressed using zip compression technology and can be up to 75% smaller in some cases. When you open and save a file, it unzips and zips automatically.
- **Recovery from file damage:** Files are structured modularly so that different data components are kept separately. Files can be opened even if one element is damaged.
- **More privacy:** The Document Inspector can remove hidden data or personal information.
- **Compatibility with other programs:** Using a zip utility and any XML editor, you can access any Office file that has been saved in XML format.
- **Macro detection:** Office 2007 files have to be saved with an "m" (such as .docm, .xlsm, and .pptm) to contain macros.

Saving a File

It is important to save your files frequently in order to not lose work in case of power outage or other failures. When you are saving a document that you are updating, use the Save feature. The Save feature will save all of the updates you have made to your document and keep the file with its current name and in its current location. The Save As feature can be used when you are saving a document for the first time or when you want to update a file and retain the original file. When you use the Save As feature, you are prompted to choose a filename and location in the Save As dialog box.

Did You Know?

You can use the keys on the keyboard to perform many Office commands. These key combinations are called **keyboard shortcuts**. Some common shortcuts include the following:

- Ctrl + O to open the Open dialog box
- Ctrl + S to save a file
- Ctrl + P to open the Print dialog box

S TEP-BY-STEP 1.6

1. Type your name at the bottom of the letter under "Warmly," and at the top of the document before the address.

2. Click the **Office Button**, then click **Save**. Your name has been saved to the Letter file.

3. Click the **Office Button**, then click **Save As**. The Save As dialog box opens, as shown in Figure 1-9.

FIGURE 1-9
The Save As dialog box

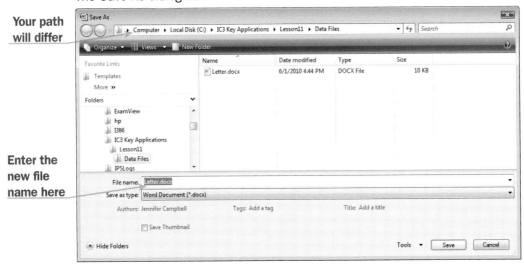

4. In the File name text box, type **Your Name Letter.docx**.

5. Click **Save**. The Save As dialog box closes. There are now two versions of the same file, but only the Your Name Letter file is open.

Previewing a File

2-1.4.2

When your document is complete and ready for distribution, you can print a hard copy of it. Before you print, you can use the Print Preview feature to verify that your page layout does not need any modifications. Previewing before you print is important as it can save paper and ink by only printing files you have reviewed. The Print Preview window can help identify that your document fits on one page or that the margins are correct, for example. You cannot edit your document in the Print Preview window, but you can return to the program window to make any necessary modifications before printing.

S TEP-BY-STEP 1.7

1. Click the **Office Button**, then point to **Print**. Printing options appear.

2. Click **Print Preview**. The Print Preview window appears, as shown in Figure 1-10.

FIGURE 1-10
The Print Preview Window

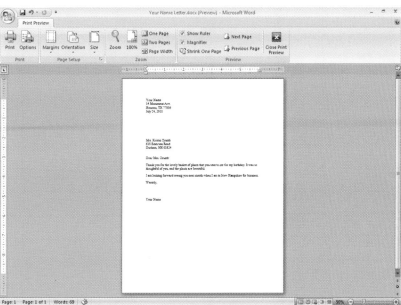

3. Verify that the letter fits on one page and that there are no other areas to fix.

4. Click **Close Print Preview** to return to the Word window.

Printing a File

2-1.4.3

When your document is complete and ready for distribution, you can print a hard copy of it. There are many options available for printing, including changing the quality, choosing color or black and white, and selecting a printer if you are connected to more than one. The Print dialog box can be used to make any modifications or verifications to your printing options. You can also choose the Quick Print option, which will print with the default settings. Your Print dialog box and options will vary depending on the printer setup. If you are working in a lab, verify with your instructor or lab manager that it is okay to print. You can use the Print Preview feature to verify that your page layout does not need any modification. Always make sure to save your document before printing it, and if necessary, put your name on the file to distinguish it.

S TEP-BY-STEP 1.8

1. Click the **Office Button**, then point to **Print**. Printing options appear.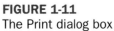

2. Click **Print**. The Print dialog box appears, as shown in Figure 1-11.

FIGURE 1-11
The Print dialog box

Your dialog box may differ

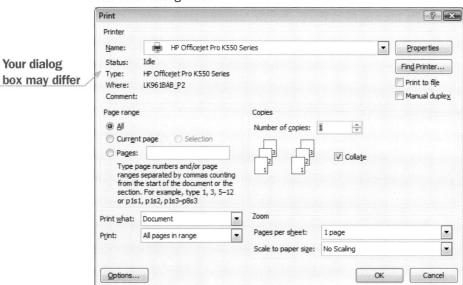

3. Verify that the printer listed is correct, then click **Print** if told to do so by your instructor, or click **Cancel** to close the dialog box without printing.

4. The **Your Name Letter** file is printed.

Closing Files and Exiting Programs

2-1.1.2
2-1.2.9

Closing a file puts it away for later use but leaves the program window open. Exiting a program shuts it down, freeing up memory and resources for your computer to perform other tasks. When closing a file or program, you will be prompted to save any changes to your files that you have made since your last save.

S TEP-BY-STEP 1.9

1. You should have two files open in Word: Document1, and Your Name Letter. Your Name Letter should be the active file.

2. Click the **Office Button**, then click **Close**. If prompted to save changes, click **Yes**. The Your Name Letter file closes, and Document1 appears.

3. Click the **Office Button**, then click **Exit Word**. When prompted to save changes to Document1, as shown in Figure 1-12, click **No**. Word is now closed.

FIGURE 1-12
Message box

Getting Help

2-1.1.3
2-1.1.4

There are many resources available to you when you need assistance in performing tasks. The Microsoft Office Word Help button opens the Word Help window. Using the Help window you can browse topics, search by keyword, and print any topics. If you are connected to the Internet, you can access content available from Office Online.

S TEP-BY-STEP 1.10

1. Open **Microsoft Office Word 2007**.

2. Click the **Microsoft Office Word Help** button. The Word Help window opens, as shown in Figure 1-13.

> **Did You Know?**
>
> You can also open the Help window at any time by pressing [F1].

FIGURE 1-13
The Word Help window

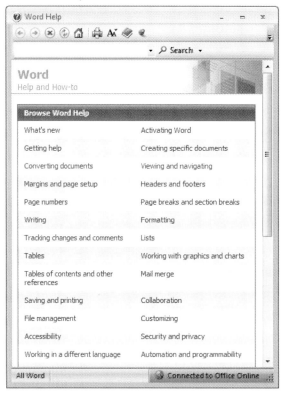

3. Click the **Getting help** link.

4. Click any topic in the Getting help section. Read the topic.

5. Press the **Back button** to return to the Getting help topic list.

6. Press the **Forward button** to return to the previous help topic.

7. Type **Saving a file** in the Search text box, then click the **Search** button.

8. Click the topic **Save a file**. Read the topic.

9. Click the **Close** button on the Word Help window.

10. Exit Microsoft Word.

SUMMARY

In this lesson, you learned:

■ Microsoft Office 2007 is a suite of several applications or programs.

■ Some of the programs available in Microsoft Office are Word, Excel, Access, PowerPoint, and Outlook.

■ Each program has a different purpose, but they all share common elements such as the Ribbon.

■ You can open new files, save files with the same name or a different name, and print files. Before you print a file, you should save it and preview it.

■ Some of the ways you can customize the view to suit your needs include Minimizing the Ribbon, changing the zoom, and adding buttons to the Quick Access Toolbar.

■ A variety of help resources are available when you need to learn more about any topic.

VOCABULARY *Review*

Define the following terms:

Application	Mini toolbar	Save/Save As
Closing	Operating system	ScreenTip
Dialog box launcher	Print	Scroll bars
Exiting	Program window	Status bar
File extension	Quick Access Toolbar	Suite
Help	Ribbon	Zoom
Help desk		

REVIEW *Questions*

SCREEN IDENTIFICATION

Identify the screen elements.

FIGURE 1-14
Microsoft Office Word 2007 window

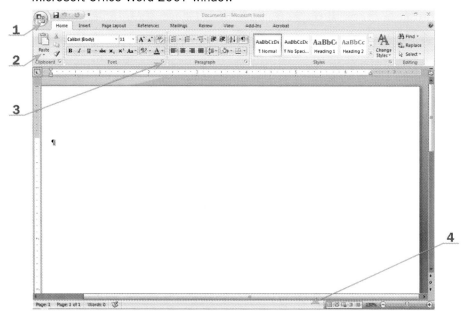

1. _____

2. _____

3. _____

4. _____

MULTIPLE CHOICE

Circle the correct answer.

1. Microsoft _____ is a database program.
   - **A.** Word
   - **B.** Access
   - **C.** Excel
   - **D.** PowerPoint

2. Microsoft _____ is a spreadsheet program.
   - **A.** Word
   - **B.** Access
   - **C.** Excel
   - **D.** PowerPoint

3. Microsoft _____ is a presentation graphics program.
    A. Word
    B. Access
    C. Excel
    D. PowerPoint

4. The _____ contains tabs that organize command buttons into groups.
    A. Quick Access Toolbar
    B. Office Button
    C. Ribbon
    D. Status bar

5. To learn more about a button's function, read the _____ that appears when you position the pointer over it.
    A. ScreenTip
    B. Toolbar
    C. Ribbon
    D. Status

TRUE/FALSE

Circle T if the statement is true or F if the statement is false.

T   F   1. The Save feature can be used to save a file with a different name.

T   F   2. The Help window can access online content.

T   F   3. Microsoft Word is used to store data in fields and records.

T   F   4. Microsoft Publisher is a desktop publishing program.

T   F   5. Microsoft Windows Vista is an operating system.

T   F   6. When working with text, sometimes a task-sensitive toolbar called the Ribbon appears.

HANDS-ON REVIEW

1. Open Microsoft Office Word 2007 using the Start menu.

2. Click each tab on the Ribbon to see the different commands. Click the Page Layout tab. In the Page Setup group, click the dialog box launcher. Close the Page Setup dialog box.

3. Add and delete a button from the Quick Access toolbar.

4. Change the zoom level to 200%. Change the zoom level to 50%. Return the zoom level to the original level.

5. Open the file Letter.docx from your Data Files. Add your name and today's date to the top of the letter, then save it as **Today Letter.docx**.

6. Preview the document.

7. Open the Print dialog box, then print the document if told to do so by your instructor. Otherwise, close the Print dialog box.

8. Open the Word Help window. Click a topic in the list, then read the results. Click the Back button. Close the Word Help window.

9. Close the Today Letter.docx file, then exit Word.

PROJECTS

PROJECT 1-1

1. Open Microsoft Excel.

2. Click each tab to see the different commands available in Excel.

3. Open at least one dialog box using a dialog box launcher.

4. Type text in one of the cells in the program window, then select the text. If the Mini toolbar appears, note the options that are available.

5. Close the file and Excel without saving changes.

PROJECT 1-2

1. Open Microsoft PowerPoint using the Start menu.

2. Click each tab to see the different commands available in PowerPoint.

3. Open the PowerPoint Help window, and read a topic.

4. Use the Office Button to open the file **Presentation.pptx** from your Data Files.

5. Save the file as **Your Name Presentation.pptx**.

6. Close the file and PowerPoint.

 TEAMWORK

Make a list of the different Microsoft Office programs available on your lab or individual computers. For each program, come up with a description of a file you might create using that program. For example, you might use PowerPoint to create a presentation and print handouts to accompany a speech you are giving.

CRITICAL *Thinking*

ACTIVITY 1-1

You want to find out more about the Print Preview window and its usefulness. Open Microsoft Word Help and search for Print Preview. Make a list of several things that Print Preview can help you to identify and fix before you print your document.

WORD PROCESSING BASICS

VOCABULARY

Comment

Deselect

Draft layout

Font

Full Screen Reading view

Insertion point

Nonprinting character

Outline view

Pixels

Placeholder

Print Layout view

Screen resolution

Scroll bar

Select

Show/Hide ¶

Template

Theme

Thumbnail

Toggle button

Track changes

Web Layout view

Zoom level

Once you have opened Word, you can start creating your document by typing directly in a new, blank document or using a preformatted template. There are many ways to navigate through your document using keyboard shortcuts and scroll bars. Selecting text is important when editing and applying formatting to text, which you'll learn about in a later lesson. To refine your documents, you may need to view nonprinting characters such as paragraph marks, spaces, and tabs. To revise a document, you can turn on the Track Changes feature so that all of your edits will be marked. You can also add comments, or margin notes, to a document.

Creating a New Document

When you start Word, a new blank document automatically opens. By default, this document is called Document1. The next new document you create during the Word session is Document2, and so forth. You should save a document before you start working with it in order to keep any changes you make.

2-1.1.1
2-1.1.6

If you are already working in Word and you want to start a new document, you can use the New Document dialog box to choose a blank document or select from a number of templates. Templates are preformatted documents you can use as a basis for forms, gift certificates,

Note

To automatically open a new, blank document, press **Ctrl + N**.

resumes, and more. When you click a category in the New Document dialog box, **thumbnails**, or small icons, of the available templates appear in the middle pane. Templates include sample text called placeholder text, which you need to replace with your own content.

S TEP-BY-STEP 2.1

1. Start Word. A new, blank document, called Document1, opens.

2. Click the **Office Button**, then click **New**. The New Document dialog box opens.

3. Click **Installed Templates** in the left pane. The New Document dialog box displays thumbnails, as shown in Figure 2-1. Your template choices may vary.

FIGURE 2-1
The New Document dialog box

These templates are available from Microsoft Office Online. You must be connected to the Internet to access them.

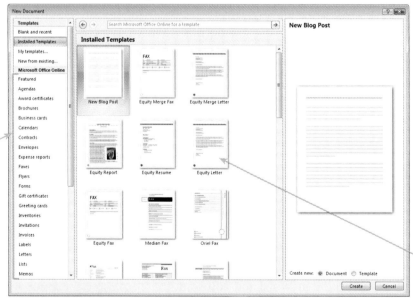

Equity Letter template thumbnail

4. Click the **Equity Letter** thumbnail, then click **Create**. The Equity Letter template opens for editing and is called Document2, as shown in Figure 2-2.

STEP-BY-STEP 2.1 Continued

FIGURE 2-2
New document based on the Equity Letter template

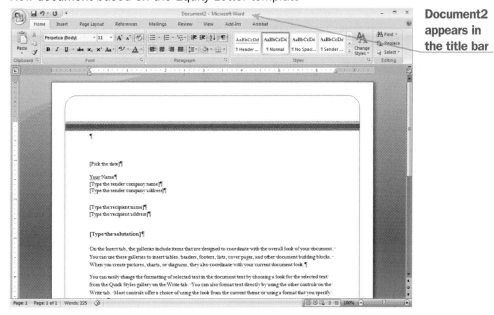

Document2
appears in
the title bar

5. Close Document2 without saving changes. Leave Word and Document1 open for the next Step-by-Step.

Entering Text in a Document

In Lesson 1, you entered text by typing your name in a document. Now you will type several lines of text in different areas in a document. You can tell where the text you type will appear by looking at the insertion point, which is a blinking line. You can move the insertion point to another place in your document by clicking the new location.

To insert a line break, press the Enter key. To indent lines, press the Tab key. It is important to use these keys to make line breaks and indents. Although you could indent a line of text by pressing the spacebar multiple times, you will not be able to control the consistency of the indented lines as you would if you press the Tab key. If you used spaces or tabs to move to a new line, you will not be able to control paragraph formatting. If you changed the font, font size, or margins, your text may not appear as you intended.

Documents can be as short as a few words or as long as hundreds of pages. When you have more text than fits on your screen, you can use the scroll bars to see additional content. Using the scroll bars adjusts the view up or down but does not move the insertion point.

2-1.3.2

Computer Concepts

The amount of information shown on your screen is called **screen resolution**. Screen resolution measures the number of **pixels**, or dots that make up graphic images, in rows and columns. The figures in this book were captured using a resolution of 1024×768. If your resolution is different, you will be able to see more or less than what is shown in a figure.

S TEP-BY-STEP 2.2

1. Type **today's date** in Document1, then press **Enter** twice. There is a blank line between the date and the insertion point.

2. Press **Tab**. The insertion point moves to the right, leaving an indentation.

3. Type the two paragraphs of text shown in Figure 2-3. Press **Enter** once in between the paragraphs, and press **Tab** to indent the second paragraph.

FIGURE 2-3
Text to type

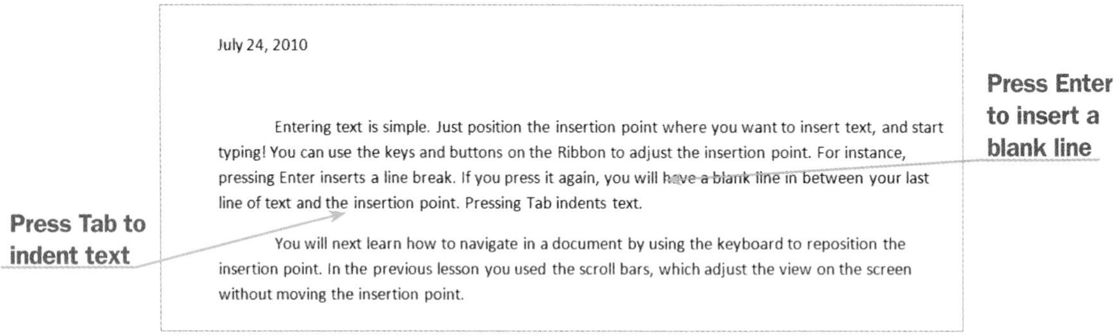

July 24, 2010

Press Enter to insert a blank line

       Entering text is simple. Just position the insertion point where you want to insert text, and start typing! You can use the keys and buttons on the Ribbon to adjust the insertion point. For instance, pressing Enter inserts a line break. If you press it again, you will have a blank line in between your last line of text and the insertion point. Pressing Tab indents text.

Press Tab to indent text

       You will next learn how to navigate in a document by using the keyboard to reposition the insertion point. In the previous lesson you used the scroll bars, which adjust the view on the screen without moving the insertion point.

4. Press **Enter** three times. Type **Your Name**, then press **Enter**.

5. Depending on your screen resolution, you may not be able to see all of the text you have typed. If you can still see all of the text, press **Enter** several more times until you can no longer see the date at the top.

STEP-BY-STEP 2.2 Continued

6. Use the scroll bars to move back to the top of the document until you can see the date.

7. Scroll back to the bottom to view the insertion point.

8. Save the document as **Entering Text.docx**. Leave Word and the document open for the next Step-by-Step.

Moving Through a Document

The insertion point can be moved by clicking the mouse wherever you need to insert and format text. There are also many keyboard shortcuts that quickly move the insertion point to a new position, as shown in Table 2-1. Being familiar with these positioning tools can help you to make edits to your document efficiently and accurately. If there are extra line breaks at the end of a document, pressing Ctrl + End will position the insertion point before the last line break instead of after the last line of text, indicating to you that you need to delete the extra line breaks.

STEP-BY-STEP 2.3

1. Press **Ctrl + End**. The insertion point moves to the end of the document.

2. Press **Ctrl + Home**. The insertion point moves to the beginning of the document.

3. Press **End**. The insertion point moves to the end of the line.

4. Press the **down arrow** to move down a line, then press the **up arrow** to move up a line.

5. Press **Page Down**, then press **Page Up**. The insertion point moves down and back up on the screen. The exact location will vary depending on your screen resolution.

6. Press the **right arrow** twice to move the insertion point two characters to the right.

7. Press the **left arrow** twice to move the insertion point two characters to the left.

8. Click at the beginning of the third line of the first paragraph.

9. Press **Ctrl + right arrow** three times, then press **Ctrl + left arrow** three times.

10. Press **Ctrl + End**. Close the document but leave Word and open for the next Step-by-Step.

TABLE 2-1
Navigating through a document

KEYBOARD SHORTCUT	MOVES THE INSERTION POINT...
Ctrl + Home	To the beginning of the document
Ctrl + End	To the end of the document
Home	To the beginning of the line
End	To the end of the line
Page Up	Up one screen
Page Down	Down one screen
Arrow keys	One character to the left or right, or one line up or down
Ctrl + left arrow key	One word to the left
Ctrl + right arrow key	One word to the right

Selecting Text

In order to edit or format text, you first need to select it. You can use the mouse to drag the cursor over the text you want to select, or you can use any of the options in Table 2-2 to select portions of your document.

2-2.1.2

Once text is selected, you can press Delete to remove the text, start typing to overwrite the text, or apply formatting options from the Ribbon or using keyboard shortcuts. If you select the wrong portion of text, you can click anywhere outside of the text to deselect it.

TABLE 2-2
Selecting portions of documents

TO SELECT...	DO THIS
A word	Double-click the word
A sentence	Click anywhere in the sentence, press and hold Ctrl, then click again
A paragraph	Click anywhere in the paragraph, then triple-click
All of the text in a document	Press Ctrl + A
A line of text	Position the pointer in the left margin next to the line, then click
One character at a time	Click to the left or right of the first character to select, press and hold Shift, then press the left or right arrow as many times as necessary to select each character in that direction
Placeholder text	Click anywhere in the placeholder

S TEP-BY-STEP 2.4

1. Open the file **Job Letter.docx** from your Data Files. The document opens, as shown in Figure 2-4.

FIGURE 2-4
Job Letter.docx

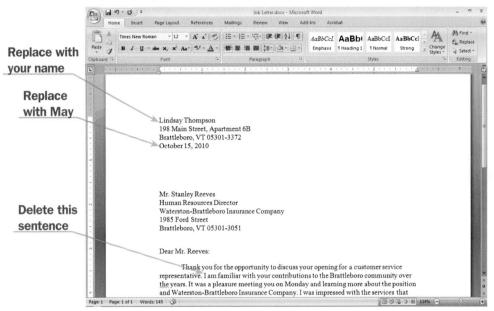

2. Position the pointer in the left margin next to *Lindsay Thompson*, then click. The line is selected.

3. Type **your name**.

4. Double-click the word *October* in the date line to select it. Type **May**.

5. Click anywhere in the second sentence of the first paragraph, press and hold **Ctrl**, then click. The second sentence is selected.

6. Press **Delete**.

7. Click anywhere in the second paragraph, then triple-click. The paragraph is selected.

8. Click anywhere outside of the second paragraph to deselect it.

9. Press **Ctrl + A** to select all of the text, then click anywhere in the document to deselect it.

10. Click to the left of the word *Respectfully*.

11. Press and hold **Shift**, then press the **right arrow** 12 times to select the entire word. *(Hint:* Do not select the comma (,).)

12. Type **Sincerely**, then save the document as **Updated Job Letter.docx** to your Data Files. Leave Word and the document open for the next Step-by-Step.

Displaying Nonprinting Characters

Formatting marks such as paragraph breaks, tabs, and spaces are nonprinting but can be viewed on the screen while working in your document. Table 2-3 lists some of the nonprinting characters for Word. Some people prefer to work with the nonprinting characters displayed, and others choose not to view them. The Show/Hide ¶ button is a toggle button, meaning that you click it once to turn the feature on and click again to turn it off.

2-1.2.4
2-2.1.1

While you could use the spacebar to move the insertion point to a new line or indent text, using the Enter and Tab keys appropriately will make sure that your document is laid out correctly. Viewing the nonprinting characters can show you potential errors, such as extra line breaks at the end of a document, that could make your document print on an extra page.

TABLE 2-3
Nonprinting characters

SYMBOL	CHARACTER
¶	Paragraph
→	Tab
•	Space
———Page Break———	Page break
↵	Manual line break

S TEP-BY-STEP 2.5

1. In the Paragraph group, click the **Show/Hide ¶** button.

2. If your screen does not display the symbols shown in Figure 2-5, press the **Show/Hide ¶** button again.

FIGURE 2-5
Nonprinting characters displayed

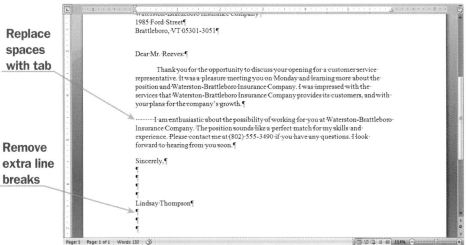

STEP-BY-STEP 2.5 Continued

3. Press **Ctrl + End**, then press **Enter**. The paragraph mark displays.

4. Press **Tab**. The tab mark displays.

5. Type a period (**.**), then press **spacebar**. Note that the space mark is raised above the period.

6. Select and delete the tab and space you added.

7. Position the insertion point at the beginning of the second paragraph. Note that instead of a tab mark, spaces were used to indent the text.

8. Select the space characters at the beginning of the paragraph, then press **Tab**.

9. Scroll to the end of the document. As shown in Figure 2-5, extra paragraph marks appear after *Lindsay Thompson*.

10. Position the insertion point before the paragraph mark after Lindsay Thompson, then press **Delete** until all of the extra line breaks are removed.

11. Save your changes. Leave Word and the document open for the next Step-by-Step.

Changing Views

Word has many different ways to view your document. You can click one of the View buttons on the status bar to change the view, as shown in Figure 2-6, or you can increase or decrease the zoom to see more or less of the document on the screen at one time.

FIGURE 2-6
Changing the view

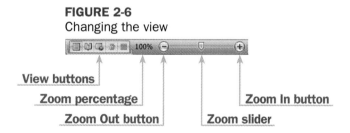

View buttons
Zoom percentage
Zoom Out button
Zoom In button
Zoom slider

Word has five different layout views. **Print Layout view** shows your text using margins and page breaks as it will appear when printed. **Full Screen Reading view** allows you to view the document without the Ribbon, ruler, or other tools, in order to optimize reading from the screen. **Web Layout view** removes the page breaks and shows how your document would appear if saved to the Web. **Outline view** allows you to see the hierarchy of your document by displaying the headings and indenting subheadings or text paragraphs. **Draft layout view** shows the page breaks as lines, allowing you to edit while viewing more of the document on the screen.

Changing the zoom is an easy way to view more or less of your document. You can change the zoom using the Zoom slider, Zoom In, or Zoom Out buttons on the status bar, as shown in Figure 2-6. The **Zoom level** indicates the percentage higher or lower than what will be printed—

100% zoom shows exactly what will appear when a document is printed. To see more on the screen, choose a lower zoom. To see less text but have the text appear larger, use a higher zoom.

S TEP-BY-STEP 2.6

1. Look at the view buttons on your status bar. The one that is selected appears indented and has an orange tint.

2. If necessary, click the **Print Layout** button to select Print Layout view.

3. Click the **Full Screen Reading view** button. See Figure 2-7. *Note:* The Full Screen Reading view does not show the pages as they print. It may show your document on one or two pages regardless of the number of pages in the document.

FIGURE 2-7
Full Screen Reading view

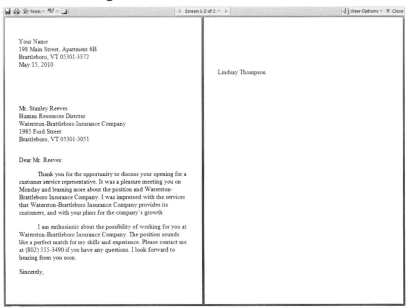

4. Press **Escape** to return to Print Layout view, click the other view buttons on the status bar, then click the **Print Layout button**.

5. Note the Zoom level. Drag the **Zoom slider** to the left and right to change the Zoom.

6. Double-click the **Zoom percentage**. In the Zoom dialog box, return the zoom level to the original percentage.

7. Save your changes and close the document. Leave Word open for the next Step-by-Step.

Use Track Changes and Add Comments

An important word processing skill is the ability to edit and review work. When you edit a document, you can use the **track changes** feature to keep track of the insertions, deletions, and formatting changes you make. This is important if you are reviewing another person's work so that they can see all of the changes that you made.

Using commands on the Review tab on the Ribbon, you can move through the document, automatically advancing to the next change, and choose to accept or reject each change individually. You can also choose to accept or reject all comments at once. Options on the Review tab also allow you to choose what changes to show: you can choose to not display any formatting changes, for instance, but to show all insertions and deletions.

To add a note without affecting the text, you can use the **comments** feature. Comment balloons can be attached to specific text, and they are used to pose questions to the author or make your own notes. When comments are visible in the document, the screen adjusts to the left in order to show the comments on the right.

2-2.1.9
2-2.1.20

Did You Know?

There can be several reviewers for any document. Each reviewer has a unique color assigned to the edits he or she makes. A reviewer's initials are used to keep track of who is making the comments.

Note

Balloons are used to show comments and can also be used to show text edits and formatting changes. To change the balloon options to match the steps in this Step-by-Step, on the Review tab in the Tracking group, click the **Balloons** button, then click **Show Only Comments and Formatting in Balloons**.

Trends in Technology

A COMPUTER IS NOT A TYPEWRITER

Back in the late 1880s, Mark Twain was one of the first authors to submit a type-written manuscript to a publisher. Typewriters were cutting-edge technology back then and remained popular long after the first PCs appeared in homes in the late 1980s. Typewriters and computers share the QWERTY keyboard (named for the first six letters in the top row), making it easy to go from one side to the other. People who learned to type on a typewriter are able to continue their work more efficiently using a computer. You may not have ever used a typewriter, but you are probably familiar with the old rule to insert two spaces after a period or colon when typing. This rule is no longer needed, as many electronic typewriters and all word processing programs, such as Microsoft Word, automatically adjust the spacing after a period or colon. Word processing programs have many advantages over typewriters. They allow you to make edits to the text and layout of your document electronically, before ink touches paper. You can make sure that your document fits on a specific number of pages, keep track of the number of words, and even see spelling and grammar mistakes as you type.

STEP-BY-STEP 2.7

1. Open the file **Reviewing.docx** from your Data Files.

2. Click the **Review** tab on the Ribbon. The Track Changes feature is already turned on. The Review tab contains the tools you need to edit documents, as shown in Figure 2-8.

FIGURE 2-8
Document with tracked changes and comments

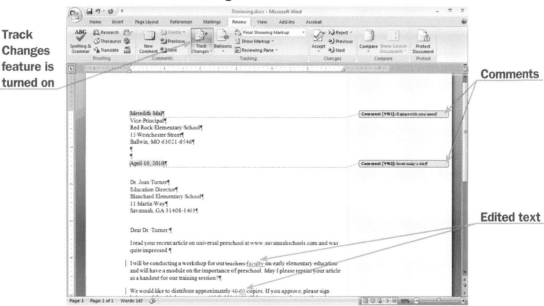

3. In the Tracking group, click the **Show Markup** button, as shown in Figure 2-9.

FIGURE 2-9
Show Markup options

4. Click each of the features selected in Figure 2-9 if they do not contain a check mark.

5. Scroll through the document, noting the changes.

6. Position the insertion point at the top of the document, type **your name**, then press **Enter**. Your name appears underlined, indicating that it has been inserted.

7. Select the line containing the text **Meredith Mai**, then press **Delete**. The deleted text appears crossed-out.

8. Select the date at the top of the document, then type **today's date**. The deleted date appears crossed-out, and the new date appears underlined.

STEP-BY-STEP 2.7 Continued

9. Click the comment next to the date, then click the **Delete** button in the Comments group on the Review tab. Delete the comment next to your name. Now that you have inserted the date and your name, you no longer need the comment as a reminder. The document returns to a view without a side margin.

10. Click the deleted word, **teachers**, in the second paragraph.

11. In the Changes group, click the **Accept** button arrow, then click **Accept and Move to Next**. The change is no longer marked, and the inserted word, *faculty*, is selected.

12. In the Changes group, click the **Accept** button. The default Accept option is *Accept and Move to Next*. The deleted number, *40*, is selected.

13. In the Changes group, click the **Reject** button arrow, then click **Reject and Move to Next**. The change is no longer marked, and the added number, *60*, is selected.

14. In the Changes group, click the **Reject** button arrow, then click **Reject Change**. The change is no longer marked, and the insertion point remains in place.

15. In the Changes group, click the **Accept** button arrow, then click **Accept All Changes in Document**. The changes are no longer marked, as shown in Figure 2-10.

FIGURE 2-10
Document with changes accepted

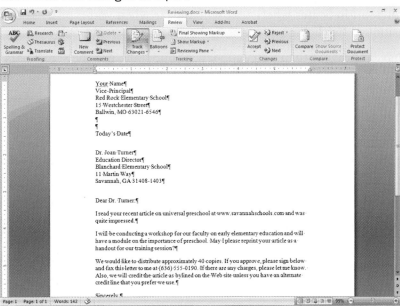

16. Position the insertion point anywhere in the first paragraph of text, then in the Comments group, click the **New Comment** button.

17. Type **your name** in the Comment balloon, then click anywhere in the document to deselect it. The comment appears in the margin, as shown in Figure 2-11.

STEP-BY-STEP 2.7 Continued

FIGURE 2-11
New comment added

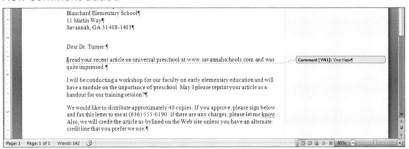

18. Save the document as **Preschool Letter.docx**, close the document, then exit Word.

> **Computer Concepts**
>
> Keep in mind other people's feelings when editing their work. Phrase your comments in the form of a suggestion or question, and involve the author(s) in the revision process.

SUMMARY

In this lesson, you learned the following:

- You can create a new document by typing into a blank document or by using a template as the basis for a new document. Templates can be used to apply consistent formatting and graphics among multiple documents.

- The insertion point indicates where text will appear when you type it. The insertion point can be repositioned by clicking or by using keyboard shortcuts.

- When you have more text than you can view at one time, use the scroll bars to view up or down without changing the position of the insertion point.

- There are many ways to select text that you want to edit or delete. You can use the keyboard, mouse, or a combination of methods.

- Tab, space, and paragraph marks are all examples of nonprinting characters. Viewing nonprinting characters can ensure that the layout and formatting of your document is correct.

- There are many views in Word that you can use, depending on your needs. You can choose to view more or less of a document on the screen by changing the zoom level.

- You can keep track of edits made in your document, and accept and reject changes.

- Comments allow you to make notes in a document without affecting the text.

VOCABULARY *Review*

Define the following terms:

Comment	Pixels	Template
Deselect	Placeholder	Theme
Draft layout	Print Layout view	Thumbnail
Font	Screen resolution	Toggle button
Full Screen Reading view	Scroll bar	Track changes
Insertion point	Select	Web Layout view
Nonprinting character	Show/Hide ¶	Zoom level
Outline view		

REVIEW *Questions*

SCREEN IDENTIFICATION

Identify the screen elements.

FIGURE 2-12
Screen identification

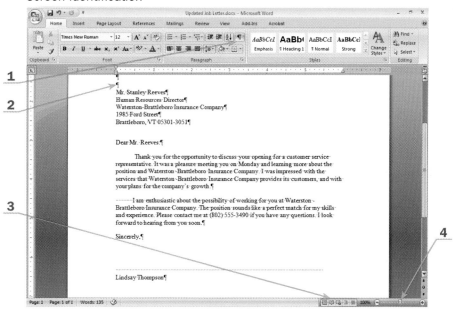

1.

2.

3.

4.

MULTIPLE CHOICE

Circle the correct answer.

1. The _____ feature adds notes to a document without affecting text.
    - A. Comments
    - B. Track Changes
    - C. Toggle
    - D. Placeholder

2. A(n) _____ button is used to turn a feature on and off.
    - A. accept
    - B. select
    - C. toggle
    - D. placeholder

3. A _____ is text you need to replace with your own.
    - A. comment
    - B. template
    - C. toggle
    - D. placeholder

4. Tab and paragraph marks are examples of _____.
    - A. toggle buttons
    - B. nonprinting characters
    - C. track changes
    - D. placeholders

TRUE/FALSE

Circle T if the statement is true or F if the statement is false.

T   F   1. You can accept or reject all changes in a document at once.

T   F   2. Pressing Ctrl + N opens the New Document dialog box.

T   F   3. The Show/Hide ¶ button is a toggle button.

T   F   4. To reposition the insertion point, use the scroll bars.

T   F   5. Pressing Ctrl + A selects all of the text in a document.

T   F   6. Triple-clicking selects an entire line of text.

T   F   7. Press End to move to the end of the document.

HANDS-ON REVIEW

1. Open Word. A new, blank document opens.

2. Type at least one paragraph (three lines or longer) in the document.

3. Press **Ctrl + End** to go to the last line in the document, press **Enter,** then type **your name.**

4. In the paragraph you typed, practice selecting a single word, a sentence, a line, and the entire paragraph.

5. Display and hide nonprinting characters.

6. Change the view to Full Screen Reading view. Change to Print Layout view.

7. Turn on Track Changes, then add and delete some text from the paragraph you typed.

8. Add a comment that includes your name and the date, then save it as **My Document.docx**.

PROJECTS

PROJECT 2-1

1. Create a new document using one of the Letter templates.

2. Replace the placeholder text with your own information.

3. Select a sentence, delete it, then type a new sentence.

4. In another sentence, select a single word, then replace it with another word.

5. Use the Shift key and the arrow keys to select portions of another word.

6. Close the new document without saving changes.

PROJECT 2-2

1. Open a one-page document you created in a previous class or lesson.

2. Turn on Track Changes and display nonprinting characters.

3. Save the document as **My Edits.docx**.

4. Make several edits by inserting and deleting text.

5. Add two comments: one with your name and the other with today's date.

6. Accept or reject all of the edits and delete the comments, then turn off Track Changes.

7. Save and close the document.

 TEAMWORK PROJECT

Exchange a one-page document with a partner. Using Track Changes and comments, practice editing each other's document diplomatically. Exchange the edited files, and make sure you understand the changes that were made to your document and how to implement the changes.

CRITICAL*Thinking*

ACTIVITY 2-1

Templates allow you to use preformatted documents that include sample graphics, fonts, text, and layouts. Open the New Document dialog box, and note the different categories of templates available. Choose a template to use to create a new document. In the new document, write a paragraph about the benefits of using templates. Include specific examples based on the template you have chosen. Save the document as **Templates.docx**.

EDITING AND FORMATTING DOCUMENTS

One of the advantages of word processing software is the ability to make changes to your document before it is printed. **Editing** text refers to changes you make to the content. In order to edit text you must not only understand basic selecting and typing features, but you need to learn how to move text from one location to another in a document. You also need to be able to search for text and make replacements to some or all instances of the search text.

Formatting is making enhancements to the text to make it stand out. As you have seen when looking at templates, there are different **fonts**, or text styles, that you can apply for different effects. You can also apply text formatting options such as **bolding**, *italics*, or <u>underlines</u>, and even change the color or add a shadow to text. **Paragraph formatting** is another way to improve the look of your document by adjusting the line spacing to add more space between lines or automatically insert space between paragraphs.

After you have made your text and formatting changes, you need to proof your document. Word has a built-in tool to check the spelling and grammar of your document. You can use the Print Preview feature you learned about in Lesson 1 to make sure that the layout of the document is correct and that it all fits on a certain number of pages. You can then make any adjustments to the document before printing it.

Delete and Insert Text

2.1.3.1

To remove one character at a time while you are typing and editing, you can use the Delete and Backspace keys. The Delete key is used when you want to remove characters that appear directly after the insertion point. The Backspace key is used to remove characters that appear directly before the insertion point. These keys are good to use when deleting small amounts of text such as a single character or word, or a portion of a word. You can also use either key to remove selected text.

> **Did You Know?**
>
> You can also remove characters by typing over them using **overtype mode**. As you type each character, it replaces the next character. Overtype mode should be used when you are replacing text with a similar amount of new text. To activate overtype mode, click the Office Button, then click Word Options. Click Advanced in the Word Options task pane, then click the Use the Insert key to control overtype mode check box to select it. To start or stop overtype mode, click the Insert key.

STEP-BY-STEP 3.1

1. Start Word and open the document **Itinerary.docx** from your Data Files. The document appears as shown in Figure 3-1.

2. On the Home tab, click the **Show/Hide ¶** button in the Paragraph group, if necessary, to display the nonprinting characters.

FIGURE 3-1
Itinerary.docx

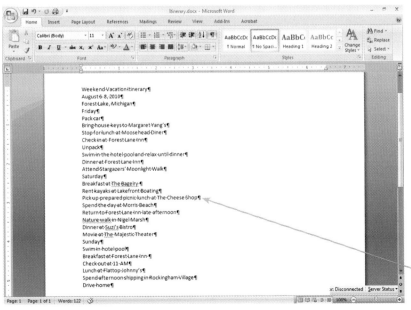

Your document may not show the non-printing characters by default

STEP-BY-STEP 3.1 Continued

3. Scroll to and click to position the insertion point at the beginning of the line *Nature walk in Nigel Marsh*.

4. Scroll to and click to position the insertion point before the words *11 AM* in the fourth line from the bottom.

5. Press **Delete** five times. 11 AM is now deleted.

6. Type **12 AM**.

7. Press **Backspace** twice, then type **PM**.

8. Save the document as **Edited Itinerary.docx**.

9. Leave Word and the document open for the next Step-by-Step.

> **Computer Concepts**
>
> Word marks potential misspellings and grammar mistakes on the screen. Words that do not appear in the dictionary that comes with Word have red wavy lines underneath them. Potential grammar mistakes, such as incorrect verb tenses or repeated words, have green wavy lines underneath them. You will learn how to review and fix these mistakes later in this lesson.

Cut, Copy, and Paste Text

All Office programs share the Office Clipboard. The **Office Clipboard** stores up to 24 items. You can cut or copy clipboard items created in an open file and then paste them elsewhere in the current file, or in another Office program file. The Clipboard can store text selections from one character to several pages in length. It can also store graphics that are embedded in your document.

2.1.3.3

The cut, copy, and paste commands are used together to remove or copy text from a document and insert it in another location. The **Cut** command removes the selection from its current location and copies it to the Clipboard. Cut is used when you want to relocate an item. The **Copy** command keeps the selection in its current location but also copies it to the Clipboard. Copy can be helpful when you have a repeated word or text that you want to insert in multiple locations in your document. The **Paste** command is used to insert Clipboard items. You can view the Clipboard to see the items that are stored to it. Unless you have the Clipboard displayed, you can only paste the most

> **Did You Know?**
>
> The keyboard shortcuts for the Cut, Copy, and Paste commands are **Ctrl + X** (Cut), **Ctrl + C** (Copy), and **Ctrl + V** (Paste).

recently cut or copied item. When the Clipboard exceeds 24 items, the first clipboard item is deleted. The Clipboard is shown in Figure 3-2.

FIGURE 3-2
The Clipboard

Clipboard contents include data from other programs

S TEP-BY-STEP 3.2

1. Position the pointer in the margin next to the line *Bring house keys to Margaret Yang's*, then click to select the line.

2. In the Clipboard group, click the **Copy** button. The selected text is copied to the Clipboard but remains in its current location.

3. Position the insertion point at the beginning of the last line *Drive home*.

4. In the Clipboard group, click the **Paste** button. The selected text is copied to the new location.

5. Edit the copied text to read **Pick up house keys from Margaret Yang's**.

6. Position the pointer in the margin next to the line *Rent kayaks at Lakefront Boating*, then click to select the line.

7. In the Clipboard group, click the **Cut** button. The selected text is copied to the Clipboard and removed from its current location.

STEP-BY-STEP 3.2 Continued

8. Position the insertion point at the beginning of the line of text *Spend the day at Morris Beach.*

9. Click the **Paste** button to insert the text in its new location. The document appears as shown in Figure 3-3.

FIGURE 3-3
Itinerary.docx after cutting, copying, and pasting

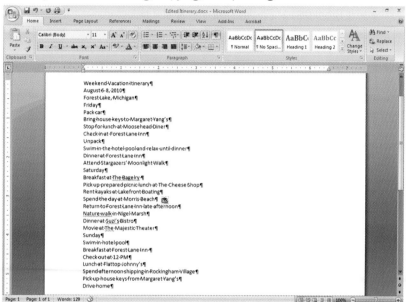

10. Save your work, then leave the document and Word open for the next Step-by-Step.

> **Did You Know?**
>
> You can use the Windows Clipboard to copy and paste one item at a time from one computer application to another.

Use Drag and Drop

The drag-and-drop feature lets you move or copy selected text or items to a new location using the mouse. You use the mouse to drag items, and when you release the left mouse button, the items are dropped in their new location. Items that are moved or copied using drag and drop are not copied to the Clipboard.

To use drag and drop to move an item, you first select it, position the mouse pointer over the item, click the left mouse button, then move the pointer to the new location. You can also use drag and drop to copy an item by selecting it, positioning the pointer over the item, pressing **Ctrl**, clicking the left mouse button, then moving the pointer to the new location.

Drag and drop can be less accurate than Cut and Paste. It is best to use when you want to move or copy text to a new location that is close to the current location and when you will not need to copy that item again.

2.1.3.3

STEP-BY-STEP 3.3

1. Select the text *Breakfast at Forest Lane Inn.*

2. Position the pointer over the text, click the left mouse button, then move the pointer to the beginning of the line *Swim in hotel pool.* The mouse pointer changes to the Move text pointer.

3. Release the left mouse button. The text is inserted in its new location.

4. Make sure the text *Breakfast at Forest Lane Inn* is still selected.

5. Press and hold **Ctrl**, then drag the beginning of the line *Pick up prepared picnic lunch....* The mouse pointer changes to the copy pointer.

6. Release the mouse button. Delete the line *Breakfast at The Bagelry.* The text appears in both locations, as shown in Figure 3-4.

FIGURE 3-4
Edited Itinerary.docx after dragging and dropping

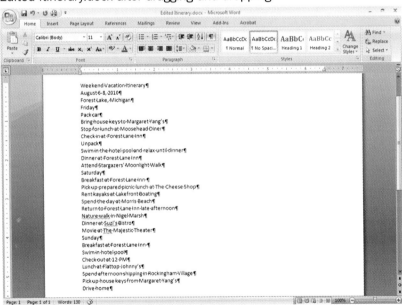

7. Save your work, then leave the document and Word open for the next Step-by-Step.

Find, Replace, and Insert Text

When you want to look for or change all instances of a word or phrase, you can use the Find tool to locate all instances and the Replace tool to replace all found instances with the same text. These features can be used to change any text, such as replacing the company name in a cover letter you want to accompany your resume during a job search.

2.1.3.5
2.1.3.6
2.2.1.7
2.2.1.8

Both tools use a dialog box to ask for more information before they can perform the action. When a dialog box opens, you can make selections and move to the next option by pressing Tab. Click OK to apply the changes or start the action, or click Cancel to close the dialog box without making any changes.

STEP-BY-STEP 3.4

1. Press **Ctrl + End**, then press **Enter**.

2. In the new line you created, type **your name**, then press **Ctrl + Home**.

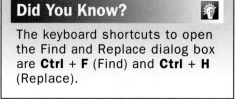

Did You Know?

The keyboard shortcuts to open the Find and Replace dialog box are **Ctrl + F** (Find) and **Ctrl + H** (Replace).

3. On the Home tab in the Editing group, click the **Find** button. The Find and Replace dialog box opens with the Find tab active, as shown in Figure 3-5.

FIGURE 3-5
Find and Replace dialog box

4. In the Find what text box, type **your name**, then click **Find Next**. Your name appears selected at the bottom of the document.

5. Click **Cancel** to close the Find and Replace dialog box, then click outside your name to deselect it, if necessary.

6. Select the text *Forest Lane Inn*, press **Ctrl + C** to copy it to the Clipboard, then deselect the text, if necessary.

7. In the Editing group, click the **Replace** button. The Find and Replace dialog box opens with the Replace tab active.

8. In the Find what text box, press **Ctrl + V** to insert *Forest Lane Inn*.

9. Press **Tab** to move to the Replace with text box, then type **Forest Lake Inn**.

10. Click **Replace All**.

STEP-BY-STEP 3.4 Continued

11. Click **Yes** in the message box to continue searching the document from the beginning, if necessary. Click **OK** in the message box, then close the Find and Replace dialog box. All instances of *Forest Lane Inn* are replaced with *Forest Lake Inn*, as shown in Figure 3-6.

FIGURE 3-6
Document after Find and Replace

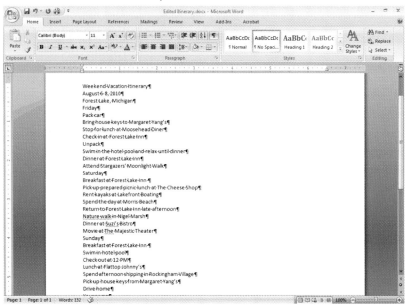

12. Save your work, then leave the document and Word open for the next Step-by-Step.

Change the Font

The document Edited Itinerary.docx that you have been using in this lesson contains all of the necessary content but is difficult to read and use. Adding text formatting will not only make the document attractive but will help to make it more readable.

There are many ways to change the text formatting in a document. For example, you can apply a new font or text style. Table 3-1 shows several examples of fonts. Each font has a set of characteristics, such as curves, angles, and serifs, that are applied to each character. Serifs are lines at the end of strokes on a letter. Fonts with lines, such as Century Schoolbook, are called serif fonts, and fonts that have no lines at the end of them, such as Arial, are called sans serif fonts. Serif fonts are thought to make long passages of text easier to read. Script fonts, such as Bradley Hand ITC and Edwardian Script, look like calligraphy or handwriting. The default fonts for Word are Calibri (sans serif) and Cambria (serif).

Computer Concepts

The **Mini-toolbar** is a task-specific toolbar, meaning that it only appears when text is selected. In addition to appearing on the Ribbon, most of the formatting options used in this lesson are available on the Mini-toolbar. To use the Mini toolbar, select the text you want to format, position the pointer over the dimmed Mini-toolbar to activate it, then click the button you want.

Font sizes are measured in **points**. Increasing or decreasing the font size is another method for distinguishing text. You can apply effects such as bolding, italics, and underlining, or change the font color.

Sets of formatting attributes are saved as styles and are named with suggested uses. You can apply a style by clicking the buttons in the Styles group on the Home tab, as shown in Figure 3-7.

> **Did You Know?**
>
> The keyboard shortcuts to apply formatting to selected text are **Ctrl + B** (Bold), **Ctrl + I** (Italic), and **Ctrl + U** (Underline).

FIGURE 3-7
Styles group

Style group

The alignment of text specifies how the text is spaced between the margins. Text can be aligned to the right or left margin, centered, or justified. **Justified** text appears evenly spaced between the left and right margins.

You can copy a set of formatting options to apply to another area of text or to multiple areas. The **Format Painter** is a tool that copies the formatting of selected text. When the pointer is placed over another area in your document, it changes to a paintbrush, indicating that you can apply the formatting attributes to the selected text. Clicking the Format Painter button once enables you to copy the formatting attributes to one other text area. To format multiple selections, double-click the Format Painter button, then click or select the text you want to format.

> **Computer Concepts**
>
> Live Preview is another feature new to Office 2007. When choosing formatting options for selected text, the selected text displays with the formatting options as you position the mouse over them. This enables you to see how the formatting options will display before you select them.

2.1.3.8
2.2.1.18

TABLE 3-1
Different font styles

FONT NAME
Calibri
Cambria
Arial
Century Schoolbook
Bradley Hand ITC
Edwardian Script

$\int$ TEP-BY-STEP 3.5

1. Press **Ctrl + Home**, select the first three lines of text in the document, click the Home tab, then in the Font group, click the **Bold** button. The text appears thicker.

2. With the first three lines of text still selected, in the Font group, click the **Italic** button. The text appears slanted.

3. In the Font group, click the **Underline** button. A line appears under the text.

4. Click the **Underline** button again to remove the line. The font buttons are toggle buttons, so clicking again removes the effect.

Did You Know?

Overusing font changes and effects can distract from the text you are trying to highlight and can make your document difficult to read. It is better to use one or two effects to distinguish text and to use one or two complementary fonts in your document.

5. In the Font group, click the **Font** list arrow, then click **Arial Black**. The font changes to Arial Black, a sans serif font.

6. In the Font group, click the **Font Size** list arrow, then click **16**. The font size increases from 11 pt to 16 pt.

7. In the Font group, click the **Font Color** button list arrow, then in the Standard Colors section of the menu, click **Blue**. The font color changes to blue.

8. In the Paragraph group, click the **Center** button. The text is now center-aligned.

9. Select the text *Friday*, then in the Styles group, click the **Heading 2** button in the Styles gallery. The text appears light blue, bold, and larger.

10. With the text *Friday* still selected, double-click the **Format Painter** button in the Clipboard group.

11. Position the pointer over the text *Saturday*. When the pointer changes to the format paint pointer, select the text **Saturday**.

12. Position the pointer over the text *Sunday*. When the pointer changes to the format paint pointer, select the text **Sunday**, then click the **Format Painter** button to turn it off. The document looks much better, as shown in Figure 3-8.

STEP-BY-STEP 3.5 Continued

FIGURE 3-8
Formatted document

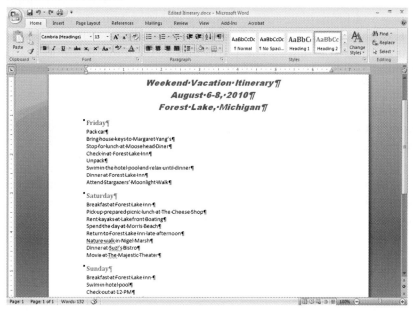

13. Save your work, then leave the document and Word open for the next Step-by-Step.

 Working in a Connected World

DESKTOP PUBLISHING

Using Microsoft Word you can create complex multipage documents. **Desktop publishing (DTP)** software, such as Adobe PageMaker, QuarkXPress, and Microsoft Publisher, provides more sophisticated tools to create newsletters, flyers, and other publications. Using a computer and any kind of DTP software, anyone can learn the page layout skills needed to create publications.

People who lay out newspapers or create product packaging, flyers with cutouts, signage, and other large- and small-scale projects are called DTP professionals. DTP professionals do more than page layout, and they need to have a background in or understanding of marketing, multimedia, graphic design, and printer specifications. They are often hired as in-house staff or on a freelance basis by companies to use combinations of their skills and create promotional materials. A DTP professional understands how a project gets from the idea stage (what do we want to create and what message should it have) to the finished product in a customer's hands. A bachelor's or associate's degree is often required for these types of jobs. Most DTP professionals have taken classes in marketing and graphic design.

Undo and Redo Actions

Word keeps track of the actions you make while working in your document. Each keystroke you make or button you click is recorded and can be undone and redone. This feature is useful when editing and formatting documents. For instance, you can apply a type of formatting such as bold to text, then immediately undo it if you don't like the effect. You can also undo and redo typing changes that you make. The Undo and Redo buttons are available on the Quick Access toolbar.

The Undo feature is used to reverse the actions you have performed, starting with the most recent task. You can use the Undo feature to reverse one action or several actions at a time.

2.1.3.4

The Redo feature is used to repeat a task you have undone. If you have not undone any actions, the Redo feature is not available and appears dimmed. You can only redo tasks in the order in which they were undone.

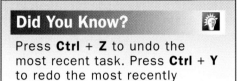

Did You Know?

Press **Ctrl + Z** to undo the most recent task. Press **Ctrl + Y** to redo the most recently undone action.

S TEP-BY-STEP 3.6

1. Click the **Undo** list arrow on the Quick Access toolbar. The list of actions you have performed appears, as shown in Figure 3-9.

FIGURE 3-9
List of recently performed actions

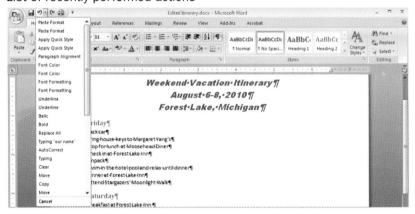

2. Click **Paste Format** from the list that appears.

3. Click the **Redo** button on the Quick Access toolbar. The formatting is reapplied.

4. Click the **Undo** button on the Quick Access toolbar. The last action is reversed and the formatting is removed.

5. Click the **Redo** button again. The formatting is reapplied.

6. Save your work, then leave the document and Word open for the next Step-by-Step.

Use Paragraph Formatting

Paragraph formatting includes adding or moving page breaks, using tabs, and adjusting the space between lines of text. You can also choose options such as the amount of space that appears after paragraphs and indentations for the beginning of a paragraph.

Consistency is an important consideration when formatting a document. Applying the same formatting options to each of the days of the week in the Edited Itinerary.docx file, as you did in the previous Step-by-Step, gives each day equal visual importance. Applying consistent para-graph formatting, such as line spacing, makes your document easier to read. To use the Format Painter to apply paragraph formatting, you must select the paragraph mark at the end of a line.

2.2.1.3
2.2.1.4
2.2.1.10
2.2.1.11

Word has rulers that you can display to help adjust the paragraph formatting. Tabs are markers on the horizontal ruler that you can adjust to change the paragraph or line indentation. See Table 3-2 for the different tab types available. To add a new tab, click the tab indicator at the top of the vertical ruler until the tab type displays, then click the horizontal ruler to set the tab. You can move an existing tab by dragging it to a new position on the ruler.

> **Computer Concepts**
>
> **White space** is the term used in desktop publishing and word processing to indicate the blank areas of the page. It is important to consider the amount of white space in your document. Too little white space makes your document difficult to read; too much white space can be distracting and can make it difficult for your eye to know where to go next.

TABLE 3-2
Tab types

NAME	TAB	USED TO
Left tab	└	Mark where a line or paragraph will start from the left margin
Right tab	┘	Mark where a line or paragraph will start from the right margin
Center tab	┴	Mark where the center of a line or paragraph will be
Decimal tab	┴	Align numbers from a decimal point
Bar tab	│	Insert a vertical bar through the current paragraph at the tab position
First line indent	▽	Set the indentation for the first line of a paragraph
Hanging indent	⌂	Set the indentation for the second and all other lines of a paragraph

S TEP-BY-STEP 3.7

1. Click the **View** tab, then in the Show/Hide group, click the **Ruler** check box to select it, if necessary. Rulers appear at the top and left side of the document window.

2. Press **Ctrl** + **A** to select all of the text in the document.

STEP-BY-STEP 3.7 Continued

3. Click the **Home** tab, then in the Paragraph group, click the **Line spacing** button, click **1.5** on the menu, then deselect the text. The space between each line is increased, as shown in Figure 3-10.

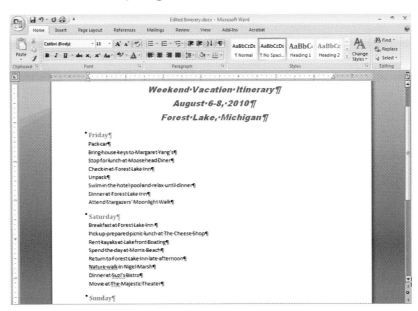

4. Press and hold **Ctrl**, then click the word *Friday*. Make sure that you do not select the paragraph mark at the end of the line.

5. Click the **Line spacing** button, then click **Add Space After Paragraph** on the menu.

6. With the text still selected, in the Clipboard group, double-click the **Format Painter** button

7. Use the format painter pointer ▱I to apply the paragraph formatting to the lines **Saturday** and **Sunday**. Press **Esc** to deselect the Format Painter. Additional line spacing helps to set each day apart.

8. Make sure that the left tab is showing at the intersection of the two rulers, as shown in Figure 3-11. If necessary, click the tab indicator until the left tab appears.

Left tab

STEP-BY-STEP 3.7 Continued

9. Select the text in between *Friday* and *Saturday*, then click the horizontal ruler at the .5" mark, then press **Tab**. The activities for Friday are indented.

10. Click the **Format Painter** button, then use the format painter pointer to copy the indentation to the lines under Saturday and Sunday, then press **Esc**. The paragraph formatting is complete, as shown in Figure 3-12.

FIGURE 3-12
Format Painter applied

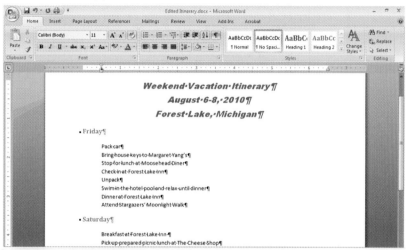

11. Save and close **Edited Itinerary.docx**, then leave Word open for the next Step-by-Step.

Apply Bullets, Numbering, and Outlines

Bullets and numbers can help to distinguish the items in a list. Bulleted lists are used when the items are of equal importance or do not need to appear in a particular order, such as a list of product features. Bullets are small characters, such as dots, that appear before each item. Numbered lists indicate an order of sequence or importance, such as directions or a Top 10 list.

To apply bullets or numbers to an existing list, select all of the items in the list, then use the Bullets and Numbering buttons on the Home tab in the Paragraph group. You can also apply bullets and numbering before you type your list. By separating the items with a line break, each item you type will have a bullet in front of it. To create a new numbered list, type 1., press the spacebar, then start typing your list. Word will automatically create a numbered list for you. To end your list, press Enter twice.

You have many options for both bulleted and numbered lists. You can create a custom bullet or choose any symbol to be a bullet. You can choose upper or lowercase letters, Arabic numbers (1, 2, 3, and so on) or Roman numerals (I, II, II, and so on) for a numbered list.

2.2.1.5
2.2.1.6

Outlines indicate a hierarchy, or structure, of elements. The Multilevel List button is used to create an outline by assigning levels to lines of text. Text that is higher in the structure appears larger and to the left. Lines also have a numeric or alphabetical indicator. Figure 3-13 shows an example of an outline.

FIGURE 3-13
Sample outline

```
1)  Introduction
    a)  Who we are
    b)  What we do
        i)   Philanthropy
        ii)  Membership
        iii) Community
2)  Outstanding Members
    a)  Past
        i)   State Senator Gary Fordham
        ii)  Dr. Janet Percy
        iii) Joe Lee, Esq.
    b)  Present
        i)   Mayor Beverly Goldberg
        ii)  Dr. Ari Kumar
        iii) George Benson, merchant
    c)  Future
        i)   You!
3)  How you can join
    a)  Sponsorship
    b)  Commitment
    c)  Introductory period
```

STEP-BY-STEP 3.8

1. Open the document **Packing.docx** from your Data Files, then save it as **Packing and Directions.docx**.

2. Select the seven lines of text under *To pack*.

3. On the Home tab in the Paragraph group, click the **Bullets** button. Bullets appear before each item in the list.

4. With the bulleted list still selected, click the **Bullets** button list arrow, then click the **black square** in the Bullet Library section of the menu. The bullets change to squares.

5. Select the six lines of text under Directions.

6. In the Paragraph group, click the **Numbering** button. Numbers appear before each item in the list.

7. Position the insertion point at the end of item 6, then press **Enter**. The number *7*, followed by a period, appears before the insertion point in the new line, as shown in Figure 3-14.

STEP-BY-STEP 3.8 Continued

FIGURE 3-14
Numbered list continues

8. Type **16 Andrea Road is on the right** in the new line, then press **Enter** three times. Numbering is no longer selected on the blank line.

9. In the Paragraph group, click the **Multilevel List** button arrow, then click the **second option** in the first row of the List Library, as shown in Figure 3-15.

FIGURE 3-15
Multilevel list options

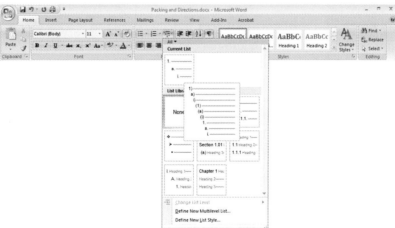

10. Type **Introduction**, then press **Enter**.

11. Press **Tab** to indent the text, then type **Who I am**.

12. Press **Enter**, then type **What I do**, then press **Enter**.

13. Press **Shift + Tab**, then type **Background**. The multilevel list is promoted one level.

STEP-BY-STEP 3.8 Continued

14. Type the rest of the list shown in Figure 3-16, pressing **Tab** to decrease the level, and **Shift** + **Tab** to move up a level.

FIGURE 3-16
Multilevel list

¶
1)→ Introduction¶
   a)→ Who·I·am¶
   b)→ What·I·do¶
2)→ Background¶
   a)→ Education¶
   b)→ Early·employment¶
   c)→ Teaching·experience¶
3)→ Fields·of·study¶
   a)→ Engineering¶
      i) → Civil¶
      ii)→ Mechanical¶
   b)→ French·language¶
   c)→ Journalism¶

15. Save your work, close the document, then leave Word open for the next Step-by-Step.

Check Spelling and Grammar

The Spelling & Grammar tool can be used to help proof your document. Word's built-in dictionary identifies possible misspellings and grammatical errors as you type. Proper nouns, such as people's names, are often identified as misspellings. You can choose to add a name you frequently use to the dictionary, or instruct the Spelling & Grammar Checker to ignore the word. The AutoCorrect tool fixes common typing mistakes, such as *annd* to *and* automatically as you type.

You can keep track of document statistics such as page count and Word count. Some of this information displays on the status bar, but you can also view the Word Count dialog box to display other statistics. This feature can be very helpful when you need to create a document that has a minimum or maximum word count.

> **Did You Know?**
>
> The Word dictionary contains English-language words that are frequently used. It is very comprehensive but may not include some words that you personally use every day. For instance, many professional or medical terms, foreign language terms, slang, acronyms, and Instant Message terms such as *rotfl* (Rolling On The Floor Laughing) are identified as errors in Word. Different dialects—for example, British English versus American English—present some words with different spelling. You can create a custom dictionary in Word that includes your frequently used terms or specifies the dialect or language.

2.1.3.7
2.2.2.19
2.2.1.21

These tools can help you create a professional, error-free document, but they are not a substitute for proofreading your document yourself. Proofreading means looking through the document as your intended audience will. Proofreading can catch or fix things such as using the wrong word, which if it is spelled correctly, Word may not identify.

STEP-BY-STEP 3.9

1. Open the document **Proofing Letter.docx** from your Data Files. Scroll through the document, noting the red and green wavy lines that appear.

2. Press **Ctrl + Home** to position the insertion point at the beginning of the document.

3. On the Review tab in the Proofing group, click the **Spelling & Grammar** button. The Spelling and Grammar dialog box appears, as shown in Figure 3-17.

FIGURE 3-17
Spelling and Grammar dialog box

4. The first error Word identifies is **Maison**. Click **Ignore All** because this is a proper noun.

5. Click **Change** to accept the next four changes that Word identifies, then click **Close** in the dialog box. The spelling and grammar in the document has been fixed.

6. Read through the document. In the second paragraph, click after the word *earl*, and type **y** to change *earl* to *early*.

STEP-BY-STEP 3.9 Continued

7. Press **Ctrl** + **End**, press **Enter**, type **yuo**, then press the **spacebar**. AutoCorrect changes from *yuo* to *You*. The document appears as shown in Figure 3-18.

FIGURE 3-18
Spelling and grammar corrected

8. Select **You**, then type **Your Name**.

9. Click the Review tab, and in the Proofing Group, click the **Word Count** button. The document statistics display in the Word Count dialog box. Click **OK** to close the dialog box.

10. Save the document as **Proofed Letter.docx**, close the document, then leave Word open for the next Step-by-Step.

Prepare a Document for Printing

Before you print a document, you should verify that it looks the way you want it to appear when printed and that all of the elements you want to appear are there. Formatting a document for printing involves using the Print Preview feature to identify areas that you want to change, such as adding or removing page breaks, inserting the date, or inserting any special formatting characters.

Adding or removing page breaks can help to balance the information that appears on each page in a multipage document. You can choose to add a page break on the first page to increase the amount of text that appears on the second page, for instance. Page breaks can also help to ensure that certain sections of text are kept together on one page (a heading with its corresponding paragraph, for instance).

Word includes many special formatting characteristics and symbols that you can add to your document. In addition to text characters such as letters and numbers that are associated with different fonts, you can add characters that are mathematical or currency-related and symbols such as the copyright © symbol.

You can also insert the current date and time. This action can let the reader know when a document was last saved, opened, or modified before it was printed. You can set the date and time to update automatically when a document is opened or to set a static date and time that does not change.

You learned the basics of printing in Lesson 1. You can specify many other printing options such as how to print from another printer, make additional copies, and set the print quality or colors. A printer can handle multiple print jobs at a time. By default, jobs are printed in the order in which they are sent to the printer. You can manage the jobs by cancelling, pausing, and deleting them. Common printing errors include running out of paper or starting a job when the printer is offline. Table 3-3 lists some printing errors and how to fix them.

2.1.4.1
2.1.4.2
2.1.4.3
2.1.4.4
2.1.4.5
2.2.1.7
2.2.1.8
2.2.1.12

TABLE 3-3
Troubleshooting printing errors

ERROR	SOLUTION
Error messages display	Write down the error message. Consult the printer manual or your instructor or lab manager to see if the error is identified; follow the suggested steps to fix the problem.
Printer is offline	If you are connected to a printer through a network, check to see that the cables are connected. If you have a wireless network, check that the printer is connected to the network hub.
Printer driver is incorrect	Drivers are software programs that communicate between software and devices. If your driver is not compatible with your program or device, contact your printer manufacturer for an updated driver.
Document does not print	Check to see that the printer is on and has paper. Also make sure that you selected the correct printer in the Print dialog box.
Document doesn't print correctly	Always use Print Preview before printing your document. If you still encounter problems, check the paper size you have selected and that the printer memory is sufficient for your job. You can also print a test page to make sure that the printer is working correctly.

STEP-BY-STEP 3.10

1. Open the document **Preview Letter.docx** from your Data Files. Save it as **Finished Letter.docx**.

2. Click the **Office Button**, point to **Print**, then click **Print Preview**. Your document appears as it will when printed.

STEP-BY-STEP 3.10 Continued

3. On the **Print Preview** tab in the Preview group, click the **Next Page** button. The second page appears as shown in Figure 3-19.

FIGURE 3-19
Second page in Print Preview

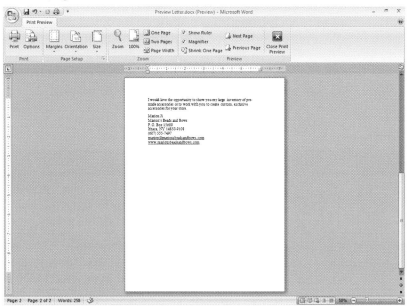

4. Using the **One Page** and **Two Pages** buttons in the Zoom group, view the pages side by side, then one at a time.

5. On the Print Preview tab, click the **Close Print Preview** button.

6. Click at the beginning of the line *Please contact me*, click the **Insert tab**, then in the Pages group, click **Page Break** to add a page break. This keeps the header with the paragraph of text.

7. Click at the end of the first line in the document. In the Symbols group, click the **Symbol** button. Click the ™ symbol. The trademark symbol is added.

8. Click after **Morgan's Crafts**. Type **(c)**. The text changes to the copyright symbol, ©.

9. Select the date in the third paragraph of the document, then press **Delete**. In the Text group, click the **Date & Time** button.

10. Click the third option in the Date and Time dialog box, then click **OK**.

11. Click the **Office** Button, point to **Print**, then click **Print**. The Print dialog box opens, as shown in Figure 3-20.

STEP-BY-STEP 3.10 Continued

FIGURE 3-20
Print dialog box

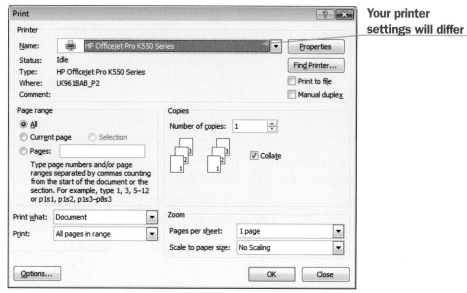

Your printer
settings will differ

12. Choose any appropriate print options, verify with your instructor that it is OK to print, then click **OK**. If you are not able to print, click **Cancel** in the Print dialog box and skip Step 13.

13. On the task bar, click the Printer symbol to open the Print manager, shown in Figure 3-21. Close the Print manager.

FIGURE 3-21
Print manager

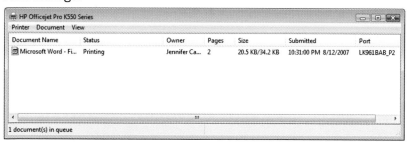

14. Save and close the document, then exit Word.

SUMMARY

In this lesson, you learned:

■ The Delete and Backspace keys can be used to remove text from your document.

■ The Clipboard stores text that you copy or remove using the Cut and Copy features. You can insert items from the Clipboard using the Paste feature.

■ To quickly move text to a nearby location in your document without adding an item to the Clipboard, use the drag-and-drop feature.

■ You can search for text to locate or replace it in your document. You can choose to replace all instances of a word or phrase in order to make a consistent change.

■ Text effects such as bolding and underlining can help make text stand out. You can also change the size or color of text to add emphasis.

■ Any task that you perform can be undone. You can undo tasks one at a time or undo several tasks at the same time. Once you have undone a task, you can choose to redo it.

■ Paragraph formatting options include adding space between each line in your document and inserting space before or after a specific line. You can also adjust how lines are spaced from the margins.

■ Adding bullets and numbers to a list can help distinguish each item. Outlines are helpful when you have a specific hierarchy for your document.

■ Checking the spelling and grammar of your document is an important step when proofing. You should also take the time to read through your document before you print it.

■ Previewing your document is the first step in preparing your proofread document for printing. You can adjust page breaks and add the date or special symbols and characters.

■ You can choose to print multiple copies of your document, change the printer, solve printing problems, and manage multiple print jobs at once.

VOCABULARY *Review*

Define the following terms:

AutoCorrect	Format Painter	Redo
Bulleted list	Justify	Replace
Cut	Mini-toolbar	Ruler
Copy	Numbered list	Script
Desktop publishing (DTP)	Office Clipboard	Serif
Dialog box	Outline	Sans serif
Drag-and-drop	Overtype mode	Spacebar
Editing	Paragraph formatting	Tab
Find	Paste	Undo
Fonts	Points	White space
Formatting	Proofreading	

REVIEW*Questions*

SCREEN IDENTIFICATION

Identify the screen elements.

FIGURE 3-22
Screen identification

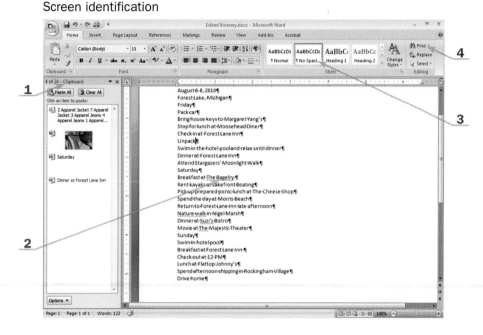

1. _____

2. _____

3. _____

4. _____

MULTIPLE CHOICE

Circle the correct answer.

1. The _____ key removes characters one at a time from the left of the insertion point.
   A. Overtype
   B. Delete
   C. Backspace
   D. Enter

2. The _____ stores text and formatting for future use.
   A. Driver
   B. Dictionary
   C. Clipboard
   D. Save

3. The _____ is the blank areas in your document.
   A. Clipboard
   B. White space
   C. Ribbon
   D. Desktop

TRUE/FALSE

Circle T if the statement is true or F if the statement is false.

T   F   1. Italics are an example of text formatting.

T   F   2. Font size is measured in points.

T   F   3. A line at the end of a character stroke is called a sans serif.

T   F   4. When more information is needed before an action can be completed, a dialog box opens.

T   F   5. The Format Painter is used to copy text to insert in a new location.

HANDS-ON REVIEW

1. Open the file Recipe.docx. Using the Delete key, remove the word **family** from the first paragraph.

2. Using keyboard shortcuts, cut the line of text **Serves 6** and paste it under the date so that it is the third line.

3. Use drag and drop to move the paragraph that begins *While the soup simmers* to be the second paragraph under the heading Directions.

4. Find and replace all instances of **Rice** to **Couscous**.

5. Change the font of the recipe title to bold, centered, and red. Increase the font size of the title text to 16.

6. Undo the last two actions, then redo them.

7. Change the line spacing to 1.5. Apply bolding and add space before the lines **Soup, Dumplings**, and **Directions**.

8. Add a bullet of your choice to the lists under Soup and Dumplings. Add letters to the list under Directions. (*Hint:* Use the Numbering button.)

9. Check the spelling and grammar in the document. Accept all suggestions.

10. Preview your document, then close Print Preview. Add a page break before Directions. Set the date and time at the top of the document to update automatically when the document opens.

11. Specify to print four copies of your document, but do not print them. Click Cancel in the Print dialog box.

12. Save the document as Edited Recipe.docx.

PROJECTS

PROJECT 3-1

1. Open the document Letter.docx from your data files and save it as Cover Letter.docx.

2. Use the text-formatting skills you learned in the lesson to add emphasis to the text in the document.

3. Adjust the line spacing and indentation of the text in the document.

4. Read the list of job experiences, and decide whether it would be better to make it a bulleted or numbered list, then do so.

5. Check the spelling and grammar, then preview your document.

6. Make any adjustments to the formatting to make the document fit on one page.

7. Save Cover Letter.docx.

PROJECT 3-2

1. Open the document Summer Vacation.docx from your data files and save it as NYC Vacation.docx.

2. Use drag and drop to move the text *New York City* to be the second line.

3. Use Cut and Paste to move the line that begins *The highlight* to be after the line that begins *We took advantage.*

4. Use Find and Replace to change the second instance of **New York City** to **Manhattan.** Do not change the first instance.

5. Save NYC Vacation.docx.

CRITICAL *Thinking*

ACTIVITY 3-1

In a blank Word document, type one paragraph about the importance of each of the topics listed below. Include the reasons why you should do each action and the benefit to the readers of your documents. Proof, spell check, and apply formatting to the document. Save the document as **Formatting and Printing.docx.**

1. Text formatting.

2. Paragraph formatting.

3. Proofreading and previewing your document.

ACTIVITY 3-2

1. Print and review the hard copy of the document **Spelling and Grammar.docx**.

2. Circle any spelling and grammar errors that you find.

3. Run the Spelling and Grammar tool.

4. Compare the errors you found with the errors found by Word.

5. Make a list of the items identified by Word as errors that you would not correct.

6. Make a list of the items you identified as errors that Word did not identify.

7. Make any additional corrections, then save it as Proofed Invitation.docx.

 TEAMWORK

As a group, come up with a document that describes the differences between the following terms:

- Bulleted lists *versus* numbered lists
- Cut and paste *versus* drag and drop
- Text formatting *versus* paragraph formatting
- Serif fonts *versus* sans serif fonts

USING TABLES

Estimated Time: 1.5 hours

OBJECTIVES

Upon completion of this lesson, you should be able to:

- Insert a table and enter text
- Modify rows and columns
- Format a table
- Create and modify a table grid
- Modify tables
- Convert text to a table

VOCABULARY

Ascending

AutoFit

Border

Cell

Column

Contextual tab

Descending

Draw table

Embedding

Eraser

Formula

Header

Insert Table

Integrate

Linking

Merge

Orientation

Quick Tables

Realignment

Row

Shading

Split

Table

Table Styles

Tables organize information in horizontal rows and vertical columns. Information is contained in cells, which are the intersections of rows and columns. Tables can include a header row or column that describes the data displayed in the row or column. An example of a table is shown in Figure 4-1.

In Figure 4-1, the top row and the far-left column (blue with white text) are the header row and column, respectively. They are formatted to stand out so that it is easy to distinguish them from the table data. The other cells in the table contain the table data. You can either read a row across to see all of the data for that particular item or you can read a column from top to bottom to see the different data in that column.

FIGURE 4-1
Sample table

Item #	Category	Title	Size	Quantity	Price
1	Bow	Daisies & Dots	One size	6	$4.00
2	Bow	Dalmatian	One size	6	$4.00
3	Bow	Back to School	One size	6	$4.00
4	Headband	Orange & Pink	One size	2	$10.00
5	Headband	Lavender	One size	1	$8.00
6	Leotard	Flowers & Lace	6/7 (Small)	1	$20.00
7	Leotard	Pretty Princess	6/7 (Small)	1	$20.00
8	T-shirt	Pink & Rainbow	5T	1	$10.00

Header row — *Cell* — *Row* — *Column*

When you work with data in a table, you may need to modify the table. You can sort the data in a table alphabetically and add or delete rows and columns. You can also move tables to another location in the document.

To change the effect of the table, you can add formatting. **Table Styles** apply borders, shading, and text effects to a table. You can also apply formatting manually. Text can also be adjusted to a cell border or **realigned** so that it reads top to bottom instead of left to right. Rows and columns can be resized to fit the data. The table in Figure 4-1 has been formatted with **shading** to distinguish the rows, while **borders** distinguish the header row and the top and bottom of the table. The blue column and row indicate that they contain identifying information.

There are many ways to insert a table. You can use the **Insert Table** button to choose the number of rows and columns for your table. Using the **Draw Table** command and the **Eraser** tools can help you create a table that fits your precise need. If you have text that is separated logically using tabs, commas, or paragraph marks, you can convert it to a table.

Insert a Table and Enter Text

Before inserting a new table, you should think about the data you want to include in it. When you are fairly certain about the number of columns and rows you want to insert, and if you will be typing your data directly into the table, you can use the Insert Table feature. The Insert Table feature creates a grid of evenly sized columns and rows.

2-2.2.1
2-2.2.2

After your table is created, you can enter data in the table. Press Tab and the arrow keys to navigate in the table. Later, you can modify the table to insert or delete columns or rows.

STEP-BY-STEP 4.1

1. Start Word. A new, blank document opens.

2. Type **Inventory Sheet** at the top of the document, then press **Enter**. The title of your table is Inventory Sheet. You are now ready to insert the table.

3. Click the **Insert** tab, then in the Tables group, click the **Table** button. The Insert Table menu opens.

4. Drag to insert a table with four rows and four columns. While you are selecting the rows and columns in the gallery, make sure *4x4 Table* appears at the top of the gallery, as shown in Figure 4-2. Your table is inserted with equally sized rows and columns.

STEP-BY-STEP 4.1 Continued

FIGURE 4-2
Insert Table menu

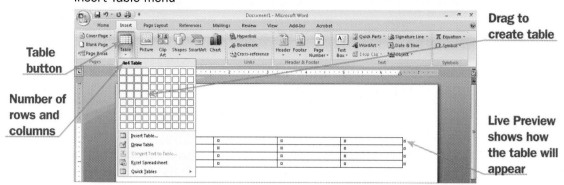

5. Click in the first cell in the top row to position the insertion point if necessary, then type **Inventory Number**.

6. Press **Tab**, type **Item Description**, press **Tab**, type **Price**, press **Tab**, then type **Quantity**.

7. Press **Tab** to move to the first cell in the second row, then use Figure 4-3 to complete the rest of the table.

FIGURE 4-3
Text inserted into table

Inventory·Sheet¶

Inventory·Number¤	Item·Description¤	Price¤	Quantity¤	¤
149¤	Red·t-shirt¤	$14.00¤	34¤	¤
150¤	Green·t-shirt¤	$14.00¤	20¤	¤
151¤	Blue·and·yellow·t-shirt¤	$16.00¤	45¤	¤

¶

8. Save the document as **Inventory Sheet.docx**, then leave the document and Word open for the next Step-by-Step.

Modify Rows and Columns

When creating tables, you can add or delete rows and columns to fit the data you need to enter. To add a row onto the end of your table, place the insertion point in the last cell, then press Tab. A new row is automatically created.

To modify a table, or a selection of columns or rows, you must know how to select portions of a table. Table 4-1 outlines different selection methods.

TABLE 4-1
Table selection methods

TO SELECT	DO THIS	POINTER
The entire table	Position the pointer over the top-left corner of the table, and click the Table Select button ⊞	
A row	Position the pointer to the left of the row and click	⬈
Multiple rows	Position the pointer to the left of the top or bottom row of the range, click, then drag up or down to select the range	⬈
A column	Position the pointer above the column and click	↓
Multiple columns	Position the pointer above the left or right column of the range, click, then drag left or right to select the range	↓

You are not restricted to adding rows onto the end of a table. If you want to insert a new column or row in between a current row or column, use the Table Tools Layout tab. You can choose to add rows above or below the current row or to the left or right of the current column.

2-2.2.3

Modifying the height of rows or width of columns can help to size them appropriately based on the amount of data in each cell. You can change the height or width of the entire table, certain rows or columns, or choose to size the cells to fit their contents. Using the AutoFit feature means that as cell contents and formatting change, the columns and rows will adjust accordingly.

Did You Know?

Contextual tabs, such as the Table Tools Layout tab, appear on the Ribbon only when certain actions or selections are made. They provide context- and task-specific tools and buttons.

STEP-BY-STEP 4.2

1. Position the pointer above the column **Inventory Number**, then when the pointer changes to a black down arrow, click to select the column. Use the tips in Table 4-1 throughout this Step-by-Step to select different parts of the table. The column is highlighted, and the Table Tools Layout and Table Tools Design contextual tabs are active, as shown in Figure 4-4.

STEP-BY-STEP 4.2 Continued

FIGURE 4-4
Table Tools Layout and Table Tools Design contextual tabs activated

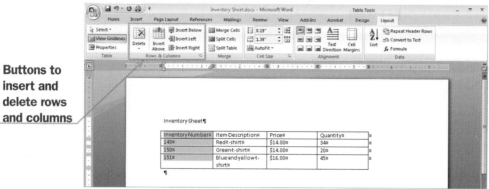

**Buttons to
insert and
delete rows
and columns**

2. Click the **Table Tools Layout** tab, if necessary, then in the Rows and Columns group, click the **Insert Right** button. A new column appears in between the Inventory Number and Item Description columns.

3. Click in the top row of the new column, type **Color**, then press the **down arrow**.

4. Press the **down arrow** to enter the color information: **Red**, **Green**, **Blue and yellow**, and **Purple**.

5. Position the insertion point in the last cell of the table, then press **Tab**. A new row is inserted.

6. Enter the following data in the new row and press **Tab** to move between cells: **152**, **Purple**, **Purple polka dot t-shirt**, **$16.00**, **18**.

7. Position the pointer to the left of the **149** row, click to select the row. On the **Table Tools Layout** tab in the Rows & Columns group, click the **Insert Above** button. A new row is inserted.

8. Enter the following data in the new row, pressing **Tab** to move between cells: **148**, **Brown**, **Brown t-shirt**, **$14.00**, **29**.

9. Position the pointer in between the Price and Quantity columns, click, then use the pointer to drag the column divider to the left so that the Price column cell contents fit precisely in the column. You manually adjusted the size of the column, and the table appears as shown in Figure 4-5.

FIGURE 4-5
New column inserted, row added, and column widths adjusted

Inventory·Sheet¶

Inventory·Number¤	Color¤	Item·Description¤	Price¤	Quantity¤	¤
148¤	Brown¤	Brown·t-shirt¤	$14.00¤	29¤	¤
149¤	Red¤	Red·t-shirt¤	$14.00¤	34¤	¤
150¤	Green¤	Green·t-shirt¤	$14.00¤	20¤	¤
151¤	Blue·and·yellow¤	Blue·and·yellow·t-shirt¤	$16.00¤	45¤	¤
152¤	Purple¤	Purple·polka·dot·t-shirt¤	$16.00¤	18¤	¤

¶

**Enter text in
new column**

STEP-BY-STEP 4.2 Continued

10. On the Table Tools Layout tab in the Cell Size group, click the **AutoFit** button, then click **AutoFit Contents**. The columns in the table adjust to fit their contents, as shown in Figure 4-6.

FIGURE 4-6
Columns AutoFitted

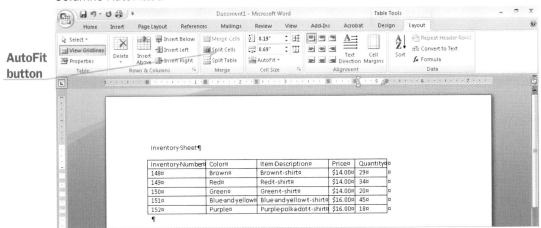

11. Save the document, then leave the document and Word open for the next Step-by-Step.

Format a Table

Adding formatting to a table can help to define the header row. Borders can distinguish one row or column from another. Shading is another tool that can help to set your table apart from the rest of your document and make it more readable.

You can use all of the formatting techniques you learned about in Lesson 3, including changing the font type, color or size; adding enhancements, such as bold and italics; and adjusting the alignment to the center or edges of the columns. Changing the text orientation will make the text read from top to bottom.

As always, keep in mind the readability of your table. Formatting should be used to clarify, define, and enhance your table, but it should not be used as a distraction.

> **Did You Know?**
>
> You can select a row, column, cell, or the entire table by clicking the Select button in the Table group on the Table Tools Layout tab, then clicking an option.

2-2.2.4

STEP-BY-STEP 4.3

1. Select the title of the table, **Inventory Sheet**. Using the buttons in the Font and Paragraph groups on the Home tab, format the title as **Bold**, **16-point**, and **Centered**.

2. Select the first row of the table, click the **Table Tools Design** tab, click the **Shading** button arrow in the Table Styles group, then click the **Orange** color box under Standard colors.

STEP-BY-STEP 4.3 Continued

3. With the first row still selected, format the row as **Bold** and **12-point**. The column widths adjust to fit the increased font size of the first row.

4. With the first row still selected, click the **Table Tools Layout** tab. In the Alignment group, click the **Text Direction** button, drag the row's bottom divider to resize to fit the contents if necessary, then deselect the row. Resize column 1, if necessary. The text in the first row reads from top to bottom, as shown in Figure 4-7.

FIGURE 4-7
Formatting applied to table

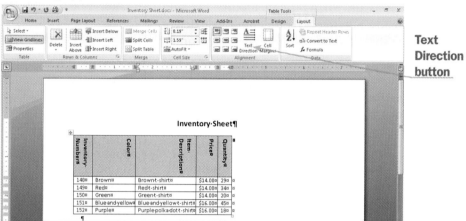

5. Select the rows **148** to **152**, then on the Home tab in the Paragraph group, click the **Align Text Right** button. The text in the selected rows is now aligned to the right border of the columns.

6. Select the entire table, then change the font to **Arial** and the color to **Blue** (under Standard Colors), resize the first row and column again if necessary, then deselect the table. The table is now formatted, as shown in Figure 4-8.

7. Save and close the document, then leave Word open for the next Step-by-Step.

FIGURE 4-8
Table formatting complete

Inventory Number¤	Color¤	Item Description¤	Price¤	Quantity¤	¤ ¶
148¤	Brown¤	Brown·t-shirt¤	$14.00¤	29¤	¤
149¤	Red¤	Red·t-shirt¤	$14.00¤	34¤	¤
150¤	Green¤	Green·t-shirt¤	$14.00¤	20¤	¤
151¤	Blue·and·yellow¤	Blue·and·yellow·t-shirt¤	$16.00¤	45¤	¤
152¤	Purple¤	Purple·polka·dot·t-shirt¤	$16.00¤	18¤	¤

Inventory·Sheet¶

Create and Modify a Table Grid

You can use the drawing and eraser tools to create and modify a table. These tools become available when you click the Insert Table button on the Insert tab in the Tables group. The drawing tools are useful when you are creating tables with rows and columns of different sizes. The Rulers can help size and position the table cells as you are drawing them.

Once the table is drawn, you can modify it using the tools you already practiced. You can add or delete rows, format the table, and adjust the sizing of columns and rows.

The Eraser button is available on the Table Tools Design tab in the Draw Borders group. When you click the Eraser button, the pointer changes to an eraser, which you can use to delete column and row borders in the table.

You can also merge and split cells. **Merging** cells combines two cells into one. **Splitting** cells adds a divider and creates multiple cells from one. The Eraser and Draw Table tools are one way to split and merge tables.

2-2.2.1
2-2.2.3

Did You Know?

You can apply a simple mathematical **formula** to data in a Word table, such as **=SUM(Above)**, which totals the values in the column above. To do so, place the insertion point in the blank cell below or to the right of where you want to insert the formula. On the Table Tools Layout tab in the Data group, click the Formula button. The Formula dialog box opens. Enter a new formula or accept the suggested formula, then click OK.

Did You Know?

Similar to using a template, you can insert a preformatted table, such as a calendar, into your document using **Quick Tables**. To do so, click the Insert tab, then in the Tables group, click the Table button. On the Insert Table menu, point to Quick Tables, then click an option in the gallery.

Trends in Technology

INTEGRATING DATA FROM OTHER PROGRAMS

The programs in the Microsoft Office 2007 suite all work together. Not only do they share a common interface and tools such as the Ribbon, dialog boxes, and the Office Button, but you can also **integrate** or insert and edit data from one program to another.

A spreadsheet is an Excel document. Like a Word table, it separates data into cells, rows, and columns. Excel is used to perform mathematical functions such as creating sums and data analysis such as comparisons and projections.

Integrating data from other programs saves you time and reduces errors. Instead of retyping data from an Excel spreadsheet into a Word table, you can copy the cells from Excel and paste them into Word. There are two ways to paste the cells: linking and embedding. **Linking** data means that the information is still connected to the source file and that any updates made to the source file (in this case, an Excel spreadsheet) will also be made to the Word file. **Embedding** data means that the information is copied into the destination file without any connection to the source, and changes made to the source will not be updated in the destination file.

S TEP-BY-STEP 4.4

1. Press **Ctrl + N**. A new, blank document opens.

2. If the Rulers are not displayed, click the **View** tab, then in the Show/Hide group, click the **Ruler** check box to select it.

3. Click the **Insert** tab, in the Tables group, click the **Table** button, then click **Draw Table** from the 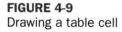 menu. The pointer changes to a pencil.

4. Position the pointer at approximately **1 inch** on the horizontal ruler and at **1.5 inches** on the vertical ruler, then draw a cell approximately **2 inches** wide and ½ **inch** high, as shown in Figure 4-9.

FIGURE 4-9
Drawing a table cell

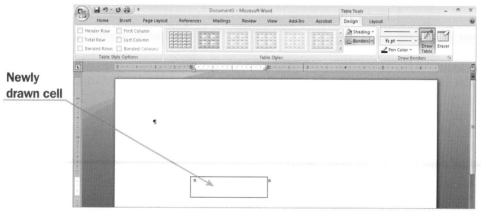

Newly drawn cell

5. Insert a second column to the right of the cell you just created by drawing a new cell approximately **1 inch** wide and ½ **inch** high.

6. Draw a second row approximately ¼ **inch** high with two cells the same width as the first row, then place the insertion point in the last cell.

7. Press **Tab** three times to insert two new rows.

8. Use the Draw Table pointer to split the cells in the first column into two columns, each approximately **1 inch** wide, as shown in Figure 4-10.

STEP-BY-STEP 4.4 Continued

FIGURE 4-10
Cells split

New column
divider

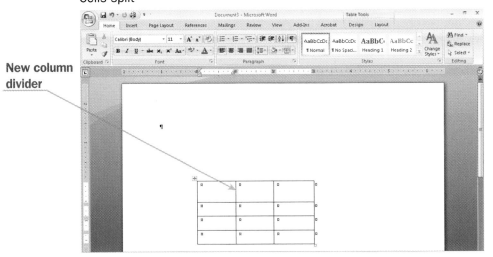

9. Click the **Table Tools Design** tab if necessary, then in the Draw Borders group, click the **Eraser** button. The pointer changes to an eraser.

10. Click the **dividers** between each column in the first row. The first row is now one cell.

11. Enter the table data shown in Figure 4-11.

FIGURE 4-11
Data entered into the table

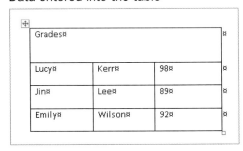

12. Save the document as **Grading Table.docx**, then leave the document and Word open for the next Step-by-Step.

Modify Tables

Table Styles are a quick way to apply coordinated formatting effects to your table. Using font formatting, cell alignment, borders, and shading, Table Styles change the look of your table.

You can reposition the table in your document by selecting it and dragging it to another location.

To specify the order of table data, you can sort it. Sorting can either be ascending (A–Z or 1, 2, 3) or descending (Z–A or 3, 2, 1).

2-2.2.5
2-2.2.4

STEP-BY-STEP 4.5

1. Click anywhere in the table, click the **Table Tools Design** tab if necessary, then in the Table Styles group, click the **second style** (ScreenTip, "Light Shading").

2. Click the **third style** (ScreenTip, "Light Shading–Accent 1"), then notice the changes.

3. Click the **fourth style** (ScreenTip, "Light Shading–Accent 2"). The table appears as shown in Figure 4-12.

FIGURE 4-12
Table Styles applied

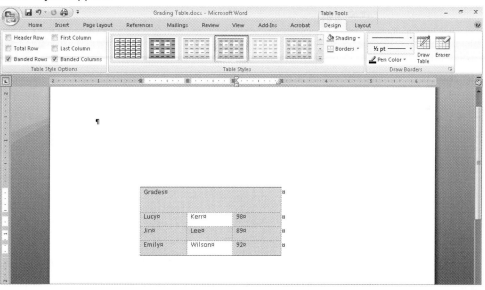

4. Position the pointer over the Select Table button at the upper-left corner of the table, click, then drag the table toward the right margin until the left border of the table is at approximately **1 inch** on the horizontal Ruler. The table is moved.

5. Select the three rows under Grades, click the **Table Tools Layout** tab, then in the Data group, click the **Sort** button.

STEP-BY-STEP 4.5 Continued

6. In the Sort dialog box, click the **Sort by** list arrow, click **Column 3**, change the Type to **Number**, if necessary, make sure the **Ascending** option button is selected, then click **OK**. Deselect the table. The data is sorted, as shown in Figure 4-13.

7. Save and close the document, then leave Word open for the next Step-by-Step.

FIGURE 4-13
Table moved and data sorted

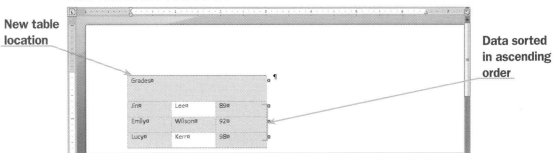

New table location

Data sorted in ascending order

Converting Text to a Table

2-2.2.1

Table data can also be converted back to text. When you convert table data to text, you need to specify how the cell data will be separated (commas, line breaks, tabs, and so on). When typing text that is to be converted to a table, do not add extra tabs or spaces to make the text for the columns align properly. Adding extra spaces or tabs will cause your table to be converted with extra columns, and the columns will not align.

STEP-BY-STEP 4.6

1. Press **Ctrl + N**. A new, blank document opens.

2. Type **Month**, press **Tab**, type **Family**, press **Tab**, type **Snack**, then press **Enter**.

3. Type **January**, press **Tab**, type **Johnson**, press **Tab**, type **Popcorn**, then press **Enter**.

4. Type **February**, press **Tab**, type **Chi**, press **Tab**, type **Fruit**, then press **Enter**.

5. Type **March**, press **Tab**, type **Akbar**, press **Tab**, then type **Crackers**.

6. Select the four lines of text, then on the Insert tab, in the Tables group, click the **Table** button, then click **Convert Text to Table**.

STEP-BY-STEP 4.6 Continued

FIGURE 4-14
Text converted into a table

Month¤	Family¤	Snack¤	¤
January¤	Johnson¤	Popcorn¤	¤
February¤	Chi¤	Fruit¤	¤
March¤	Akbar¤	Crackers¤	¤

¶

7. In the Convert Text to Table dialog box, click the **Tabs** option button. Verify that the table will have 3 columns, click **OK**, then deselect the table. The data is separated into a table grid, as shown in Figure 4-14.

8. Select the table, click the **Table Tools Layout** tab, then in the Data group click the **Convert to Text** button.

9. In the Convert Table To Text dialog box, click the **Commas** option button, click **OK**, then deselect the table. The data is separated by commas and now appears on separate lines, as shown in Figure 4-15.

10. Save the document as **Snacks.docx**, then close the document and exit Word.

FIGURE 4-15
Table converted into text

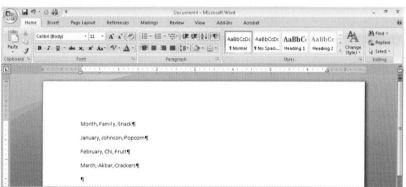

SUMMARY

In this lesson, you learned:

- A table is a grid that organizes data into rows and columns. The intersection of a row and column is called a cell.

- You can create a table using three methods: the Insert Table button to specify the number of rows and columns, the Draw Table and Eraser tools to create rows and columns of different sizes, and converting text separated by commas or tabs into a table.

- You can enter text in a cell by clicking in it and typing. The Tab key moves the insertion point to the next cell, and the arrow keys move up and down in a table.

- You can select a row or range of rows, a column or range of columns, or the entire table at once.

- Rows and columns can be easily added or deleted. The column width and row height can be changed manually or set to adjust automatically as changes to text or formatting are applied.

- Formatting table text is done using the same tools you learned in Lesson 3. You can apply text effects, change the font color or size, or realign and change the orientation of text.

- Cells can be split or merged.

- Table Styles are formatting specifications such as borders, shading, and font effects that create a professional-looking table.

- Tables can be moved to a new location in the document by dragging them.

- Table data can be sorted to specify the order in which data in a column appears. Data can be sorted in ascending or descending, alphabetical or numerical order.

- Text can be converted into a table, and data in a table can be converted into text.

VOCABULARY *Review*

Define the following terms:

Ascending	Embedding	Orientation
AutoFit	Eraser	Quick Tables
Border	Formula	Realignment
Cell	Header	Row
Column	Insert Table	Shading
Contextual tab	Integrate	Split
Descending	Linking	Table
Draw table	Merge	Table Styles

REVIEW *Questions*

SCREEN IDENTIFICATION

Identify the screen elements.

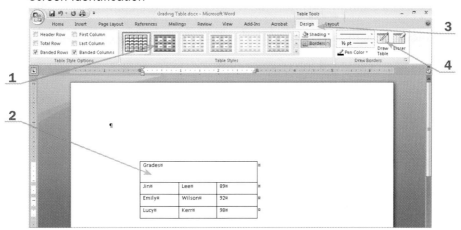

FIGURE 4-16
Screen Identification

1. _____

2. _____

3. _____

4. _____

MULTIPLE CHOICE

Circle the correct answer.

1. A _____ is the intersection of a row or column.
   A. grid   C. table
   B. cell   D. spreadsheet

2. When the Draw Tables feature is active, the pointer appears as _____ .
   A. ✛   C. ✏
   B. ↻   D. 👆

3. All of the following are ways to create a table except _____ .
   A. Converting text separated   C. Inserting a Table Style
      by commas   D. Drawing a table
   B. Using the Insert Table button

4. Press _____ to move to the next cell in a table.
   A. Tab   C. Down arrow
   B. Enter   D. Shift

5. _____ creates one cell from two.

    A. Splitting   **C.** Converting

    B. Connecting   **D.** Merging

TRUE/FALSE

Circle T if the statement is true or F if the statement is false.

T   F   **1.** To select a column, position the pointer above the column, then click.

T   F   **2.** Tables can be moved around in the document by dragging.

T   F   **3.** A cell can be divided into two or more cells.

T   F   **4.** Data sorted from A-Z is in descending order.

T   F   **5.** The Eraser tool deletes data.

HANDS-ON REVIEW

1. Open a new, blank document. Use the Insert Table button to create a 3×3 table. Enter the text shown below:

FIRST NAME	LAST NAME	TEAM
Julio	Ignazio	Blue Stars
Mia	Hardy	Yellow Moons

2. Press **Tab** to insert a new row and enter **Sarah, Jones, Blue Stars.** Adjust the column widths to AutoFit to the text.

3. Enter a new column called Goals at the right of the table. Use the down arrow to enter **4, 7,** and **6.**

4. Format the table text as **Arial, 12-point.** Make the first row bold.

5. Use the Draw Table tool to add a new row to the bottom of the table with the same column widths as the first four rows. Enter **Brian, Hu, Yellow Moons,** and **9.**

6. Apply a Table Style of your choice to the table.

7. Drag the table so that the top border of the table is at approximately **3 inches** on the vertical ruler and centered between the left and right margins.

8. Sort the data in the Goals column in descending order.

9. Convert the table to text separated by commas. Convert it back to a table and reapply the formatting.

10. Save the document as **Soccer Teams.docx,** then close the document.

PROJECTS

PROJECT 4-1

1. Open the document **Plant Table.docx**.

2. Print the table, then identify the following:
   a. A split cell.
   b. A merged cell.
   c. Realigned text.
   d. The column used to sort the data and the order in which the data was sorted.

PROJECT 4-2

1. Create a new, blank document.

2. Use the Draw Table feature to create a table with three ½-inch-high rows and three columns. Make the first two columns one inch wide and the third column ½ inch wide.

3. Position the insertion point in the last cell, then press **Tab**.

4. Apply a Table Style of your choice.

5. Enter your own data in the table.

6. Save the document as **My Table.docx**.

 TEAMWORK

Divide the terms in the vocabulary list evenly among the members of your team. Each team member should create flash cards for his or her terms that have the definition on one side and the term on the other side. Practice quizzing each other until you are familiar with all of the terms in the lesson.

CRITICAL *Thinking*

ACTIVITY 4-1

Create a new Word document saved as **Table Options.docx**. Insert a new table with two columns and three rows. In each cell in the first column, type the three ways you can create tables. In the second column, describe each method. Apply the style of your choice to the table, then save and close the document.

ADDING FEATURES TO MULTIPAGE DOCUMENTS

Documents that span multiple pages, such as reports and newsletters, need to be easy to read and navigate. Columns separate text vertically on a page or in an article into two or more parallel paths. Headers and footers run along the top and bottom margins of the pages in your document, and they contain information such as the title of the document, page number, date, and other relevant identifying information.

Applying text styles and templates to your document can help to create a cohesive look and feel. Borders and shading make the document visually interesting and help to separate sections of text or the header or footer. Using clip art, graphic files saved to your hard drive or downloaded from the Internet, and drawing tools, you can add and modify graphics to illustrate text.

When a document contains references to other works or when you want to add a clarification to text, you can add footnotes and endnotes. Footnotes are sequential notes at the bottom of the page on which the citation or explanation appears. Endnotes are also sequential, but they are compiled into a list that appears on the last page of a document.

You can also add a table of contents, listing a document's section titles and page numbers. Word enables you to create a table of contents automatically by searching for the styles and headings applied to your document. As the document changes, Word updates any new headings and page references.

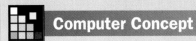

Computer Concept

PLANNING A MULTIPAGE DOCUMENT

Any project, regardless of size, should start with a planning session. This can take a few minutes or several days, depending on the complexity of the document you are creating. During the planning stage for a multipage document, you should ask the following questions:

1. *What information needs to be included?* Identify the title, all text you will need, and the anticipated length of your document.
2. *How will I differentiate the parts of my document?* Consider adding formatting, page numbers, headers, footers, and section headings.
3. *Will anyone else be writing portions of the document?* Contact these people and discuss the timing, length, and shared style elements in the information they will be providing.
4. *Is any artwork going to be added?* Gather or create the graphic files you will need, make sure you have permission to use them or are using them legally, and check the file sizes.

Use the answers to the above questions to plan the layout of the elements including all articles and graphics, formatting, and other information. A sample document plan is shown in Figure 5-1.

FIGURE 5-1
Sample table

Element	Page	Author	Notes
Header	All but page 1		Include 3 columns: 1. Chelsea Park Restoration Committee 2. Volume 1, Issue 1 3. February 2010
Footer	All but page 1		Just page number
Title1			**Chelsea Park Restoration Committee Newsletter**
List: Board Members	3	Janet	
Article: From the President	1	Janet	**Add Trees clip art**
Article: Chelsea Park History	1	Abner	
Article: Restoration Plans	1-2	Linda	**Add graphic Layout.bmp**
Article: Fundraising	2	Christina	**Add sun shape**
Article: Publicity	3	Janet	**Add drawn object**

Apply Styles

Styles are a way of creating consistent formatting among text with a similar importance. You can apply a Title style to the title of your document and other styles, such as Heading 1, Heading 2, and so on, to each level of heading in a document. Normal style is used for the body text of your document.

The style you are currently using is highlighted in the Styles group on the Home tab, as shown in Figure 5-2. To apply a new style, click the Styles button for the style you want to apply or click the More button to open the Styles gallery. The new style you choose will be applied to the paragraph where you place the insertion point or to selected text or paragraphs.

While there are many style options available to you, you can also create and name a new style or modify an existing style. To create a new style, select the formatted text, click the More button in the Styles group, then click Save Selection as a New Quick Style.

FIGURE 5-2
Styles group on the ribbon

Current style

Click to open the Styles gallery

2-2.1.17

Once styles have been assigned, you can apply a Quick Style set to your document by clicking the Change Styles button in the Styles group. A Quick Style set will change all of the attributes of the document based on the style to which text has been assigned. Styles can also be used to create a table of contents, which you will learn about later in this lesson.

STEP-BY-STEP 5.1

1. Open the document **Newsletter.docx**. A two-page newsletter opens without any formatting. The Normal style is applied to all of the text in the document.

2. Select the first line in the document, click the **More** button in the Styles group on the Home tab, then click the **Title** style. The text is formatted as dark blue, 26-point Cambria font.

3. To make the title fit on one line, change the font size to **20-point**, then click anywhere in the title to deselect it. The title text appears as shown in Figure 5-3.

FIGURE 5-3
Title formatted

STEP-BY-STEP 5.1 Continued

4. Select the line **From the President**, then click the **Heading 2** style in the Styles group on the Home tab. Click the More button, if necessary, to access additional styles.

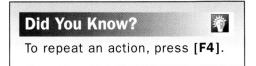

Did You Know?

To repeat an action, press **[F4]**.

5. Select the following lines and apply the **Heading 2** style to them: **Chelsea Park History**, **Restoration Plans**, **Fundraising**, and **Publicity**.

6. Select the following lines and apply the **Heading 3** style to them: **Board Members**, **Restoration Timeline**, and **Ways to Contribute**.

7. Select the line *Site map of new Chelsea Park*, then format it with **Dark Red** (under Standard Colors), **Italics**, and **12-point** font. (*Hint*: Use commands in the Font group.)

8. With the line still selected, click the **More** button in the Styles group, then click **Save Selection as a New Quick Style**. The Create New Style from Formatting dialog box opens.

9. Enter **Caption1** in the Name text box, then click **OK**.

10. Press **Ctrl + Home**, click the **Change Styles** button in the Styles group, point to **Style Set**, then click **Distinctive**. The document appears as shown in Figure 5-4.

11. Save the newsletter as **Committee Newsletter.docx**, then leave the document and Word open for the next Step-by-Step.

FIGURE 5-4
Distinctive Quick Style set applied

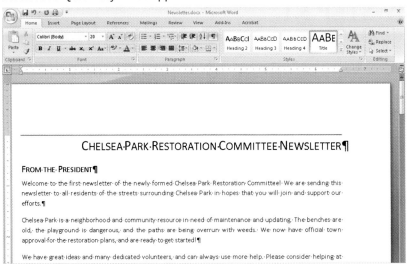

Use Columns and Insert Breaks

When you look at a newspaper or Web page, you will see that many, if not all, articles are separated into columns. Using Word, you can apply multiple columns to your entire document, or you can use section breaks so that portions of your page or document have different numbers of columns.

Section breaks can also be used to make text appear on a new page or to create sections with different pagination, headers or footers, paragraph formatting, or layout options. Table 5-1 lists the different types of breaks that you can add to your document. Section breaks control the paragraph formatting in the section before the break. When you delete a section break, the formatting of the section following is applied to the text.

When you apply certain paragraph formatting options to selected text, section breaks are automatically inserted into your document before and after the selection.

Did You Know?

You can choose paragraph formatting options such as numbers of columns when inserting a new page into your document.

TABLE 5-1
Section and page breaks

BREAK TYPE	USED TO
Next page	Start the new section on the next page of your document, such as for a new chapter.
Continuous	Start the new section on the same page of your document. This is useful when applying columns to a section of a page.
Even page or **Odd page**	Start a new section on the next even-numbered or odd-numbered page. In a document with many chapters, this helps to start all chapters on a left- or right-hand page.

STEP-BY-STEP 5.2

1. Scroll down and click the beginning of the line, **Chelsea Park History**.

2. Click the **Page Layout** tab, then in the Page Setup group, click the **Breaks** button.

3. In the Section Breaks section on the Breaks menu, click **Next Page**.

4. Click the beginning of the *Site map of the new Chelsea Park* caption line, then insert a **Continuous** break. The articles on the history and restoration plans are their own section now, which allows you to apply formatting to only that section.

5. Scroll up, make sure the insertion point is in the section containing the *Chelsea Park History* or *Restoration Plans* article, then on the **Page Layout** tab in the Page Setup group, click the **Columns** button.

6. Click **Two** on the Columns menu. The section is formatted in two columns.

STEP-BY-STEP 5.2 Continued

7. Click before the *Restoration Plans* heading line, click the **Breaks** button, then click **Column**. The two columns appear, as shown in Figure 5-5.

FIGURE 5-5
Two columns applied

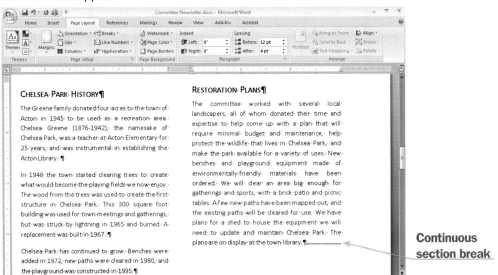

Continuous section break

8. Scroll to page 3, select the paragraph under the *Publicity* article (but not the header or the line beginning *The next meeting...* below the paragraph), apply **two columns**, deselect the text, then press **Enter** before the last line. Continuous section breaks are automatically inserted, and the third page of your document appears as shown in Figure 5-6.

FIGURE 5-6
Section breaks inserted

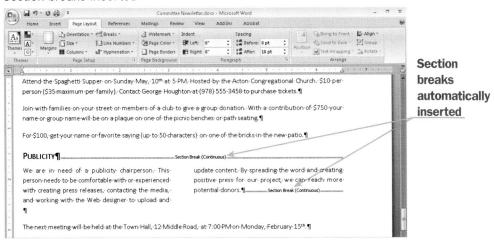

Section breaks automatically inserted

9. Save your work, then leave the document and Word open for the next Step-by-Step.

Add Headers and Footers

Headers and footers can help to identify elements such as a page title, page numbers, and in the case of a newsletter, the volume and date of the publication. You can choose to have a footer and header appear on every page, in certain sections only, or to appear on all but the first page. If your document will be printed on facing pages, you can have a different header and footer for the right- and left-hand pages.

Header and footer text are separate from the body of your document. When headers and footers are inserted into your document, they will appear dimmed while you work on the main part of your document. In order to edit or modify them, you can double-click the header or footer to activate it. Changes you make will apply to the document or section as appropriate.

The top margin of the document is reserved for the header text, and the bottom margin is reserved for the footer. Using the Insert tab and the buttons in the Header & Footer group, you can choose a preformatted header. You can also double-click the top or bottom margin to activate the header or footer. Preformatted options are used to create columns or automatically insert formatted page numbers, for instance. Many preformatted headers and footers contain placeholders, which you worked with when using templates. To change placeholder text, click on the placeholder to select it, then start typing.

2-2.1.13
2-2.1.14

When you insert page numbers into a header or footer, they will update automatically when you add or remove content. You can choose a preformatted page number option, then modify the formatting.

S TEP-BY-STEP 5.3

1. Click the **Insert** tab, then in the Header & Footer group, click the **Header** button.

2. From the Header menu, click **Blank (Three Columns)**. The header is active.

3. Click the first placeholder, then type **Chelsea Park Restoration Committee**.

4. Click the second placeholder, then type **Volume 1, Issue 1**.

5. Click the third placeholder, then type **February 2010**.

6. Select all of the text in the header, format the text with **italics**, then double-click the document to deselect the header. The header appears as shown in Figure 5-7.

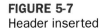

FIGURE 5-7
Header inserted

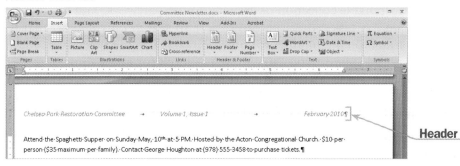

STEP-BY-STEP 5.3 Continued

7. Double-click the **bottom margin** of the second page to activate the footer. The footer is blank and contains no placeholders.

8. On the **Insert tab** in the Header & Footer group, click the **Page Number** button.

9. Point to **Current Position**, then click **Accent Bar 1**. The page number, 2, is inserted, and page numbers appear in the footer of all three pages in your document.

10. Scroll to page 1, double-click the **footer** if necessary, click the **Header and Footer Tools Design** tab, click the **Different First Page** check box in the Options group, then deselect the footer. Page 1 no longer has a page number or header.

11. Go to page 2, then scroll to the footer. It is dimmed, and the page number appears as shown in Figure 5-8.

12. Save your work, then leave the document and Word open for the next Step-by-Step.

FIGURE 5-8
Footer with page number

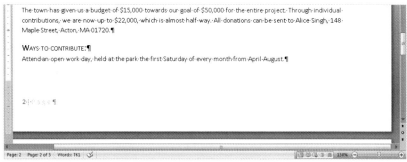

Insert and Modify Clip Art and Other Graphics

Inserting Graphics

Illustrating the text in your document with graphics can help to inform the reader or provide visual interest to your document. You can insert and resize the graphic files that you have stored on your computer, such as the clip galleries that come with Office 2007, or use pictures that you have taken with a digital camera and copied to your computer.

Clip art is a searchable collection of drawn graphics, artwork, and photography that is available using the Clip Art task pane. You can choose to search only clip art that is stored on your computer or to search on the Internet for other clip art. The file types available are clip art, photographs, movies, and sounds; you can choose to search for all or some of these. To search for a selection of graphics you can use to support your text, enter a keyword, such as "airplane," in the Search for text box, then click Go. Thumbnails of the available clip art will display in the task pane, as shown in Figure 5-9. Click the selection to insert it.

The Drawing tools allow you to insert simple shapes, such as circles and squares, and more complex symbols and shapes including banners, stars, and hearts.

FIGURE 5-9
Clip Art task pane

Modifying Graphics

2-1.3.9
2-1.3.10
2-1.3.11

Once you have chosen the graphic(s) to include, you need to place them and edit them to fit your document. When a graphic is selected, gray handles appear on its edges. These handles indicate that the graphic is active and can be modified. You can use the handles to resize or move the graphic to a new location. When a graphic is selected, the Drawing Tools contextual tabs are available. You can use the buttons on these tabs to resize, add a border, and crop or remove portions of the graphic.

Computer Concepts

CONSIDERING FILE SIZES

The file size of your document is the amount of space it uses in your computer for storage and memory. File sizes are measured in KB (kilobytes) or MB (megabytes). A larger file size means that the file uses more computer resources to store, edit, and send it by e-mail or the Internet.

One way to monitor the size of your document is to pay attention to the file size of graphics that you insert. You can view the file size in the Insert Picture dialog box. Click **Views** in the dialog box, then click **Details**. If the size does not show, right-click any column in the right pane, then click **Size**.

STEP-BY-STEP 5.4

1. Click the end of the *Site map of the new Chelsea Park* caption, then press **Enter**.

2. Click the **Insert** tab, then in the Illustrations group, click the **Picture** button and navigate to your Data Files. The Insert Picture dialog box opens, as shown in Figure 5-10. The Layout.bmp file is only 226 KB, so the file size won't make your document too large.

FIGURE 5-10
Insert Picture dialog box

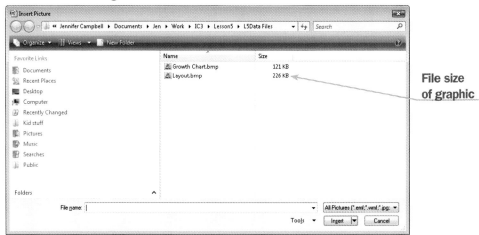

3. Click **Layout.bmp**, then click **Insert**. The site map appears in the document.

4. If the ruler is not visible, click the **View** tab, then in the Show/Hide group, click select the **Ruler** check box.

5. Position the pointer over one of the corner handles, then drag a handle to resize the graphic until the right margin is at the **4-inch** mark on the ruler, as shown in Figure 5-11.

FIGURE 5-11
Graphic inserted and resized

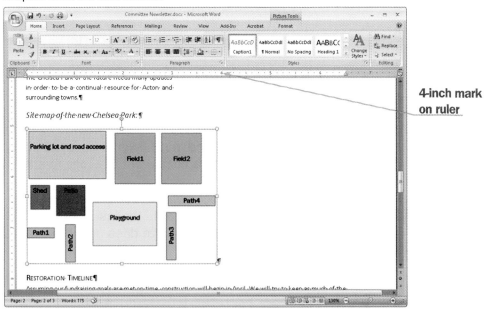

STEP-BY-STEP 5.4 Continued

6. Position the insertion point at the bottom of the page before the section break on page 1, press **Enter**, click the **Insert** tab, then in the Illustrations group, click **Clip Art**. The Clip Art task pane opens.

7. Type **tree planting** in the Search for text box, click the **Results should be** list arrow, verify that the **Clip Art** check box is selected, then click **Go**. Your results may vary depending on whether or not you are connected to the Internet. If the clip art shown in Figure 5-12 is not available, choose another related image.

8. Click the **image** shown in Figure 5-12, then close the task pane. The clip art is inserted into the document.

FIGURE 5-12
Clip art search results

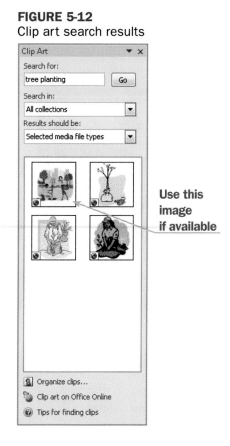

Use this image if available

STEP-BY-STEP 5.4 Continued

9. Click the **More** button in the Picture Styles group, click **Double-Frame, Black**, click the **Home** tab, then in the Paragraph group, click the **Center** button, and deselect the graphic. The inserted clip art appears as shown in Figure 5-13.

FIGURE 5-13
Picture Style applied and graphic centered

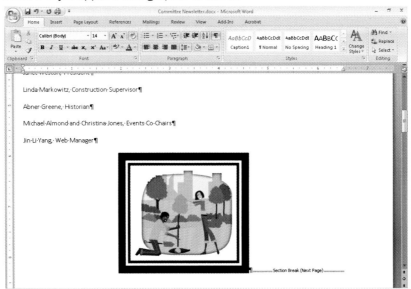

10. Scroll to the article *Ways to Contribute*, click **Shapes** on the Insert tab, then in the Basic Shapes section of the Shapes gallery, click **Sun**.

11. Use the pointer to draw a sun to the right of the article.

12. On the Drawing Tools Format tab in the Size group, click the **Shape Height** text box, type **1.25**, click the **Shape Width** text box, then type **1.25**.

13. Click the **Shape Fill** button arrow in the Shape Styles group, click **Yellow** under Standard Colors, click the **Text Wrapping** button in the Arrange group, then click **Tight**.

14. Position the shape as shown in Figure 5-14, then deselect it.

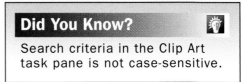

Did You Know?

Search criteria in the Clip Art task pane is not case-sensitive.

FIGURE 5-14
Shape inserted and modified

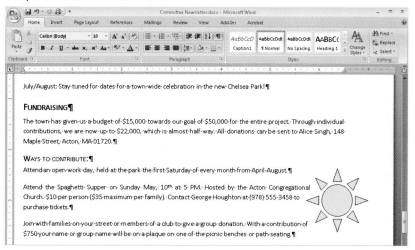

15. Save your work, then leave the document and Word open for the next Step-by-Step.

 **Ethics in Technology**

UNDERSTANDING COPYRIGHT LAW

Copyright refers to the legal protections afforded a creative work, such as a book, song, computer program, or piece of art. Copyright law protects a category of **intellectual property**, which includes the range of what someone can create, manufacture, invent, or design.

Copyright attaches to a work as soon as it is created in a fixed medium. You have probably seen symbols such as © (copyright), ® (registered trademark) or ™ (trademark pending). These symbols mean that the company or individual has registered their product or work with the appropriate government office. You may also see a note or disclaimer such as "This work is the property of John Doe and may not be reproduced without permission."

Even without these symbols or messages, a work is still protected by copyright or trademark law. It is illegal to reproduce artwork, make copies of pages of a book, or download music without the permission of the owner or unless you have purchased the right to do so, such as by purchasing a song online. The responsibility to obtain permission lies with the person who would like to use the work.

On the Internet, there are many sources for free music, graphics, and other media that can be used to enhance documents or for your personal use. You should always check the copyright status and terms of use before downloading or copying anything from the Internet. It is also important to cite the source and give proper credit for any material you use from the Internet, even if you have permission from the copyright holder. However, be aware that giving credit is never a substitute for obtaining permission.

Add Borders and Shading

Adding a border to the bottom of the footer and the top of the header can help to separate them from the document. You can also separate columns with border lines and add lines around a text box.

A text box is an object that contains text but that can be resized, moved, and repositioned like a graphic. Text boxes can contain any text but are often used in newsletters to set aside a quotation from an article, called a **pull quote**, or a **sidebar**, which highlights additional information that is related to the text.

Shading formats an area of text with grayed or colored tint. Headers or boxes of text sometimes have shading applied to them in order to set them apart.

2-2.1.16

STEP-BY-STEP 5.5

1. Double-click the **header** on page 2 or 3 to activate it.

2. Click the **Home** tab, then in the Paragraph group, click the **Border** list arrow, then click **Bottom Border**. Your Border list arrow might differ based on previous use. A line is inserted below the header, as shown in Figure 5-15.

FIGURE 5-15
Border applied to header

3. Click the **footer** to activate it, then select the text.

4. On the **Home** tab in the Paragraph group, click the **Border** list arrow, click **Top Border**, then deselect the footer. A line is inserted above the footer.

5. On page 3, select the last line, click the **Shading** button arrow in the Paragraph group, then click **Light Green** under Standard Colors.

6. Scroll to page 1, click at the beginning of the word **Sincerely**, click the **Insert** tab, then in the Text group click the **Text Box** button, then click the **Simple Text Box** option.

7. Type **Since 1965, over 400 community celebrations and events have taken place in Chelsea Park**.

8. Click the **More** button in the Text Box Styles group, then click the **Colored Fill, White Outline—Accent 1** style in the top row.

9. Click the **Home** tab, select the text in the text box, then format it with **bold**, **white**, **centered**, and **Italics**. Resize and position the text box as shown in Figure 5-16.

STEP-BY-STEP 5.5 Continued

FIGURE 5-16
Text box inserted and formatted

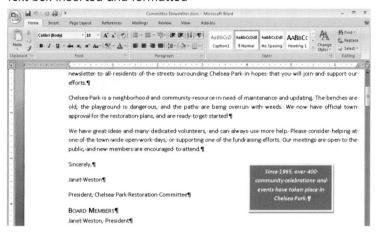

10. Save and close the document, then leave Word open for the next Step-by-Step.

Add Footnotes and Endnotes

Footnotes and endnotes are often used in documents, such as reports, to provide clarification or to cite the source of information. When quoting or using information from another source such as a book, Web site, or article, you should credit and identify the source. This is necessary to give credit to the person who conducted the research or wrote the material you are using. It also gives your document credibility: by supporting your text with outside sources, your report becomes a more reliable source of information instead of just a collection of your thoughts. A citation should include the author(s), the title of the work (book, Web site, or periodical and article name), the date published, and the page(s) referenced.

Did You Know?

There are many different styles for citing sources. Your school or business may prefer a certain style such as *The Chicago Manual of Style* or another industry-specific resource.

To create a footnote or endnote, select the text or position the insertion point after where you want the citation to appear. Click the References tab, then in the Footnotes group, click the Insert Footnote or Insert Endnote button, then type the citation information. The References tab is shown in Figure 5-17.

FIGURE 5-17
References tab

Next to the text you are citing, a number for the footnote or endnote will appear in superscript or raised font. Like page numbers, footnotes and endnotes are automatically renumbered as your text is modified or added to.

2-2.1.15

You can choose to have footnotes appear at the bottom of the page or below the text they reference. Endnotes can appear at the end of the document or section. To change references from footnotes to endnotes or vice versa, or to specify the location of footnotes or endnotes, click the dialog box launcher in the Footnotes group on the References tab, make the appropriate selections in the Footnote and Endnote dialog box, then click OK. You can also choose other numbering formats, symbols, or alphabetical options to sequentially differentiate your notes.

S TEP-BY-STEP 5.6

1. Open the document **Report.docx**, then save it as **Committee Report.docx**. The report is five pages long.

2. Scroll to Page 3, then click the end of the fourth paragraph under *Progress*.

3. Click the **References** tab if necessary, then in the Footnotes group, click the **Insert Footnote** button. The insertion point moves to the bottom of the page. The footnote is number 1.

4. Type **See Minutes from Acton Town Meeting # 431, 12/15/09**.

5. Scroll to Page 2, then click the end of the second paragraph under *Chelsea Park History*.

6. Click the **References** tab, then in the Footnotes group, click the **Insert Footnote** button. The insertion point moves to the bottom of the page. The footnote is number 1, and the footnote you added in step 3 becomes footnote 2.

7. Type **Abner Greene,** *History of Acton* **(iUniverse, 2006) 150–172**. Make sure to italicize the book title, as shown in Figure 5-18.

FIGURE 5-18
Footnotes added

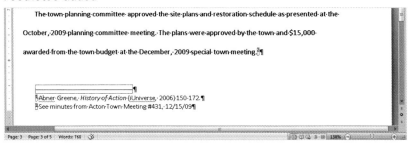

8. Click the **dialog box launcher** in the Footnotes group. The Footnote and Endnote dialog box opens.

9. Click **Convert**, click **OK** in the Convert Notes dialog box, then close the Footnote and Endnote dialog box. The footnotes are now endnotes on page 5.

STEP-BY-STEP 5.6 Continued

10. Click the Footnotes **dialog box launcher** again, click the **Endnotes** option button if necessary, verify that **End of document** is selected, click the **Number format** list arrow, click the **A, B, C** option, then click **Apply**. The dialog box closes, and the numbered footnotes become lettered endnotes, as shown in Figure 5-19.

FIGURE 5-19
Lettered endnotes

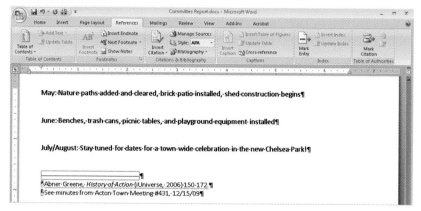

11. Save your work, then leave the document and Word open for the next Step-by-Step.

Create a Table of Contents

A table of contents usually appears at the beginning of a report, book, or other multipage document. It is used to identify the chapters or sections and where to find them. It is a great reference tool, and using Word, you can generate a table of contents using headings. The table of contents can be updated to reflect additional or deleted headings or a page location that has changed since the table of contents was generated.

There are different formats you can choose when adding a table of contents. You can also choose to add different sublevels using heading styles.

STEP-BY-STEP 5.7

1. Scroll to page 1 of the report, and place the insertion point before the page break.

2. Click the **References** tab, in the Table of Contents group, click the **Table of Contents** button, then click **Automatic Table 1**. A table of contents displays with entries and page numbers for all text formatted with the Heading 1 style. Scroll up to view the table of contents, if necessary.

3. Click the **Home** tab, scroll to page 2, apply the **Heading 1** style to the title *Board Members*, scroll to page 4, then apply the **Heading 1** style to the title *Restoration Timeline*.

STEP-BY-STEP 5.7 Continued

4. Scroll to page 1, click anywhere in the table of contents, click the **Update Table** button that displays at the top of the table of contents, click the **Update entire table** option button in the Update Table of Contents dialog box, then click **OK**. The table of contents is updated to reflect the new headings, as shown in Figure 5-20.

FIGURE 5-20
Updating the table of contents

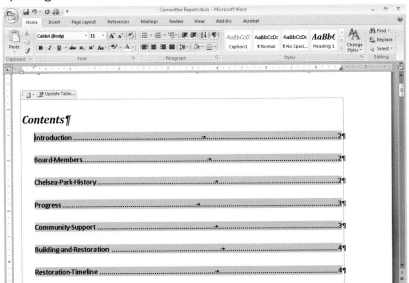

5. Scroll in the document, insert page breaks before the **Community Support** and **Building and Restoration** headings, scroll to page 1, then update the table of contents. The page references are updated, as shown in Figure 5-21.

6. Save your work, then leave the document and Word open for the next Step-by-Step.

FIGURE 5-21
Table of contents updated

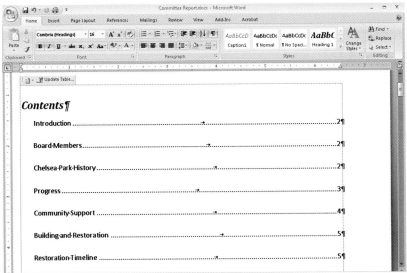

Enhance Text

Y ou have learned many different ways to edit, format, and proof the text in your documents. Word offers other tools to polish the text in your document and to add and edit your text more efficiently.

The Thesaurus can help choose the most appropriate word and to vary the word choice in your document. A **thesaurus** is a reference tool that displays **synonyms**, or words with the same meaning. You can use the Thesaurus to find synonyms for a selected word or to search for a word.

AutoComplete is a tool that finishes words as you type them. AutoComplete entries for days of the week and for months are built into Word. When you type the first few letters of an AutoComplete entry, a ScreenTip appears with the word. To use AutoComplete, press Enter to have Word finish typing, or keep typing to overwrite the entry.

Quick Parts are **building blocks** of frequently used text that you can insert. To create a new Quick Part, select the text you want to reuse, and include the paragraph mark after the text to include paragraph formatting. Click the Quick Parts button in the Text group on the Insert tab, then click **Save Selection to Quick Part Gallery**. The name you save it as will appear on the Quick Parts menu to be used in the rest of your document.

STEP-BY-STEP 5.8

1. Scroll to the top of page 2, then select the word **create** in the first line under the heading.

2. Click the **Review** tab, then in the Proofing group, click the **Thesaurus** button. The Research task pane opens, and the Thesaurus presents a list of choices, as shown in Figure 5-22.

FIGURE 5-22
Thesaurus

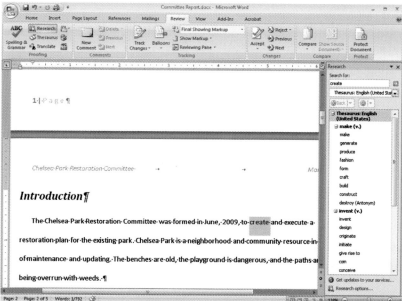

STEP-BY-STEP 5.8 Continued

3. Scroll if necessary, click the **list arrow** next to **establish** in the Thesaurus, click **Insert**, then close the Research task pane. The word is replaced in the document.

4. In the introductory paragraph, select the text **Chelsea Park Restoration Committee**.

5. Click the **Insert** tab, then in the Text group click the **Quick Parts** button, then click **Save Selection to Quick Part Gallery**. The Create New Building Block dialog box opens.

6. Click **OK** to accept the defaults in the dialog box and to save the text as a Quick Part.

7. Position the insertion point at the beginning of the line *Board Members*.

8. In the Text group, click the **Quick Parts** button, then click the **Chelsea Park** entry from the gallery, as shown in Figure 5-23. The text is inserted.

> **Did You Know?**
>
> To access a menu of synonyms, right-click a word in your document, then point to Synonyms. Choose a word from the short-cut menu, or click Thesaurus to open the Thesaurus.

FIGURE 5-23
Inserting a Quick Part

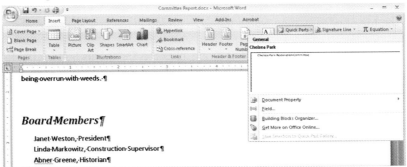

9. Use the Format Painter to change the formatting of *Chelsea Park Restoration Committee* to match the rest of the line, if necessary.

10. Save and close the document, do not save changes to the Building Blocks if prompted, then exit Word.

SUMMARY

In this lesson, you learned:

- Styles are used to create consistent formatting and to assign levels to text in order to apply Quick Sets or create a table of contents.

- Columns create parallel lines of text and are often used in newspapers and other publications.

- Section breaks can be continuous or move text to the next page or the next odd or even page. They are used to apply separate paragraph formatting or pagination to parts of your document.

- Headers and footers are information that appears in the top and bottom margins of pages. You can insert page numbers or other identifying information in all of the pages in your document, to certain sections, or to all but the first page of your document.

- You can illustrate your document by inserting graphic that you save, create, or download.

- Clip art graphics enhance your document; they are available through a searchable task pane and can include photographs, sounds, drawings, or other objects.

- Shapes such as hearts, stars, and lines can be added, resized, and recolored.

- Borders add lines to separate text or elements such as text boxes.

- Shading fills objects or sections of text with color or tinting.

- Footnotes and endnotes are citations that provide clarification or reference the source of data or information you use in your document.

- A table of contents is a listing of headings or chapters and their corresponding page numbers. You can create one automatically and update it easily.

- The Thesaurus is used to find words with similar meanings.

- Quick Parts and Building Blocks are reusable text that can be inserted from a gallery.

VOCABULARY *Review*

Define the following terms:

AutoComplete	Footer	Shading
Border	Footnote	Sidebar
Building Block	Header	Style
Clip art	Intellectual property	Superscript
Column	Pull quote	Synonym
Copyright	Quick Part	Table of contents
Crop	Quick Style	Text box
Endnote	Section break	Thesaurus

REVIEW *Questions*

SCREEN IDENTIFICATION

Identify the screen elements.

FIGURE 5-24
Screen Identification

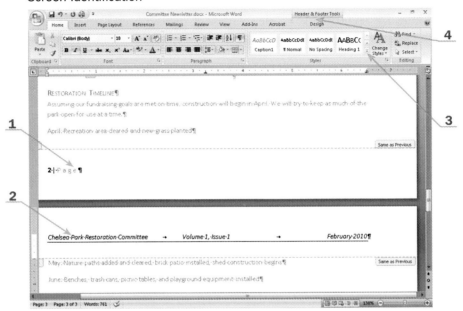

1.

2.

3.

4.

MULTIPLE CHOICE

Circle the correct answer.

1. A word with a similar meaning to another is called a _____.
    A. Building Block
    B. Thesaurus
    C. Synonym
    D. Sidebar

2. A _____ break is used to apply different formatting to a portion of text.
    A. Column
    B. Section
    C. Page
    D. Formatting

3. Newspapers often use _____ to separate text within an article.
   A. Pull quotes
   B. Breaks
   C. Sections
   D. Columns

4. Text that uses _____ formatting is raised.
   A. Superscript
   B. Shading
   C. Subscript
   D. Heading

TRUE/FALSE

Circle T if the statement is true or F if the statement is false.

T F 1. Clip art is a graphic that you download from the Internet or create and save to your computer.

T F 2. If no copyright symbol or message is visible, you can assume that the work is not protected and you can use it however you wish.

T F 3. A pull quote is a type of text box.

T F 4. A footnote is a citation that appears at the bottom of the page.

T F 5. Footnotes and endnotes are always numbered.

T F 6. A table of contents can be updated automatically.

HANDS-ON REVIEW

1. Open the document **Marketing Plan.docx** and save it as **My Marketing Plan.docx**.

2. Apply styles to the document title (Title) and all headings (Heading 1). (*Hint*: There are eight headings.)

3. Apply the Modern Style Set.

4. Insert a next page break before the heading *Targeted Consumer Demographics*.

5. Make the article *Product Definition* two columns.

6. Add the date and your name to the header, and add the page number in the footer.

7. Insert the graphic **Growth Chart.bmp** under the Market Cycle text, center it, then decrease the line space before the title to fit the graphic on page 1.

8. Add your name to a footnote anywhere under Customer Service Plan.

9. Under the Product Definition heading, choose another synonym for *comfort*.

10. Make any other changes to your document to make it fit onto two pages, then save and close the document.

PROJECTS

PROJECT 5-1

Open the file **Journal.docx**. Replace five words with synonyms of your choice. Insert a piece of clip art and a shape, and size and place them appropriately. Add your name to the footer, then save the document as **Enhanced Journal.docx**.

PROJECT 5-2

Open a multipage document that you created in another class. Add or modify headers and footers. Apply styles to the headings or add headings with the Heading 1 or Heading 2 style. Create a table of contents and add at least one footnote. Save the document as **Your Name Report.docx**.

 TEAMWORK

Choose a topic for a newsletter for a club or organization. Make a plan for the document that details the articles, types of formatting, and graphics you will include. Use a Word table to present the information. Save it as **Team Newsletter Plan.docx**.

CRITICAL *Thinking*

ACTIVITY 5-1

Open a new, blank Word document, then save it to your Data Files as **Copyright.docx**. Write a paragraph about what you have learned about copyright from this lesson. Write a second paragraph about any experience you have with respecting copyright or some rules you now know. Create a Quick Part with your name, and insert it at the end of the document. Save and close the document.

SPREADSHEET BASICS

OBJECTIVES

Upon completion of this lesson, you will be able to:

- View the worksheet window
- Navigate in a worksheet
- Select worksheet data
- Create a new worksheet
- Enter data in a worksheet
- Modify rows and columns
- Format a worksheet
- Edit cell contents

Estimated Time: 1 hour

VOCABULARY

AutoFill

Cell

Cell address

Clipboard

Column

Conditional formatting

Copy

Cut

Deselect

Formula bar

Gridline

Insertion point

Name box

Number format

Paste

Range

Row

Scroll bar

Select

Spreadsheet

Table Styles

Workbook

Worksheet

Worksheet window

Wrap

Microsoft Office Excel 2007 is a spreadsheet program that organizes data in rows and columns. As in a Word table, the intersection of a row and column is called a cell. Each cell contains one unit of data—a number, formula, or text. Excel is used to create invoices, schedules, lists, and other files that require data analysis.

Cells are grouped in a worksheet, which contains a seemingly infinite number of cells but has a maximum of 1,048,576 rows and 16,384 columns. Each Excel file is called a workbook. By default, a workbook contains three worksheets, each on its own tab. You can add or remove worksheets from a workbook as needed.

Excel contains many built-in formulas and functions that can perform calculations and analyze data. The results can be displayed in numbers or in more complex graphs and charts. Sections of cells can be set as a range. A range is a group of data that is used in calculations or formulas. An example of a range is a list of holidays that are not included as work days when creating a schedule. You will learn more about ranges, formulas, and functions in Lesson 7. You can give a range a unique name; otherwise, ranges are identified by the first and last cell in the selected area. For instance, the range **A1:B6** selects cells in columns A and B that are also in rows 1 to 6.

Applying formatting options will modify the look of your spreadsheet, which helps to differentiate the data and make it more readable. For example, shading adds definition to a row or column that serves as a heading row or totals column. You can use borders to distinguish any combination of cells, rows, or columns. Adjusting the font and formatting of cell contents is another way to enhance your worksheet. You can also adjust the height and width of rows and columns to fit the data.

View the Worksheet Window

Excel shares elements of the user interface with Word and other Office programs such as the Ribbon, dialog boxes, and scroll bars. Many of the basic program tasks, such as starting a program, and saving, opening and closing a file, are the same for all Office programs. The Microsoft Office Excel 2007 program window is shown in Figure 6-1.

FIGURE 6-1
Worksheet window

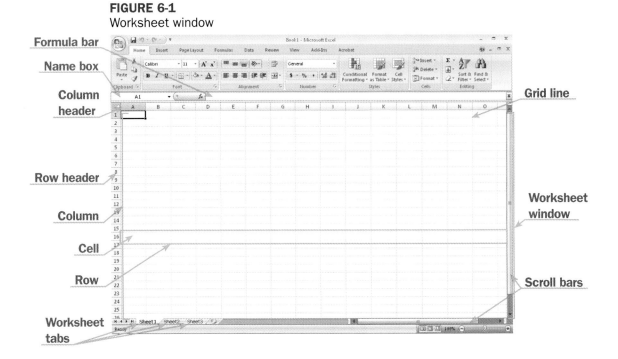

The worksheet window is the main work area where you will enter, format, and edit information. If you have more content in your spreadsheet than can be viewed on the screen at one time, use the scroll bars to move up and down in the spreadsheet.

The program window displays the current worksheet in the workbook. To move to another worksheet, click the worksheet tab at the bottom of the screen.

Rows are horizontal and are sequentially numbered, starting with 1. Columns are vertical and are alphabetical starting from A to Z. The 27th column is AA, the 28th is AB, and so on. Each cell has a unique identifier called the cell address. The cell address is the column letter and row number of the cell; the first cell in a worksheet is cell A1. The nonprinting lines that separate the cells are called gridlines.

The Name box displays the name of the active cell or range (or when multiple cells are selected, the upper-left cell in the range). When you are selecting a range, it will display the number of cells in the selection.

2-3.1.1

The Formula bar, located next to the Name box, displays the contents of the active cell. When a cell contains a formula, the calculation appears in the Formula bar. You can use the Formula bar to edit a formula or cell contents.

STEP-BY-STEP 6.1

1. Start Excel by using the **Start** button or a desktop shortcut. A new, blank workbook, called Book1, opens. The insertion point is in the first cell, cell A1.

2. Click the **Office Button**, then click **Open**

3. In the Open dialog box, locate the Data Files, then open the file **Invoice.xlsx**.

4. Click the tabs on the Ribbon to see the groups and buttons available. Note that many of the buttons on the Home tab are the same as those in Word, but the other tabs contain Excel-specific tasks.

5. Click cell **C17**. Cell C17 is at the intersection of column C and row 17.

6. Look at the Formula bar to view the formula in cell C17, as shown in Figure 6-2. The data displayed in the cell is the result of the formula. In this case, it is the sum of the cells immediately above it, cell range C13:C16.

FIGURE 6-2
Formula displayed in Formula bar

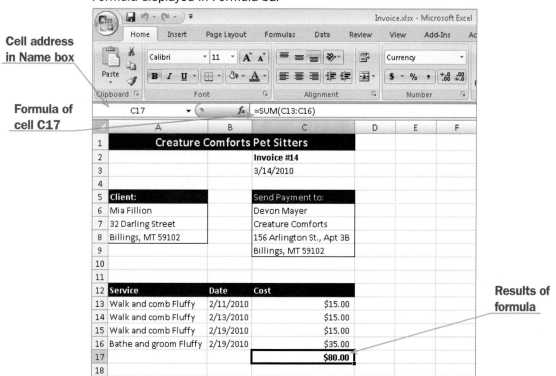

STEP-BY-STEP 6.1 Continued

7. Click cell **A5**. View the cell address displayed in the Name box.

8. Leave the workbook and Excel open for the next Step-by-Step.

Navigate in a Worksheet

The insertion point can be moved by clicking the mouse in a cell to make it active. There are also many keyboard shortcuts that quickly move the insertion point to a new position, as shown in Table 6-1. Being familiar with these positioning tools can help you to make edits to your spreadsheet efficiently.

TABLE 6-1
Navigating through a workbook

KEYBOARD SHORTCUT	MOVES THE INSERTION POINT
Ctrl + Home	To cell A1
Ctrl + End	To the bottom-right cell that contains content
Ctrl + left arrow, or **Home**	To the beginning of the row
Ctrl + right arrow	To the last cell that contains content in the row
Page Up	Up one screen
Page Down	Down one screen
Tab, or **right arrow**	One cell to the right
Shift + Tab, or **left arrow**	One cell to the left

STEP-BY-STEP 6.2

1. Press **Ctrl + End**. The insertion point moves to cell C17, the last cell in the workbook.

2. Press the **up arrow** to move to cell **C16**.

3. Press **Ctrl + Home**. The insertion point moves to cell A1. Note that cells A1:C1 are all selected because they are merged. You will learn how to merge cells later in this lesson.

4. Press **Ctrl + right arrow**. The insertion point moves to the end of the row, cell XFD.

5. Press the **down arrow** to move down a row, then press the **up arrow** to move up a row.

6. Press **Ctrl + Home**, press **Page Down**, then press **Page Up**. The insertion point moves down and back up on the screen. The exact location will vary depending on your screen resolution.

> **Did You Know?**
>
> Press **Ctrl + G** to open the Go To dialog box. Make a selection in the Go to list, or type a cell address or range name in the Reference text box, then click **OK**. The insertion point automatically moves to the specified location.

STEP-BY-STEP 6.2 Continued

7. Press **Tab** twice to move the insertion point two cells to the right.

8. Press **Shift + Tab** twice to move the insertion point two cells to the left.

9. Click the **January** worksheet tab to move to another worksheet.

10. Click the **February** worksheet tab, then leave the workbook and Excel open for the next Step-by-Step.

Select Worksheet Data

In order to edit or format content, you first need to select it. You can use the mouse to drag the pointer over the cell(s) you want to select, or use any of the options in Table 6-2 to select portions of your workbook.

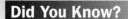

Did You Know?

You can also press **Esc** to deselect any cell or range in a worksheet.

2-3.1.2

Once a cell is selected, you can press Delete to remove any information, start typing to overwrite the cell contents, or apply formatting options by using the Ribbon or keyboard shortcuts. If you select the wrong portion of the workbook, you can click anywhere outside of it to deselect it.

TABLE 6-2
Selecting portions of workbooks

TO SELECT	DO THIS
A cell	Click in the cell
Cell contents	Click in the cell, then click in the Formula bar
A row	Position the pointer to the left of the row, then click
Multiple rows	Position the pointer to the left of the top or bottom row of your intended selection, click, then drag up or down
A column	Position the pointer above the column, then click
Multiple columns	Position the pointer above the leftmost or rightmost column of your intended selection, click, then drag left or right
All of the cells in a worksheet	Press Ctrl + A
A selection of cells	Click a cell, then drag up or down and to the left or right to select multiple cells from adjacent rows and columns
Nonadjacent cells, rows, or columns	Select a row, column, or cell(s), press and hold Ctrl, then select another row, column, or cell(s).

STEP-BY-STEP 6.3

1. Click cell **C2** to select it.

2. Click cell **C6**, select the contents of the Formula bar, then type **Your Name** in the Formula bar.

STEP-BY-STEP 6.3 Continued

3. Position the pointer above column **B**, click to select column **B**, click any cell to deselect it, drag the pointer to select columns **B–D**, then deselect them.

4. Select column **B**, press and hold **Ctrl**, then select column **D**. You have selected two nonadjacent columns.

5. Select row **3**, then select rows **2** and **4**.

6. Press **Ctrl + A** to select all of the cells in the worksheet, then click any cell to deselect them.

7. Click cell **B3**, then drag to select cells **B3:C10**, as shown in Figure 6-3.

FIGURE 6-3
Cells B3:C10 selected

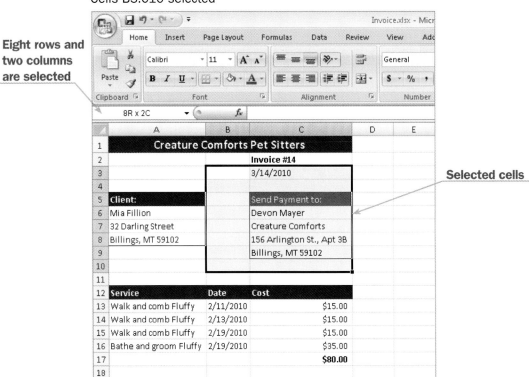

Eight rows and two columns are selected

Selected cells

8. Close the workbook without saving changes, then leave Excel open for the next Step-by-Step.

Create a New Worksheet

When you start Excel, a new, blank document opens automatically. By default, this document is called Book1. The next blank spreadsheet you create during the Excel session is Book2, and so forth. You should save a document before you start working with it in order to keep any changes you make.

If you are already working in Excel and you want to start a new workbook, you can use the New Workbook dialog box to choose a blank spreadsheet or select a template. Templates have placeholder text and are preformatted, and they also include formulas to perform the expected calculations based on the template type. When you create a workbook based on a template, the workbook is called by the template name and numbered sequentially (*TemplateName1, TemplateName2*, and so on) by default until you save it with a new name.

There are a few default templates available when Office is installed on your computer. Most of the templates are available for download from Microsoft Office Online; you must be connected to the Internet to access them. You can view these templates through the New Workbook dialog box by clicking a category in the left pane as shown in Figure 6-4, clicking a thumbnail in the far right pane, then clicking Download. After Microsoft verifies that your software copy is properly registered, Excel will download and open the template.

FIGURE 6-4
Downloading a template from Microsoft Office Online

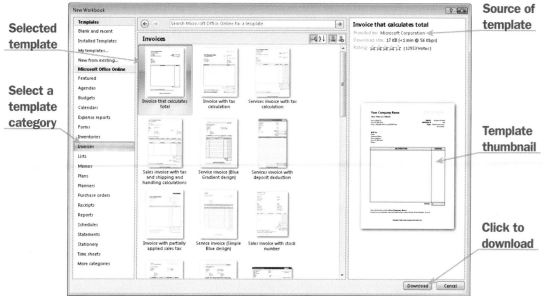

 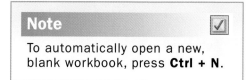

STEP-BY-STEP 6.4

2-1.2.1
2-3.1.3

1. Make sure that the new, blank workbook that you opened when you started Excel, Book1, is open.

> **Note** ☑
>
> To automatically open a new, blank workbook, press **Ctrl + N**.

2. Click the **Office Button**, then click **New**. The New Workbook dialog box opens.

STEP-BY-STEP 6.4 Continued

3. Click **Installed Templates** in the left pane. The New Workbook dialog box displays thumbnails, as shown in Figure 6-5. Your template choices may vary.

FIGURE 6-5
Applying an installed template

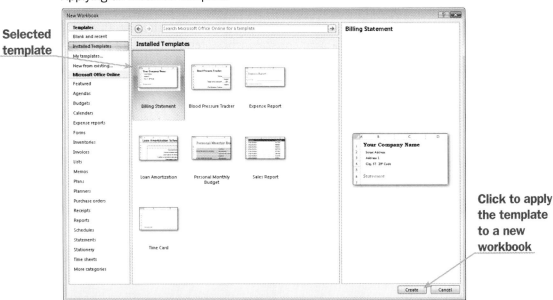

4. Click the **Time Card** thumbnail, then click **Create**. The Time Card template opens for editing and is named TimeCard1, as shown in Figure 6-6. The insertion point is in the first cell that is open for editing—in this case, cell C7. (*Note:* If the Time Card template is not available, choose another.)

FIGURE 6-6
New Time Card workbook

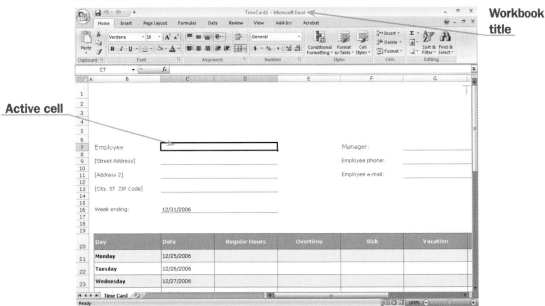

5. Close TimeCard1 without saving changes. Leave Book1 and Excel open for the next Step-by-Step.

Entering Data in a Workbook

When a cell is active (highlighted) in the worksheet, you can enter text or numbers just as you would in Word. In Excel, the insertion point, a blinking line that indicates the current position, is visible when typing information in a cell or when typing in the Formula bar.

Excel recognizes series of text as well as sequences and patterns of numbers. When you enter data such as the days of the week, or numbers in a sequence or pattern such as 1, 2, 3, or 10, 15, 20, you can use AutoFill to complete the series. For example, after typing 1, 2, 3, Excel automatically inserts 4 as the next entry.

Text that you type in Excel is usually either numeric data intended to be used in calculation, analysis, chart or graph, or text or numbers used to identify cell content, such as a table heading. Excel automatically modifies numbers to match the current number format such as date, currency, or decimal. Table 6-3 shows examples of different number formats.

> **Did You Know?**
>
> To automatically fill a column or row with the same value, type the data in the first cell, select that cell and all of the cells in the series, then press **Ctrl + D** to fill the column or click **Ctrl + R** to fill the row.

> **Did You Know?**
>
> Typing an apostrophe (') before a number or formula stores the cell contents as text.

TABLE 6-3
Number formats

FORMAT	USED FOR	USED IN A FORMULA?
General	The default number format. Usually displays numbers as they are typed but will round to decimal points or use scientific notation for numbers with large digits. *Example: 1045.99*	Yes
Number	Any numbers. You can specify decimal points, negative numbers, thousands separators, and other options. *Example: 1045.99*	Yes
Currency	Monetary numbers, using currency symbols such as £ or $. *Example: $1,045.99*	Yes
Accounting	Like currency, but it aligns the currency symbols and decimal points in columns. *Example: $1,045.99*	Yes
Date	Show the day of the week, the year, or just the day and month. *Examples: 7/15/2010; Wednesday, July 15, 2010*	Yes
Time	Shows the time to the second. *Example: 9:30:00 AM*	Yes
Percentage	Displays numbers as multiples of 100. *Example: 48%*	Yes
Fractions	Displays numbers as fractions. *Example: ½*	Yes
Scientific	Displays large numbers in exponential format. *Example: 1.00E+13*	Yes
Text	Treats numbers as text	No
Special	ZIP or Postal Codes, phone numbers, and Social Security numbers. *Example: (978) 555-6790*	No

Some number formats can be used in calculations while others, such as phone numbers, cannot. Applying the correct number format ensures that your data and formulas appear correctly.

2-3.1.3
2-3.1.5

STEP-BY-STEP 6.5

1. Click cell **A1** in Book1, type **12/17/10**, press **Tab,** then press the **left arrow**. The date format is automatically applied, as shown in Figure 6-7.

FIGURE 6-7
Date format applied

Date format is applied

Number Format list arrow

2. Press the **down arrow**, then type **Employees** in cell A2.

3. Press the **down arrow** twice, type **1** in cell A4, press the **down arrow**, then type **2** in cell A5.

4. Select cells **A4** and **A5**, point to the small, **black square** in the lower-right corner of cell A5, then when the pointer changes to a black crosshair, drag down to cell A9, as shown in Figure 6-8. AutoFill inserts the numbers 3–6 in the cells. (*Hint:* If the crosshair pointer is not active, you will move the data instead of automatically filling the cells.)

FIGURE 6-8
Using AutoFill

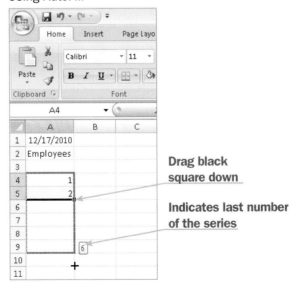

Drag black square down

Indicates last number of the series

STEP-BY-STEP 6.5 Continued

5. Make sure that cells A4 to A9 are still selected, then on the Home tab in the Number group, click the **Number Format** list arrow as shown in Figure 6-9, scroll down, then click **Text**. The numbers are left-aligned in the cells and have the Text format applied, which means that they can no longer be used as numbers in calculations.

FIGURE 6-9
Number Format menu

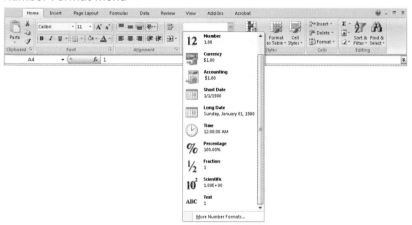

6. Type the information as shown in Figure 6-10.

FIGURE 6-10
Data for employees

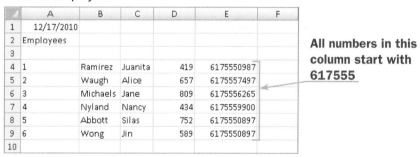

	A	B	C	D	E	F
1	12/17/2010					
2	Employees					
3						
4	1	Ramirez	Juanita	419	6175550987	
5	2	Waugh	Alice	657	6175557497	
6	3	Michaels	Jane	809	6175556265	
7	4	Nyland	Nancy	434	6175559900	
8	5	Abbott	Silas	752	6175550897	
9	6	Wong	Jin	589	6175550897	
10						

All numbers in this column start with **617555**

7. Select cells D4 through D9, then in the Number group, click the **Number Format** list arrow, then apply the **Currency** format. The entries have a dollar sign and decimal point to two places.

8. Select cells E4 through E9, then click the **dialog box launcher** in the Number group. The Format Cells dialog box opens.

STEP-BY-STEP 6.5 Continued

9. On the Number tab, click **Special** in the category list, click **Phone Number** in the Type list, as shown in Figure 6-11, then click **OK**. The entries are formatted for area code and phone number.

FIGURE 6-11
Format Cells dialog box

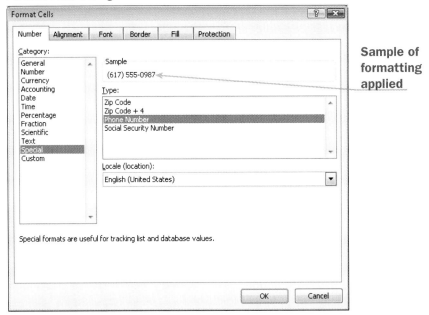

Sample of formatting applied

10. The workbook appears as shown in Figure 6-12.

FIGURE 6-12
Number formats applied

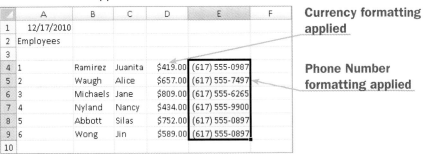

Currency formatting applied

Phone Number formatting applied

11. Save the workbook as **Employee Data.xlsx**. Leave the workbook and Excel open for the next Step-by-Step.

Careers in Technology

You will use and build your spreadsheet skills using Excel or another program in almost any office or business situation. Spreadsheets are used in a variety of ways:

- To enter, track, and analyze data
- To create and update project schedules
- To create business-related forms with formulas, such as expense reports, budgets, and invoices

No matter what your position is, from entry-level assistant, sales clerk, or manager to CEO, you will encounter spreadsheets and be called upon to create and edit them on a regular basis.

Modify Rows and Columns

When creating or editing a spreadsheet, you can adjust the columns and rows to fit your data. Changing the cell height and width ensures that your data is readable. This can be done manually by dragging the row or column dividers or by using the tools on the Page Layout tab. You can change the height and width of a single column or row, a selection of columns and rows, or the entire worksheet.

When there is more data than fits in the cell, you can wrap the data or have it appear in multiple lines. This increases the height of your row automatically without changing the width. You can also choose to AutoFit cell content so that it adjusts to changes in text and formatting.

Did You Know?

As you type, Excel makes suggestions based on content that is in the current column. Press **Enter** or **Tab** to accept the suggestion, or keep typing to overwrite it.

2-3.1.7
2-3.1.4

You can also insert new columns and rows in between current data. When you insert a new row or column, the data adjusts down or to the right in order to make room for your new row or column.

STEP-BY-STEP 6.6

1. Select column **B**, then on the Home tab in the Cells group, click the **Insert** button arrow, then click **Insert Sheet Columns**. A new column B is inserted, and the content that was in column B is moved to column C. Click anywhere in row 4, click the **Insert** button arrow, then click **Insert Sheet Rows**, as shown in Figure 6-13. A new row 4 is inserted, and the content that was in row 4 is moved to row 5.

FIGURE 6-13
Inserting rows and columns

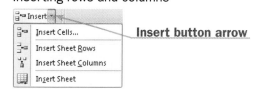

STEP-BY-STEP 6.6 Continued

2. Select rows 3 and 4, click the **Insert** button arrow, then click **Insert Sheet Rows**. Two new rows are inserted because you had selected two rows.

3. Select the new rows you just inserted, if necessary. On the Home tab in the Cells group, click the **Delete** button arrow, then click **Delete Sheet Rows**. The rows are deleted.

4. Enter the text in the new row 4 and column B, as shown in Figure 6-14. (*Hint*: Press Enter to accept the suggestions provided by Excel.)

FIGURE 6-14
Inserting text into new rows and columns

	A	B	C	D	E	F	G	
1	12/17/2010							Text for row 4
2	Employees							
3								
4	ID Number	Title	Last	First	Salary	Phone		
5	1	Assistant	Ramirez	Juanita	$419.00	(617) 555-0987		
6	2	Manager	Waugh	Alice	$657.00	(617) 555-7497		
7	3	Supervisor	Michaels	Jane	$809.00	(617) 555-6265		
8	4	Assistant	Nyland	Nancy	$434.00	(617) 555-9900		
9	5	Manager	Abbott	Silas	$752.00	(617) 555-0897		Data for
10	6	Assistant	Wong	Jin	$589.00	(617) 555-0897		column B
11								

5. Drag the divider at the top of the worksheet between columns A and B to the right. The column width increases.

6. Double-click the divider at the top of the worksheet between columns A and B. The column width adjusts to the size of the current column contents.

7. Select column D, then in the Cells group, click the **Format** button, then click **AutoFit Column Width**, as shown in Figure 6-15.

FIGURE 6-15
Format menu

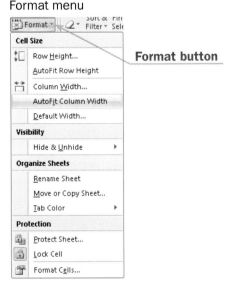

Format button

STEP-BY-STEP 6.6 Continued

8. Select row **2**, then drag the **Resize** pointer down until it is at **42.00**, as shown in Figure 6-16.

FIGURE 6-16
Changing row height

New row height → **New bottom gridline of row** →

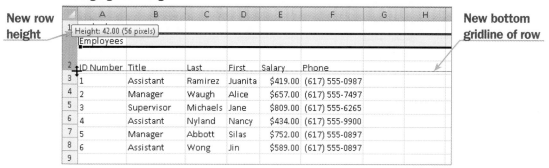

9. Select cell **A2**, click in the Formula bar, position the insertion point before the word *Employees*, type **Mercy Plumbing**, press **Spacebar**, then press **Enter**.

10. Click cell **A2**, in the Cells group, click the **Format** button, then click **Format Cells**.

11. In the Format Cells dialog box, click the **Alignment** tab, click the **Wrap text** check box, as shown in Figure 6-17, then click **OK**. The workbook appears as shown in Figure 6-18.

FIGURE 6-17
Format Cells dialog box

Click to wrap text →

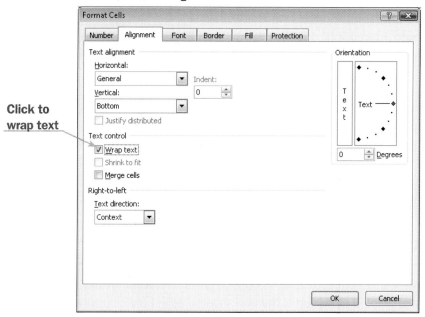

STEP-BY-STEP 6.6 Continued

FIGURE 6-18
Row 2 modified

Row height adjusted

Wrapped text

	A	B	C	D	E	F	G
1	12/17/2010						
2	Mercy Plumbing Employees						
3							
4	ID Number	Title	Last	First	Salary	Phone	
5	1	Assistant	Ramirez	Juanita	$419.00	(617) 555-0987	
6	2	Manager	Waugh	Alice	$657.00	(617) 555-7497	
7	3	Supervisor	Michaels	Jane	$809.00	(617) 555-6265	
8	4	Assistant	Nyland	Nancy	$434.00	(617) 555-9900	
9	5	Manager	Abbott	Silas	$752.00	(617) 555-0897	
10	6	Assistant	Wong	Jin	$589.00	(617) 555-0897	
11							

12. Save your work, then leave the workbook and Excel open for the next Step-by-Step.

Format a Worksheet

You can apply the same font formatting options to Excel text and data, just as you learned to do for Word text. Enhancing text by increasing the font size, adding color, or applying effects such as bolding can emphasize text in selected cells, rows, or columns or the entire worksheet. Borders outline the gridlines of cells, columns, or rows. Unlike gridlines, border lines will be visible when the workbook is printed. Shading fills a cell or selection with a color or pattern. You can also use the Undo and Redo buttons on the Quick Access Toolbar to undo or reapply any formatting or editing that you performed.

2-3.1.6
2-3.1.8

Table Styles are another way to easily apply formatting including shading, borders, and fonts. When you apply a Table Style, you are given the option of verifying the range of cells to format as a table and also whether or not to apply a header row with separate formatting. Applying a Table Style does not change the data in your table, but it can be a quick way to enhance and distinguish your data.

> **Did You Know?**
>
> You can also apply **conditional formatting**, which is formatting that changes depending on the value. You can set conditional formatting to highlight dates that are before or after a certain point or change the color of numbers that are positive or negative.

STEP-BY-STEP 6.7

1. Select cells **A4:F4**, then format the text as **bold**, **12-point**, and **Arial**. Double-click the column border between columns A and B at the top of the worksheet to adjust the column width.

2. Select cells **A4:F4** again if necessary, then on the Home tab in the Font group, click the **Fill Color** button, then click **More Colors**. The Colors dialog box opens.

3. Click the **pink color** shown in Figure 6-19, then click **OK**.

STEP-BY-STEP 6.7 Continued

FIGURE 6-19
Colors dialog box

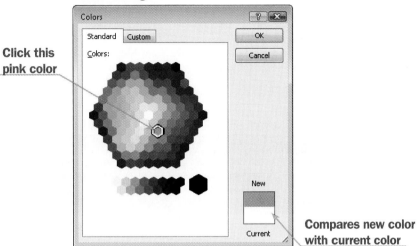

Click this
pink color

New

Compares new color
with current color

Current

4. In the Font group, click the **Border** button arrow, click **Outside Borders**, then deselect the
   cells. The selection has lines around it, as shown in Figure 6-20.

FIGURE 6-20
Font effects, border, and shading applied

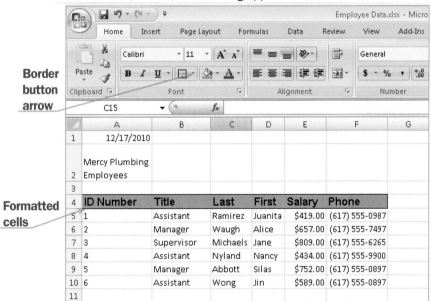

Border
button
arrow

Formatted
cells

5. Select cell **A1**, then in the Font group, click the **Italic** button.

6. In the Alignment group, click the **Align Text Left** button.

7. Select cells **A2:F2**, then in the Alignment group, click the **Merge & Center** button. The cells
   are now one cell, and the text is centered across the cell.

STEP-BY-STEP 6.7 Continued

8. Apply formatting to the rest of the worksheet as shown in Figure 6-21, then save and close the workbook.

FIGURE 6-21
Formatted table

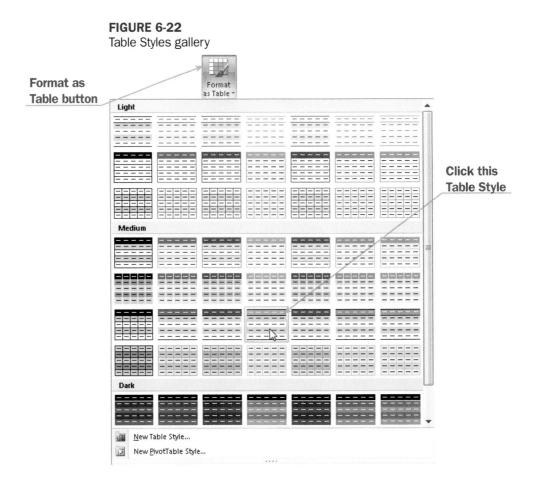

Left-aligned, italic

Dark Blue fill (Standard Colors) and White font color

Merged and centered cells and expanded row height

Light Green font (Standard Colors), 20-point Arial Black font

9. Open the workbook **Grocery List.xlsx**, then in the Styles group, click the **Format as Table** button, then click the **Table Style Medium, 18** style, as shown in Figure 6-22. The Format As Table dialog box opens.

FIGURE 6-22
Table Styles gallery

Format as Table button

Click this Table Style

STEP-BY-STEP 6.7 Continued

10. Click the **My table has headers** check box, then click **OK**.

11. Adjust the column width for column B so that all the text is visible in the cells. The workbook appears as shown in Figure 6-23.

FIGURE 6-23
Table Style applied

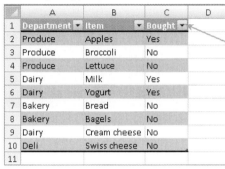

Headers have filter arrows added when the style is applied

12. Save the workbook as **Grocery List Formatted.xlsx**, close it, then leave Excel open for the next Step-by-Step.

Edit Cell Contents

The **Clipboard**, which you learned about in Lesson 3, stores data and objects that you cut or copy from one worksheet in order to paste them in another location in the current workbook, another workbook, or in a document in another application.

The cut, copy, and paste commands are used together to remove or copy text from a document and insert it in another location. The **Cut command** and the **Copy command** are used to copy a selection to the Clipboard. Cut is used when you want to relocate an item, and Copy is used to repeat data. The **Paste command** is used to insert Clipboard items. When you paste a selection that you cut, it is removed from the current location and relocated to the new location. When you paste a selection that you copied, it is kept in the current location and also inserted in the new location.

S TEP-BY-STEP 6.8

1. Open the workbook **Invoice.xlsx**, save it as **January Invoice.xlsx**, then click the **January** worksheet tab.

Did You Know?

When you copy a cell selection, you can only insert it into a cell range of the same size. When you copy a row or row(s) or a column or column(s), you can insert them in between current rows or columns.

STEP-BY-STEP 6.8 Continued

2. Select row **13**, then in the Clipboard group on the Home tab, click the **Copy** button. The row appears with a dotted line around it, as shown in Figure 6-24.

FIGURE 6-24
Copying a row

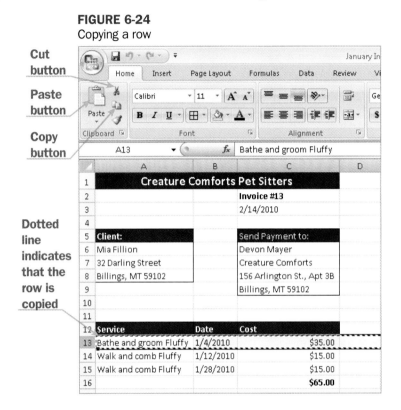

3. Right-click row **16**, then click **Insert Copied Cells**, as shown in Figure 6-25. The data from row 13 appears in row 16.

FIGURE 6-25
Inserting copied cells

4. Select cell **B16**, press **Delete**, then type **1/29/2010**.

STEP-BY-STEP 6.8 Continued

5. Select cells **C2** and **C3**, then drag them to cells **A2** and **A3**, as shown in Figure 6-26.

FIGURE 6-26
Moving cells

Outline and ScreenTip show new location

Cells selected for moving

6. Click cell **C7**, click the end of the text in the Formula bar, then type **, Inc.** so that the cell reads *Creature Comforts, Inc.*

7. Copy cell **C7**, click the **February** worksheet tab, click cell **C7**, then click the **Paste** button.

8. Click the **January** worksheet tab. The worksheet appears as shown in Figure 6-27.

9. Save and close the workbook, then exit Excel.

FIGURE 6-27
Modified invoice

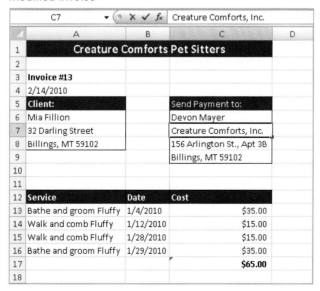

SUMMARY

In this lesson, you learned the following:

■ Excel has many of the same features as Word including the Ribbon, dialog boxes, and scroll bars.

■ Excel has several unique elements, such as the Formula bar and Name box, which are used to edit and navigate content in your workbook.

■ An Excel document is called a workbook, and it is organized in rows and columns of cells on a worksheet. Cells are the intersection of a row and column and are outlined by gridlines.

■ There are many keyboard shortcuts to quickly move to a new location in your workbook.

■ Using the mouse and keyboard shortcuts, you can select rows, columns, cells, cell contents, and nonadjacent selections.

■ You can create a workbook in three ways: insert a new blank workbook, use a template installed on your computer, or download a template from Microsoft Office Online.

■ To enter information in a workbook, type directly in a cell, type in the Formula bar, or use AutoFill to fill a series or continue a pattern.

■ Applying a number format, such as Text, Accounting, or Date, will ensure that your data appears properly and can be used in formulas or is restricted from use in calculations.

■ You can adjust the height of rows and the width of columns manually or by using AutoFit. Rows and columns can be inserted and deleted from a workbook.

■ The same formatting tools as those found in Word can be used to format the font or apply borders and shading. You can also apply a Table Style to quickly enhance data.

■ Cutting, copying, and pasting cell contents, rows, and columns are other ways to modify your workbook.

VOCABULARY*Review*

Define the following terms:

AutoFill	Formula bar	Select
Cell	Gridline	Spreadsheet
Cell address	Insertion point	Table Styles
Clipboard	Name box	Workbook
Column	Number format	Worksheet
Conditional formatting	Paste	Worksheet window
Copy	Range	Wrap
Cut	Row	
Deselect	Scroll bar	

REVIEW *Questions*

SCREEN IDENTIFICATION

Identify the screen elements.

FIGURE 6-28
Screen Identification

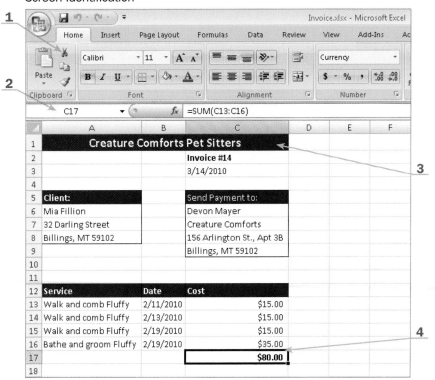

1.

2.

3.

4.

MULTIPLE CHOICE

Circle the correct answer.

1. The _____ feature is used to continue a series, such as A, B, C.
   A. AutoInsert
   B. AutoFill
   C. AutoFormat
   D. AutoComplete

2. A(n) _____ is a nonprinting line that differentiates a column, row, or cell.
   A. Border
   B. Cell address
   C. Gridline
   D. Range

3. A new blank workbook comes by default with three _____.
   A. Worksheets
   B. Columns
   C. Cells
   D. Rows

4. Use the _____ to edit cell contents.
   A. Cell address
   B. Name box
   C. Column header
   D. Formula bar

TRUE/FALSE

Circle T if the statement is true or F if the statement is false.

T   F   1. Shading is used to outline cells.

T   F   2. Pressing **Ctrl + N** opens the New Workbook dialog box.

T   F   3. Press **Tab** to move to the next cell.

T   F   4. When you choose to wrap text, it will appear in multiple lines in the same cell.

T   F   5. Pressing **Ctrl + A** selects all of the cells in a workbook.

T   F   6. Data that is formatted as text can be used in a formula.

T   F   7. Press **End** to move to the end of the workbook.

HANDS-ON REVIEW

1. Open Excel, open a new, blank workbook if necessary, practice navigating through the tabs on the Ribbon, click in the Formula bar, then use the scroll bars.

2. Navigate to cell **B3**, press **Tab** three times, then press **Ctrl + Home**.

3. Select row **3**, select column **B**, select the entire workbook, then select the range **B2:AA5**.

4. Create a new, blank worksheet using the New Workbook dialog box.

5. Enter numbers in cells **A1:A4** and **B1:B4** in the worksheet, then format the data using the **Currency** format.

6. Insert a new row between rows 1 and 2, then enter numbers in the new cells B1 and B2. Insert a new column in between columns B and C, then delete the column. Autofit the contents of the cells in columns A through C.

7. Format the cells in row 1 with bold, red Arial 16-point font. Add shading and a border to column C.

8. Copy column A, then paste it into column C. Cut row 4, then insert the cut cells into row 2.

9. Close the workbook without saving changes.

PROJECTS

PROJECT 6–1

Note: If you are not connected to the Internet, choose a template from the Installed Templates category in the New Workbook dialog box.

1. Create a new workbook by downloading one of the Inventory templates from Microsoft Office Online.

2. Replace some of the placeholder text with your own information, and enter data in at least three of the rows.

3. Select a column, delete it, then undo the deletion.

4. Close the workbook without saving changes.

PROJECT 6–2

1. Open a new, blank workbook.

2. Enter the following information starting in cell A1. Use AutoFill to complete each series.

Monday	Tuesday	Wednesday	Thursday	Friday
1	2	3	4	5
January	February	March	April	May

3. Practice navigating by clicking in the following cells: A3, B2, and D3.

4. Select row 1.

5. Select column B.

6. Select cells A1 through C3.

7. Apply any Table Style. Do not include a header row.

8. Save the workbook as **Practice.xlsx**.

TEAMWORK

Using Table 6-3, divide the number formatting types between your partner or group. For each format that you are assigned, format data in a single column. Print out the data, exchange your columns, and try to identify the formatting.

CRITICAL*Thinking*

ACTIVITY 6-1

Templates allow you to use preformatted workbooks that include sample formulas, data, formatting, and layouts. Open the New Workbook dialog box, and note the different categories of templates available. Choose a template to use to create a new workbook. Replace some of the placeholders with your own content, add your name, and apply formatting. Save it as **My Template.xlsx**.

ARRANGING WORKSHEET DATA

Once you have entered and formatted data in your worksheet, you can modify the worksheet by rearranging the data, establishing how the page is set up, and setting it up for printing.

There are several ways to arrange the data in your worksheet. You can **merge** cells to join them into one, or **split** merged cells into two or more cells. **Sorting** data arranges the cells in sequential order, such as numeric or alphabetical, and either **ascending** (A–Z or 1–25) or **descending** (Z–A or 25–1). **Filtering** data excludes certain categories of data from view without deleting them from the spreadsheet.

Changing the view of the worksheet to **Page Preview** can help to identify adjustments you want to make to page breaks, column width, row height, and more. You can also change the page setup to view the spreadsheet in **landscape** view (longer than it is wide) or in **portrait** view (taller than it is wide).

Other modifications you can make to the worksheet to make it printable include adding a **header**, or text that repeats at the top of the page, and a **footer**, or text that repeats at the bottom of each page. You can use headers and footers to identify page numbers, worksheet titles, dates, or text and graphics that you add.

When printing a worksheet, you can specify the page(s) to print and which elements to include such as gridlines to identify separations of the cells, columns, and rows.

Merge and Split Cells

Merging cells combines multiple adjacent cells into one. You can merge cells horizontally, vertically, or both. When merging cells in two directions, you must have the same number of cells selected in each column and row.

You can merge using the Merge & Center button in the Alignment group on the Home tab, which will center the data across the selection. This is useful when creating a worksheet title or header that will span the width of the data in the table or worksheet. Merge & Center is a toggle button, so to unmerge the cells, click in the merged cell, then click the Merge & Center button.

When you click the Merge & Center button arrow, you can select other options such as Merge Across. This will merge multiple columns but keep the rows separate. The Merge Cells option merges cells and aligns the data in the bottom-right of the merged cell.

2-3.1.4

The cell address of the merged cell is the address of the upper-left cell in the merged range. When you merge cells that contain data, the data in the upper-left

> **Did You Know**
>
> A **range** is a name assigned to two or more adjacent or non-adjacent cells in order to reference them in a formula without selecting the cells. To define a range, use the buttons in the Defined Names group on the Formulas tab.

section of the selection becomes the data for the merged cells. Any data in other cells is deleted, so you should verify the data before you merge. You will be prompted before the data is deleted.

Splitting cells makes one merged cell into two cells. You cannot split a cell unless it has been merged, and you can only split a merged cell into the same number of cells as were originally merged. When you split a merged cell, the data from the merged cell appears in the upper-left cell of the split area.

Figure 7-1 shows examples of merged and split cells.

FIGURE 7-1
Merged and split cells

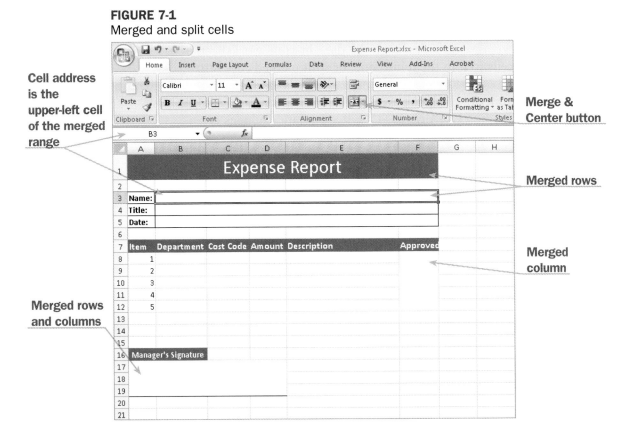

STEP-BY-STEP 7.1

1. Start Excel. In the new, blank workbook, type simple data in cells **A1:B2**, then select cells **A1:B2**.

2. On the Home tab, in the Alignment group, click the **Merge & Center** button, then click **OK** in the alert box. Cells A1, A2, B1, and B2 are merged into one new cell, A1. The data in cells A2, B1, and B2 is deleted, and the data from cell A1 is centered at the bottom across columns A and B.

3. Make sure that cell A1 is selected, click the **Merge & Center** button arrow, then click **Unmerge Cells**, as shown in Figure 7-2. The merged cell splits back into four cells, but only the data from the merged cell is retained; the data that was deleted when you merged cells A1:B2 does not reappear.

FIGURE 7-2
Merging and splitting cells

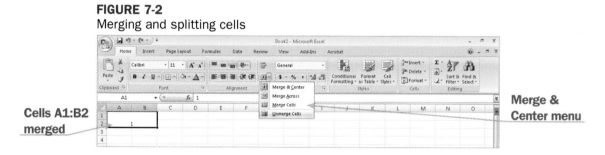

Cells A1:B2 merged

Merge & Center menu

4. Enter simple data in cells **A1:A4**, select cells **A1:A4**, click the **Merge & Center** button arrow, click **Merge Cells**, then click **OK** in the alert box. The data in cell A1 is aligned to the bottom of the merged cell.

5. Enter simple data in cells **E1:G4**, select cells **E1:G4**, click the **Merge & Center** button arrow, click **Merge Across**, then click **OK** four times to overwrite all of the data. The data in the merged cells appears right-aligned, and the worksheet appears as shown in Figure 7-3 (your data will differ).

FIGURE 7-3
Cells merged across

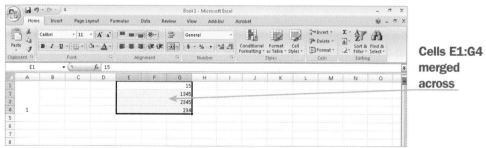

Cells E1:G4 merged across

6. Save the workbook as Merge and Split.xlsx, close the workbook, then leave Excel open for the next Step-by-Step.

Sort Data

Sorting data arranges it in a specific order such as alphabetical, numeric, or by date and time. You can choose to sort data in ascending or descending order or by choosing a custom sort. Most sorts are by column, but you can also sort by rows. You can sort data in the entire column or row, or just in a specific table of data. To identify the area to sort, select a row or column head or, in a table, click any cell in the sort column.

In Lesson 6, you formatted a worksheet area as a table. A **table** is an area that can be formatted, sorted, or filtered independently of the rest of the worksheet.

Custom sorts are used when you want to sort by multiple columns of data. Excel allows you to sort up to 64 columns of data. In addition to numbers and text, you can sort by cell color, font color, or by icon. In Figure 7-4, the data is first sorted in ascending order by Column A, then in descending order by Column B.

FIGURE 7-4
Data sorted by Column A, then Column B

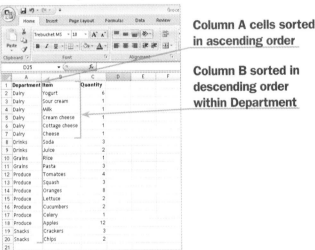

Column A cells sorted in ascending order

Column B sorted in descending order within Department

When sorting data, you have to be careful not to select multiple cells unless you only want to sort the selection. Applying the correct number format is another way to ensure that the data is sorted properly; if you have numbers in a column that are formatted as text and numbers formatted as currency, accounting, or as another format, the data will not sort properly. Excel will display a sorting error message when it identifies a potential sort issue. Table 7-1 lists common sorting problems and how to solve them.

TABLE 7-1
Troubleshooting sort errors

ERROR	SOLUTION
Merged cells	Merging can cause problems because Excel is not able to match cells into columns and rows. If you have a table of data with merged cells, you need to select the cells in the area to sort (not just the sort column or row), then identify which row/column by which to sort.
Mixed formats	Excel will sort numbers formatted as text differently than data formatted with any of the number formats that can be used in calculations (accounting, general, and so on). Make sure your data is formatted with the same format within the sort column or row.
Extra spaces	If there is a space before the data when it was entered into a cell, Excel considers the space to be the first sort character. Make sure that none of your cells contain extra spaces.
Formulas are miscalculated	If you select the wrong sort order, or if the formulas used in your cells contain relative references (cells that adjust when data is moved), you may encounter errors. Undo the sort, view the cells in the Formula bar, then attempt to fix the miscalculations.
Rows and columns are hidden	Sometimes it is helpful to hide rows and columns; this excludes them from view but does not delete them. You can tell if cells are hidden by looking for skipped column letters and row numbers.
Column headings	Excel usually identifies the top row of a table of data as the header. If the header row sorts along with the other data, undo the sort, then in the Sort dialog box, select the My data has headers check box.

STEP-BY-STEP 7.2

2-3.1.3
2-3.2.1

1. Open the workbook **Shopping List.xlsx** from your Data Files.

2. Click any cell in column **A**, then on the **Home** tab, in the **Editing** group, click the **Sort & Filter** button then click **Sort A to Z**. The cells are sorted alphabetically by department.

3. Select cells **B2:B7**, click the **Data** tab, then in the **Sort & Filter** group, click the **Sort Z to A** button. In the Sort Warning dialog box, click the **Continue with the current selection** option button, then click **Sort**. Note that only the cells in B2:B7 are sorted.

4. Click the **Undo** button on the Quick Access Toolbar, then click any cell in the range A1:C20 to deselect the data.

5. In the **Sort & Filter** group, click the **Sort** button. The Sort dialog box opens.

6. Click the **Column** list arrow, click **Department** if necessary, click the **Order** list arrow, then click **Z to A**.

STEP-BY-STEP 7.2 Continued

7. Click the **Add Level** button, click the **Column** list arrow, click **Quantity**, click the **Order** list arrow, then click **Smallest to Largest**, if necessary.

8. Click the **Move Up** arrow to move Quantity to the first criteria, as shown in Figure 7-5, then click **OK**. The workbook is sorted first by column C, then by column A, as shown in Figure 7-6.

FIGURE 7-5
Applying a custom sort

Click to add additional sort column

First sort column

Second sort column

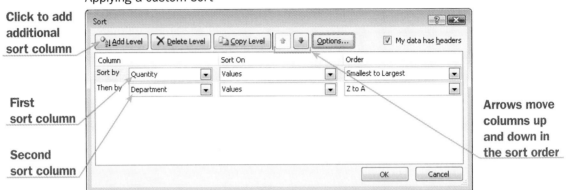

Arrows move columns up and down in the sort order

FIGURE 7-6
Data sorted by Column C, then Column A

Column A sorted in descending order within Column C sort

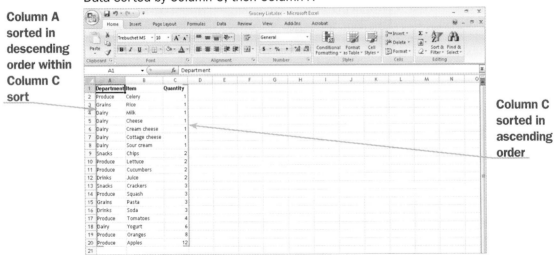

Column C sorted in ascending order

9. Save the workbook as **Sorted Shopping List.xlsx**, close the workbook, then leave Excel open for the next Step-by-Step.

Filter Data

Filtering is another way to rearrange data in a range or table in order to analyze the contents. Unlike sorting, which shows all of the data in the sort area in a specific order, filtering data will display only the data that meets certain criteria. The other data is hidden but not removed from the workbook. Figure 7-7 shows a worksheet before and after a filter is applied.

FIGURE 7-7a
Unfiltered data

Unfiltered data

	A	B	C	D	E
1	Tour Number	City	Tour Type	Start Date	Tour Leader
2	164	London	Art Gallery	9/1/2010	Brenda
3	148	New York	Bus Tour	7/6/2010	Brenda
4	150	New York	Pop Culture	7/10/2010	Brenda
5	147	San Francisco	City Walk	10/15/2010	Brenda
6	155	Tokyo	Bus Tour	9/15/2010	Brenda
7	158	London	City Walk	7/1/2010	Brian
8	151	London	Restaurant	7/6/2010	Brian
9	145	London	City Walk	9/1/2010	Brian
10	152	Munich	Restaurant	7/10/2010	Brian
11	163	Munich	Restaurant	10/15/2010	Brian
12	154	New York	Restaurant	8/15/2010	Brian
13	159	Munich	Art Gallery	7/6/2010	Hans
14	146	Munich	Art Gallery	9/1/2010	Hans
15	160	Munich	Bus Tour	9/15/2010	Hans
16	157	New York	Art Gallery	10/15/2010	Hans
17	156	Tokyo	Pop Culture	7/10/2010	Hans
18	162	London	Pop Culture	8/15/2010	Julio
19	161	San Francisco	Art Gallery	7/12/2010	Julio
20	153	San Francisco	Restaurant	9/1/2010	Julio
21	149	Tokyo	Restaurant	7/5/2010	Julio

FIGURE 7-7b
Filter applied

Filter list arrow

Data is filtered by column E

	A	B	C	D	E
1	Tour Numb	City	Tour Type	Start Date	Tour Lead
2	164	London	Art Gallery	9/1/2010	Brenda
3	148	New York	Bus Tour	7/6/2010	Brenda
4	150	New York	Pop Culture	7/10/2010	Brenda
5	147	San Francisco	City Walk	10/15/2010	Brenda
6	155	Tokyo	Bus Tour	9/15/2010	Brenda
22					

Filtered data can be copied, edited, used to create a chart, or printed.

Filters can be applied to multiple columns. Each column that you filter makes the data more specific and reduces the data displayed. Figure 7-8 shows filters applied to multiple columns.

FIGURE 7-8
Filtering by multiple columns

A2		*fx*	164	

Data is filtered by columns B and E

	A	B	C	D	E	F
1	Tour Numb	City	Tour Type	Start Date	Tour Lead	
19	161	San Francisco	Art Gallery	7/12/2010	Julio	
20	153	San Francisco	Restaurant	9/1/2010	Julio	
22						

AutoFilter is used to filter using the criteria of the current table. When you click the Filter button, filter arrows appear at the top of each column or the left side of a row. Clicking a filter arrow gives you options for filtering by one or more criteria for that column. Table 7-2 outlines different filter types.

TABLE 7-2
Filtering options

FILTER TYPE	DESCRIPTION	EXAMPLE
Comparison operator	To include data that meets a certain criteria such as **Equals**, **Before**, **After**, or **Between**	Find all dates in a schedule that are before 9/3/2010
Dynamic	Filter criteria, such as **Today**, change when you reapply the filter	Find all examples of the current date in a schedule
Cell color, font color, or icon set	Filters by cells that are colored either manually or by applying a conditional format	Find all cells that use a red font color, which is used to identify financial data that shows a loss
Filter by selection	Filters data that is equal to the contents of the active cell	Select a cell that contains the month February, then find all other cells in that column or row that also contain February
Advanced criteria	Using the same column heads in the criteria range as are in the table or sort range, enter multiple filter criteria above the range of cells or table you want to filter	To find data that meets criteria in different columns such as by Month, Salesperson, and Hourly wage
Top or bottom number	Uses values based on the cell range or table column to find the top or bottom number in a range	Find the students with the top 10 grades in a class
Blanks	Find all rows that contain a blank cell	To find areas where data is missing
Above or below average	Use a cell in a table with numeric data to calculate an average, then find the cells that are above or below the average	Find all students with passing or failing grades

STEP-BY-STEP 7.3

1. Open the file **Tour List.xlsx** from your Data Files.

2. Click the **Data** tab, then in the **Sort & Filter** group, click the **Filter** button. Filter arrows appear at the top of the column headers.

STEP-BY-STEP 7.3 Continued

3. Click the **Tour Leader** filter arrow, click the **Select All** check box to deselect it, click **Brenda**, then click **OK**. Only Brenda's tours are listed, and the filter icon appears on the filter arrow.

4. Click the **Tour Leader** filter arrow, click **Hans**, then click **OK**. Brenda's and Hans's tours are both displayed.

5. In the **Sort & Filter** group, click the **Clear** button to redisplay all data.

6. Click the **City** filter arrow, click **New York**, **San Francisco**, and **Tokyo** to deselect them, then click **OK**. Only the tours for London and Munich are shown.

7. Click the **Start Date** filter arrow, point to **Date Filters**, then click **Custom Filter**, as shown in Figure 7-9.

FIGURE 7-9
Date Filters menu

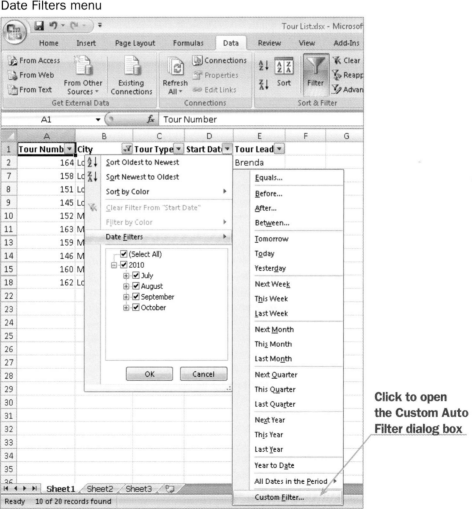

Click to open the Custom Auto Filter dialog box

STEP-BY-STEP 7.3 Continued

8. In the Custom AutoFilter dialog box, click the **Start Date** list arrow, click **is before**, click the **date** list arrow as shown in Figure 7-10, click **9/1/2010**, then click **OK**. The worksheet displays only tours for London and Munich that start before 9/1/2010, as shown in Figure 7-11.

FIGURE 7-10
Custom AutoFilter dialog box

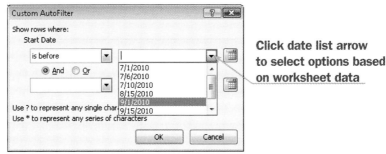

Click date list arrow
to select options based
on worksheet data

FIGURE 7-11
Custom filter applied

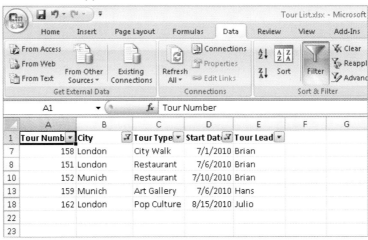

9. Save the workbook as **Filtered Tour List.xlsx**, close the workbook, then leave Excel open for the next Step-by-Step.

Add Headers and Footers

Headers and footers are text boxes that appear at the top and bottom of pages in your worksheet. You can choose to insert a custom header or a predefined header. You can also insert icons or other graphics into a header.

To add a header or footer, you can click the Page Layout View button or click the Header & Footer button in the Text group on the Insert tab, which switches the view automatically to Page Layout. To edit a header or footer, you must first switch to Page Layout view. You can change between Page Layout and Normal views using the buttons on the status bar, or by clicking the appropriate button in the Workbook Views group on the View tab.

A predefined header or footer is one that includes certain standard elements such as worksheet title, page number, or date. To include a predefined header or footer, switch to Page Layout view, click in the header or footer, then click the Header button or the Footer button in the Header & Footer group on the Header & Footer Tools, Design tab. Choose one of the header or footer options from the menu, as shown in Figure 7-12. Each header or footer element is separated by a comma on the menu.

FIGURE 7-12
Adding a predefined header element

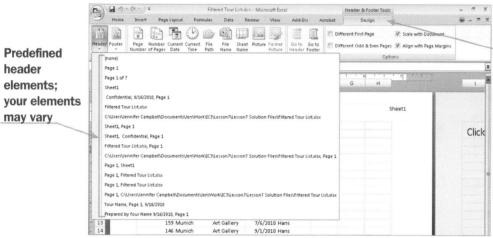

Predefined header elements; your elements may vary

Header & Footer Tools, Design tab

To include an element such as the date, page number, or a picture, use the tools in the Header & Footer Elements group on the Header & Footer Tools Design tab. When in Page Layout view, the elements you add appear as placeholders that indicate what the item is. For example, if you insert a picture, in Page Layout view you will see &[Picture] instead of the picture. Other placeholders are worksheet title &[Tab] and page number &[Page].

You can specify where and how the headers and footers should appear on pages of your worksheet. Options include the following:

- A different header or footer for odd and even pages.

- A different header or footer on the first page.

- Using the same font size and scaling as in the worksheet (useful if you are specifying a print area or instructing Excel to fit the columns or areas to fit on one page).

- Aligning the header and footer margins with the left and right worksheet margins.

Did You Know?

Ampersands (&) are used in headers and footers as nonprinting characters that differentiate elements. If you want to include an ampersand in your header or footer, you need to type two ampersands. For example, to include "Macaroni & Cheese" in a header, type **Macaroni && Cheese**.

STEP-BY-STEP 7.4

1. Open the workbook **Expense Report.xlsx**.

2. Click the **Insert** tab, then in the Text group, click the **Header & Footer** button. The Header & Footer Tools Design tab displays, as shown in Figure 7-13.

FIGURE 7-13
Header & Footer Tools, Design tab

Header area

3. In the Header & Footer Elements group, click the **Page Number** button.

4. Press **Tab**, then in the Header & Footer Elements group, click the **Sheet Name** button. The header appears as shown in Figure 7-14 with the &[Tab] placeholder for the worksheet name.

FIGURE 7-14
Finished header

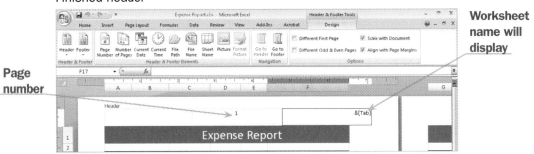

Worksheet name will display

Page number

5. In the Navigation group, click the **Go to Footer** button.

6. In the Header & Footer Elements group, click the **Picture** button, in the Insert Picture dialog box, click **Global Logo.tif** from your Data Files, then click **Insert**. The placeholder &[Picture] appears in the footer.

7. Double-click the worksheet to deactivate the footer. The logo appears in the footer, as shown in Figure 7-15.

STEP-BY-STEP 7.4 Continued

FIGURE 7-15
Finished footer

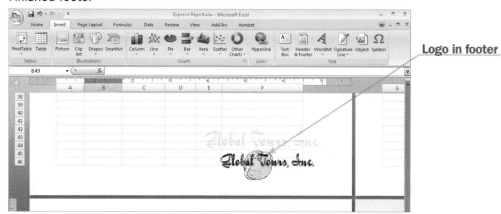

Logo in footer

8. Scroll up to view the header in Normal view. The worksheet name displays.

9. Save the workbook as **Modified Expense Report.xlsx**, then leave the workbook and Excel open for the next Step-by-Step.

Modify the Page Setup

When preparing your worksheet for printing, you can change the page orientation, scale the worksheet, add a background image, and adjust the margins of the page. Another page setup option allows you to display the gridlines and column letters and row numbers on the printed page.

Page orientation refers to whether the document is longer than it is wide, or portrait, or wider than it is in long, such as with landscape orientation. Changing the orientation to landscape allows you to fit more columns on the printed page, while portrait orientation can fit more rows. Which orientation you choose depends on how your information is set up and how you want it to appear on the page.

Adjusting the scaling of a workbook keeps the proportions of column width, row height, and font size, while making each smaller or larger to fit to the specifications.

Adding a background image or text can identify or enhance your document. In Excel, you can use a picture as a sheet background for display purposes only. A sheet background does not print, and it is not retained in an individual worksheet or in an item that you save as a Web page.

Margins are the spaces along the perimeter of a page. Changing the margins can be done using a preset margin combination or by manually dragging the margin borders to increase or decrease the margin size.

S TEP-BY-STEP 7.5

1. Click the **Page Layout** tab, then in the Page Setup group, click the **Orientation** button, then click **Landscape**. All of the columns fit on one page.

2. In the Scale to Fit group, click the **Scale** up arrow until it shows **120%**. The worksheet appears as shown in Figure 7-16.

FIGURE 7-16
Scaling applied

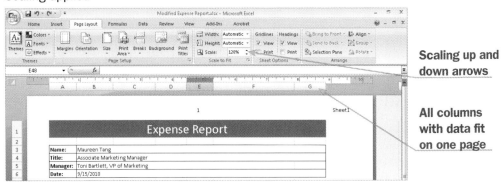

Scaling up and down arrows

All columns with data fit on one page

3. In the Page Setup group, click the **Background** button. The Sheet Background dialog box opens.

4. In the Sheet Background dialog box, click **Jetset Logo.tif** from your Data Files, then click **Insert**.

5. The logo appears tiled across the background of the worksheet, as shown in Figure 7-17.

FIGURE 7-17
Logo is tiled in the background

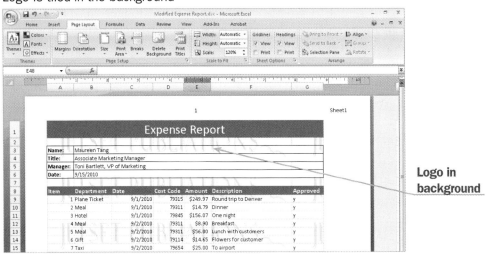

Logo in background

6. In the Sheet Options group, in the Gridlines section, click the **Print** check box. The gridlines will print on the page.

STEP-BY-STEP 7.5 Continued

7. In the Page Setup group, click the **Margins** button as shown in Figure 7-18, then click **Wide**. The margins are wider, but because you applied scaling, the worksheet still fits.

FIGURE 7-18
Changing the margins

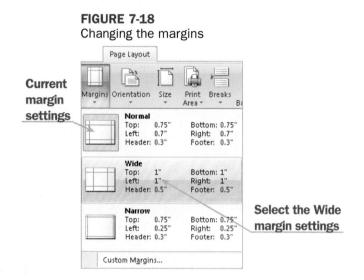

8. Save and close the workbook, then leave Excel open for the next Step-by-Step.

Preview and Print a Worksheet

2-1.4.1
2-1.4.3

Viewing a worksheet in page break preview displays blue lines that indicate where the page breaks will occur. A dotted blue line is an automatic page break that Excel has set based on the size of the page, the paper size you have selected, and the margins of the page. A solid blue line is a manual page break that you have inserted. You can drag the page breaks in any direction to change where the break occurs. When you adjust the page breaks, Excel will modify the scaling appropriately to accommodate them.

You should always preview your worksheet before printing. Print Preview displays the worksheet as it will appear when printed. In Print Preview, you can change the margins, adjust column width, and choose Page Setup options before you print your document.

In the Print dialog box, you can specify how many copies to print, change the color and page size options, and specify the printer.

STEP-BY-STEP 7.6

1. Open the workbook **Pet Sitting Invoice.xlsx**.

2. On the status bar, click the **Page Break Preview** button, click **OK** in the Welcome to Page Break Preview dialog box, if necessary. The worksheet appears as shown in Figure 7-19. (*Hint:* Scroll if necessary.)

FIGURE 7-19
Page Break Preview

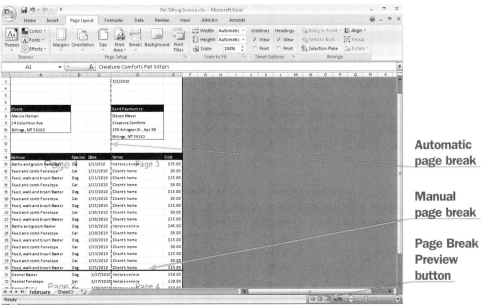

Automatic page break

Manual page break

Page Break Preview button

3. Drag the manual page break that appears between rows **30:31** to below row 35. The length of the page is now one page.

4. Click the **Office Button**, point to **Print**, then click **Print Preview**. The status bar indicates that the worksheet would print on two pages.

5. In the Preview group, click the **Next Page** button to view page 2.

6. In the Preview group, click the **Show Margins** check box, then drag the right margin toward the edge of the page a little at a time until the columns fit on one page, as shown in Figure 7-20.

STEP-BY-STEP 7.6 Continued

FIGURE 7-20
Print Preview

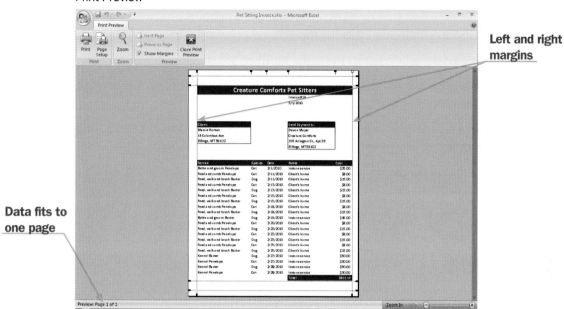

Left and right margins

Data fits to one page

Preview: Page 1 of 1

7. In the Preview group, click the **Close Print Preview** button.

8. Click the **Office Button**, point to **Print**, then click **Print**. The Print dialog box opens, as shown in Figure 7-21.

FIGURE 7-21
Print dialog box

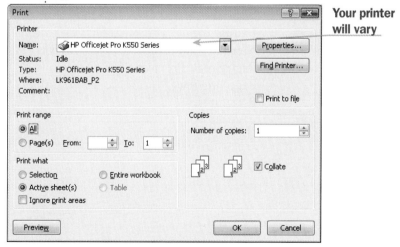

Your printer will vary

9. Select a printer if necessary, then click **OK**. The document prints.

10. Save the workbook as **Final Invoice.xlsx**, close the workbook, then exit Excel.

SUMMARY

In this lesson, you learned:

- Merging cells combines two or more cells that are in either adjacent rows or columns into one cell, or multiple columns of cells into one row.

- You can split merged cells back to the same number of cells that they were in before the merge.

- Sorting data arranges it by alphabetical, numeric, date, or another sequential order. You can also sort by row, color, graphic, or icon.

- Filtering data excludes data that meets certain criteria from view. You can exclude by multiple columns in order to further pair down the data that is shown.

- While not visible, data that is filtered remains in the worksheet and can be used to create a chart or other analysis tool.

- You can add headers and footers to include elements such as page numbers, worksheet titles, and other information. You can also add a custom header or footer.

- The page setup of a workbook can be modified by adjusting the margins, page breaks, or scaling of the worksheet.

- Previewing and printing a worksheet is an important step when finalizing your worksheet. Previewing verifies that the pages will appear as you specified in page setup view. Printing creates a printed handout of your file.

VOCABULARY *Review*

Define the following terms:

Ampersand	Header	Range
Ascending	Landscape	Scaling
AutoFilter	Merge	Sort
Descending	Page Break Preview	Split
Filter	Page Preview	Table
Footer	Portrait	

SCREEN IDENTIFICATION

Identify the screen elements.

FIGURE 7-22
Screen Identification

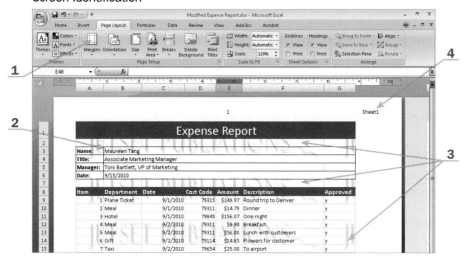

1. _____

2. _____

3. _____

4. _____

MULTIPLE CHOICE

Circle the correct answer.

1. A worksheet in _____ view is wider than it is high.
   A. Landscape
   B. Ascending
   C. Descending
   D. Portrait

2. When you _____ data, it shows only data that meets certain criteria.
   A. AutoFill
   B. Filter
   C. Sort
   D. Preview

3. When you _____ data, it rearranges it according to criteria you set.
   A. AutoFill
   B. Filter
   C. Sort
   D. Preview

4. You can adjust _____ page breaks in Page Break Preview.
   A. Manual
   B. Automatic
   C. Neither A nor B
   D. Both A and B

TRUE/FALSE

Circle T if the statement is true or F if the statement is false.

T   F   1. In Print Preview, you can adjust column widths.

T   F   2. Data sorted in descending order is sorted by A–Z.

T   F   3. Graphics that you insert in the background of a worksheet also appear when it is printed.

T   F   4. You can insert a graphic into a footer.

T   F   5. When you split cells, you can choose the number of cells in which to split the cells.

HANDS-ON REVIEW

1. Open the worksheet **Employees.xlsx**. Merge and center cells **A1:G1**. Split cells **A23:G23**.

2. Sort the data in column **B** in descending order.

3. Apply a filter to show the employees in the sales and marketing departments whose salaries are less than $752.

4. Add the page number and sheet name to the header, and add the graphic **Mercy Logo.tif** from your Data Files to the footer.

5. Modify the page setup to show gridlines when it is printed, then specify narrow margins.

6. Preview the worksheet, make any other adjustments, then print one copy of the worksheet.

7. Save the workbook as **Updated Employees.xlsx**, then close it.

PROJECTS

PROJECT 7-1

Open the worksheet **To Do List.xlsx**. Sort column B in descending order. Notice that the data does not all appear in order. Check the formatting of the data in cell **B16**, apply an appropriate number format, reapply the sort to column B (descending order). Save the worksheet as **Task List.xlsx**.

PROJECT 7-2

Open the worksheet **Monthly Expenses.xlsx**. Filter the data to show just the items purchased by Kellie. Clear the filter. Filter to show the items purchased for school between 2/8/2010 and 2/15/2010. Save the workbook as **Filtered Monthly Expenses.xlsx**.

CRITICAL *Thinking*

ACTIVITY 7-1

Open the workbook **Team Scores.xlsx**. On each of the three tabs, try to apply a sort.

- **November:** Sort ascending by column C

- **December:** Sort ascending by column D

- **January:** Sort ascending by column A

Write down errors that you notice and how you would fix them. *Hint:* column D in the December tab contains hidden rows. Save your answers in a Word document named **Sort Errors.docx**. Fix the errors, then save the workbook as **Sorted Team Scores.xlsx**.

 TEAMWORK

With a partner, create a workbook that needs adjustments in order to fit onto one page. Use the skills you learned in this lesson to modify the page setup, add a header and footer, and set the gridlines to print.

USING FORMULAS AND CREATING CHARTS

The data that you have learned to enter, edit, and format in Lessons 6 and 7 can be used to perform simple and complex calculations. The calculations in Microsoft Excel are called formulas. Tools such as AutoSum are used to perform common mathematical operations without entering a formula. Functions are used to help perform the calculations, reducing errors by guiding you through selecting the cell(s) for a calculation, mathematical operators, and function words, and inserting that information into a formula.

Formulas use a combination of mathematical operators (=, +, ×, and so on), function words such as SUM or AVG, and cell references to create the formula. Cell references can be either absolute or relative. Absolute cell references do not change even when the formula is copied to another cell; relative cell references reflect the location of the formula.

Charts are graphical representations of data. There are many different kinds of charts, such as pie, bar, and graph. Charts are used to analyze data and make conclusions.

Understand Formulas

A formula always starts with an equal sign (=), indicating to Excel that you are starting a formula. There are four potential parts of a formula: functions, operators, references, and constants.

Functions are words that Excel recognizes as part of a calculation, such as SUM, to total a range of values or AVG to find the average of a range. You will learn more about functions later in this lesson.

Types of operators include arithmetic, comparison, and reference. **Arithmetic operators** include percentages (**%**), plus signs (**+**), and asterisks (*****) to indicate multiplication. **Comparison operators** indicate criteria such as greater than (**>**), equal to (**=**), or less than or equal to (**<=**). A **reference operator** is used to indicate a range of cells, such as a colon (**:**) to reference the cell area **A5:G6**, or a comma (**,**) to reference multiple cells or ranges.

References and constants are numeric values in a formula. A **reference** can be a cell address, a range such as A5:G5, or a named range. **Constants** are numbers that do not change. For instance, if you want to double a value, you would always multiply by 2.

Excel performs calculations based on a priority of commands, not from left to right. Negative numbers

> **Did You Know?**
>
> Text is an operator that is used to join multiple references together, including text strings, numbers, or cell references.

are always read first, followed by percentages, arithmetic commands, text strings, and lastly, comparison operators. In order to remember the order of arithmetic operations, you can use the memory aid, **PEMDAS:** Please Excuse My Dear Aunt Sally, as outlined in Table 8-1.

TABLE 8-1
Order of mathematical operations

ORDER	OPERATION	DESCRIPTION	EXAMPLE
1. Please	Parentheses	Operations within the parentheses are done before being used in the rest of the formula	**(3+5)**
2. Excuse	Exponents	Powers, or exponents, such as squaring or cubing	n^2
3. My Dear	Multiplication, Division	When multiplication and division commands are both present, Excel performs them from left to right	**3*5** or **3/5**
4. Aunt Sally	Addition, Subtraction	When addition and subtraction commands are both present, Excel performs them from left to right	**3+5** or

Some examples of formulas follow:

■ =(3+A2)/5. First, Excel calculates the sum of 3 (a constant) and the value in cell **A2** (a reference), then divides the sum by 5.

■ =4+B4*C4. The values in cells **B4** and **C4** are multiplied, then 4 is added to the result.

■ =6+(D14/6)^2–500. First, the value in cell **D14** is divided by 6, then the result is squared (power of 2). Next, **6** is added to that result, and **500** is subtracted.

Create Formulas

A cell that contains a formula will display the result of the calculation. When you click a cell that contains a formula, the formula displays the Formula bar. You can use the Formula bar to edit the formula.

2-3.2.3
2-3.2.6

To reference a cell or cell range in a formula, click the cell, select the range, or type the address or name of the cell or range into the formula. For example, to create the formula =(3+A2)/5, type =(3+, then either type **A2** or click cell **A2**, and then type)/5.

STEP-BY-STEP 8.1

1. Start Excel, then open a new, blank workbook, if necessary.

2. Click cell **A1**, type **=3+5**, then press **Enter**. The result of the formula, 8, appears in cell A1.

3. Click cell **A1** again, click in the Formula bar, edit the formula to read **=3*5**, then press **Enter**. The result of the formula, 15, appears in cell A1.

4. Type and format data into the range A3:D6, as shown in Figure 8-1. (*Note:* Throughout this Lesson, apply the appropriate number format as needed to make your screen match the figures.)

FIGURE 8-1
Data to type

Result of formula: =3*5

	A	B	C	D	E
1	15				
2					
3		January	February	March	
4	Jordan	$14,870.00	$16,651.00	$13,549.00	
5	Ava	$19,097.00	$17,054.00	$ 9,743.00	
6	Nikhil	$16,884.00	$20,076.00	$10,932.00	
7					
8					

5. Click cell **B9**, type **=**, click cell **B5**, type **/**, click cell **A1**, then press **Enter**.

6. Click cell **B9**. The result of the calculation, 1273.13, appears in cell B9, and the formula appears in the Formula bar, as shown in Figure 8-2.

STEP-BY-STEP 8.1 Continued

FIGURE 8-2
Using cell references in a formula

	B9		f_x	=B5/A1		
	A	B	C	D	E	
1	15					
2						
3		January	February	March		
4	Jordan	$14,870.00	$16,651.00	$13,549.00		
5	Ava	$19,097.00	$17,054.00	$9,743.00		
6	Nikhil	$16,884.00	$20,076.00	$10,932.00		
7						
8						
9		$1,273.13				
10						
11						

Formula in Formula bar

The result of the formula

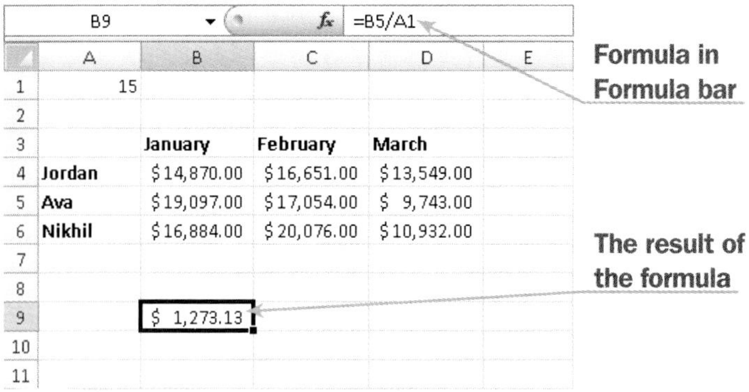

7. Click cell **C9**, type **=(C4+**, click cell C5, then type **)*2+3**. The worksheet appears as shown in Figure 8-3.

FIGURE 8-3
Typing a formula

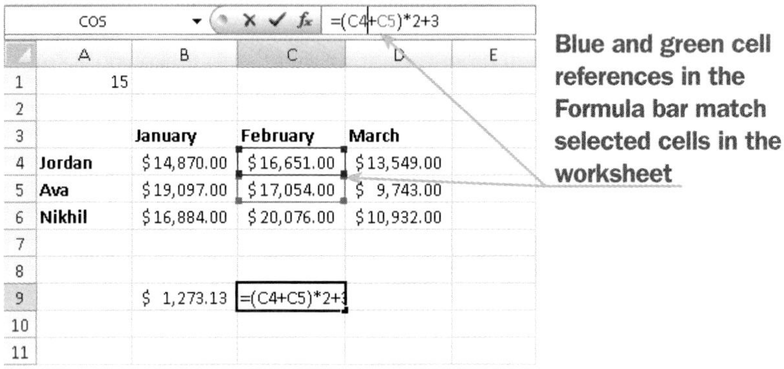

	COS		X ✓ f_x	=(C4+C5)*2+3		
	A	B	C	D	E	
1	15					
2						
3		January	February	March		
4	Jordan	$14,870.00	$16,651.00	$13,549.00		
5	Ava	$19,097.00	$17,054.00	$9,743.00		
6	Nikhil	$16,884.00	$20,076.00	$10,932.00		
7						
8						
9		$1,273.13	=(C4+C5)*2+3			
10						
11						

Blue and green cell references in the Formula bar match selected cells in the worksheet

8. Press **Enter**. The formula will be calculated by first adding the values in cells C4 and C5 (33,705.00), multiplying the sum by 2 ($67,410.00), then adding 3, which equals $67,413.00.

9. Save the workbook as **Practice Formulas.xlsx**, then leave the workbook and Excel open for the next Step-by-Step.

Use Absolute and Relative Cell References

Relative cell references are ones that change based on the location of the formula. Relative cell references are useful when you want to perform the same calculation for multiple rows or columns of data.

Relative cell references in a formula change based on the relationship of the new formula to the original formula. For example, if you enter a formula in cell A1, and then copy and paste that formula into cell A2 one row below, the pasted formula will change the cell references to one row below. Similarly, if you paste a formula in a cell four columns to the right of the original, the pasted formula will reference cells four rows to the right. For example, let's say the formula =5*C3 is in cell D3. If you copy and paste the formula in D4, it will read =5*C4.

An absolute cell reference is one that does not change no matter where you paste the formula. You might use an absolute cell reference in a formula if you want to multiply the value of each cell in column C by a value that appears in cell A3. In a formula, an absolute cell reference is noted using $ before the column letter and row number. For example, $A$3 is the absolute cell reference for cell A3. You can copy a formula that contains $A$3 into multiple columns or rows, and while any relative cell references will change, A3 will always be a part of the formula.

A **mixed cell reference** is one where either the column letter or row number is absolute but the other is relative. For example, **$A3** is a mixed reference where column A is absolute but row 3 is relative. The mixed reference **A$3** uses a relative reference for column A and an absolute reference for row 3.

2-3.2.2

Figure 8-4 shows how formulas with absolute and relative cell references change when they are copied. When the formula in cell C15 is copied to cell C16, the absolute reference stays the same, and the mixed reference updates.

FIGURE 8-4
Absolute and relative cell references

	A	B	C	D	E	
	C15		f_x =$B$3*$B6			
1			**Invoice**			Formula with absolute and mixed references
2						
3	Sales Tax		5%			Formula with relative references: =B6*C6
4						
5	Item	Quantity	Price	Cost		
6	Pencils		22 $ 0.14	$ 3.08		
7	Pens		24 $ 0.25	$ 6.00		
8	Notebooks		4 $ 2.25	$ 9.00		
9			Subotal	$ 18.08		
10			Tax	$ 0.81		Result of the formula: =$B$3*$B6
11			Total	$ 18.89		
12						
13						
14		Tax summary				
15		Pencils	0.99			Result of the formula: =$B$3*$B7
16		Pens	1.08			
17		Notebooks	0.18			
18						

$STEP-BY-STEP 8.2

1. Click cell **B11**, type **=B4*A1**, then press **Enter**. The formula contains a relative cell reference for B4.

2. Click cell **B11**, then on the **Home tab** and in the **Clipboard group**, click the **Copy** button.

3. Click cell **B12**, then in the **Clipboard group**, click the **Paste** button. The formula changes to **=B5*A2**, as shown in Figure 8-5.

STEP-BY-STEP 8.2 Continued

FIGURE 8-5
Copying a formula with relative cell references

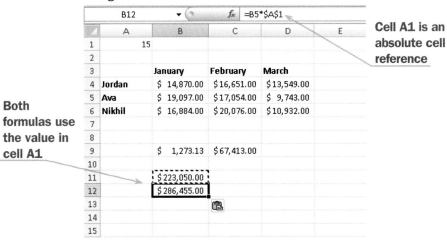

4. Press **Enter**. Because cell A2 contains no data, the result is 0.

5. Using the Formula bar, change the formula in cell B11 to **=B4*$A$1**. Cell A1 is now an absolute cell reference.

6. Copy the formula from cell B11 to cell B12. The formula in cell B12 is now **=B5*$A$1**, and because the formula uses the value in cell A1, the result is $286,455, as shown in Figure 8-6.

FIGURE 8-6
Using absolute cell references

7. Save the workbook, then leave Excel and the workbook open for the next Step-by-Step.

Use AutoSum

AutoSum is a function that is used to quickly perform a calculation on a range of cells. Using the AutoSum button on the Home tab in the Editing group, Excel will highlight the range either above or to the left of the current selection, and it will create the formula in the Formula bar using the SUM function. You can press Enter to accept the suggested range, drag to select another range, or edit the formula in the Formula bar.

2-3.2.7

You can click the AutoSum list arrow to access additional common functions that Excel can automatically calculate such as average, maximum, or minimum.

STEP-BY-STEP 8.3

1. Click cell **E4**.

2. On the **Home** tab, in the **Editing** group, click the **AutoSum** button. Dotted lines appear around cells B4:D4, as shown in Figure 8-7.   Σ

FIGURE 8-7
Using AutoSum

	A	B	C	D	E	F	G	H
COS					fx =SUM(B4:D4)			
1	15							
2								
3		January	February	March				
4	Jordan	$ 14,870.00	$16,651.00	$13,549.00	=SUM(B4:D4)			
5	Ava	$ 19,097.00	$17,054.00	$ 9,743.00	SUM(number1, [number2], …)			
6	Nikhil	$ 16,884.00	$20,076.00	$10,932.00				
7								

Formula created using AutoSum

Dotted lines surround the suggested range

3. Press **Enter**. The sum of cells B4:D4, $45,070.00, appears in cell E4.

4. With cell **E5** selected, click the **AutoSum** list arrow, click **Average**, position the mouse over cell B5, drag to select the range **B5:D5** as shown in Figure 8-8, then press **Enter**. The average of cells B5:D5, $15,298.00, appears in cell E5.

STEP-BY-STEP 8.3 Continued

FIGURE 8-8
Using the Average function

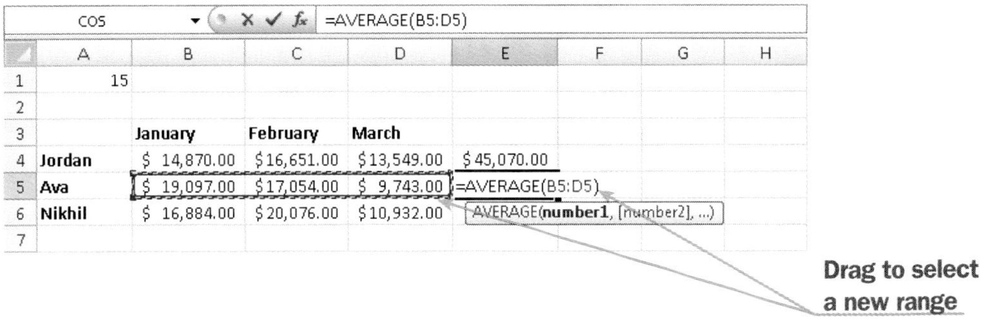

	A	B	C	D	E	F	G	H
	COS			fx	=AVERAGE(B5:D5)			
1		15						
2								
3		January	February	March				
4	Jordan	$ 14,870.00	$16,651.00	$13,549.00	$45,070.00			
5	Ava	$ 19,097.00	$17,054.00	$ 9,743.00	=AVERAGE(B5:D5)			
6	Nikhil	$ 16,884.00	$20,076.00	$10,932.00	AVERAGE(**number1**, [number2], ...)			
7								

**Drag to select
a new range**

5. Click cell **E6**, if necessary, click the **AutoSum** list arrow, click **Max**, drag to select the range **B6:D6**, then press **Enter**. The maximum of the three values, $20,076.00, appears in cell E6, and the worksheet appears as shown in Figure 8-9.

6. Save and close the workbook, but leave Excel open for the next Step-by-Step.

FIGURE 8-9
Using the Maximum function

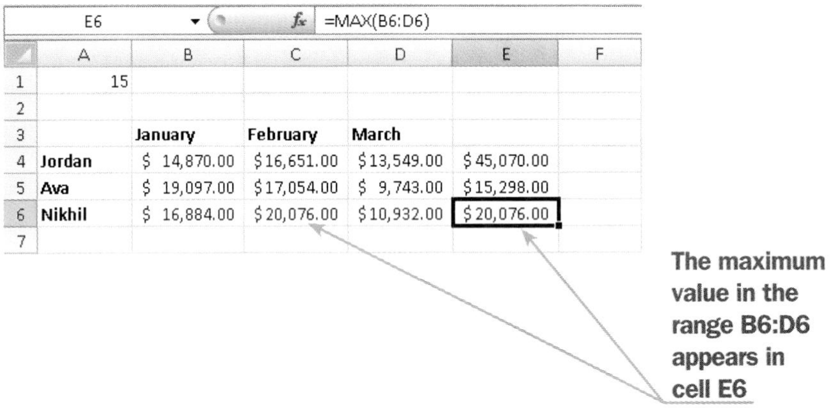

	A	B	C	D	E	F
	E6			fx	=MAX(B6:D6)	
1		15				
2						
3		January	February	March		
4	Jordan	$ 14,870.00	$16,651.00	$13,549.00	$45,070.00	
5	Ava	$ 19,097.00	$17,054.00	$ 9,743.00	$15,298.00	
6	Nikhil	$ 16,884.00	$20,076.00	$10,932.00	$20,076.00	
7						

**The maximum
value in the
range B6:D6
appears in
cell E6**

Fix Errors in Formulas

A formula that contains an error will display an error message that indicates the type of error. If a cell contains a formula with an error, a triangle will display in the top-left corner of the cell. When you see an error in a cell, you can click the cell and attempt to modify the formula based on the error message. Common error messages include #DIV/0!, #N/A, and #NAME?.

Similar to running the spell checker in Microsoft Word, you can run an Error Check on the worksheet to identify errors and to accept suggested fixes or manually edit the formula.

Many formula errors are related to incorrect syntax, or rules, that prohibit Excel from completing the calculation. Some potential syntax errors include the following:

2-3.2.8

■ Years stored as two-digit numbers such as 12/13/10, where the "10" could mean either 1910 or 2010).

■ Numbers stored as text, either with the text format applied or with an apostrophe before them, meaning that they cannot be used in a calculation.

■ Cell range references changed because rows and columns were inserted or deleted in the worksheet.

■ A formula referencing an empty cell, which returns a value of zero.

STEP-BY-STEP 8.4

1. Open the workbook **Sales Commissions.xlsx** from your Data Files.

2. Click cell **D6**, then type **=C6*B3**.

3. Copy the formula from cell **D6** to cells **D7** and **D8**. D7 displays **0** as the result, and D8 shows an error message. Depending on the format of a cell, a result of 0 can appear as a dash or a 0.

4. Click cell **D6**, change the formula to **=C6*$B$3**, then copy the formula to cell **D7**. Changing B3 to an absolute reference returns the results that you intended.

5. Click cell **D8**, then click the **Error** list arrow, as shown in Figure 8-10.

FIGURE 8-10
Fixing a formula error

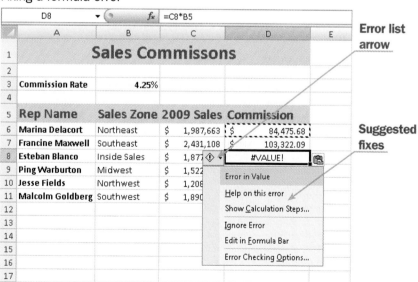

6. Click **Edit in Formula Bar**, change the formula to **=C8*$B$3**, press **Enter**, then copy the formula from cell **D6** to cells **D9:D10**. The formula is fixed.

STEP-BY-STEP 8.4 Continued

7. Click cell D11, then type **=B11*$B$3**. This produces an error, because cell B11 contains text.

8. Click the **Formulas** tab, then in the Formula Auditing group, click the **Error Checking** button. The Error Checking dialog box opens, as shown in Figure 8-11.

FIGURE 8-11
Error Checking dialog box

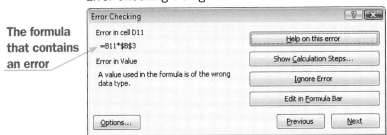

The formula that contains an error

9. Click the **Edit in Formula Bar** button, change B11 to **C11** in the Formula bar, press **Enter**, click **Resume**, then click **OK** in the Microsoft Office Excel dialog box. The worksheet appears without errors, as shown in Figure 8-12.

10. Save the workbook as **Final Sales Commissions.xlsx**, then leave the workbook and Excel open for the next Step-by-Step.

FIGURE 8-12
Worksheet after errors fixed

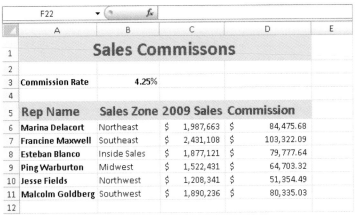

	Rep Name	Sales Zone	2009 Sales	Commission
	Commission Rate	4.25%		
	Rep Name	**Sales Zone**	**2009 Sales**	**Commission**
6	Marina Delacort	Northeast	$ 1,987,663	$ 84,475.68
7	Francine Maxwell	Southeast	$ 2,431,108	$ 103,322.09
8	Esteban Blanco	Inside Sales	$ 1,877,121	$ 79,777.64
9	Ping Warburton	Midwest	$ 1,522,431	$ 64,703.32
10	Jesse Fields	Northwest	$ 1,208,341	$ 51,354.49
11	Malcolm Goldberg	Southwest	$ 1,890,236	$ 80,335.03

Use Functions

IC3

2-3.2.4
2-3.2.5
2-3.2.6

AutoSum is an example of an Excel function. Excel also contains a Function Library, available on the Formulas tab, which groups functions into categories including Date and Time, Recently Used, Math & Trig, and Financial. Functions enable you to make calculations that help you analyze your worksheet data without having to do the math yourself.

When you click a function category in the Function Library group, a menu of formulas appears. Clicking a function usually opens a dialog box that guides you through selecting cells and ranges and inserting operators and function words, and it helps to ensure that your calculation will not produce an error.

The functions on the menu are listed by the function word and appear in all capitals. Some are easy to figure out, such as WEEKDAY, which excludes Saturdays and Sundays from a date and time formula. Others, such as ACCRINT, which calculates the accrued interest of an account, require you to have some knowledge of what you are trying to accomplish. If you are not sure what a function means, you can position the mouse over the function name on the menu to reveal a ScreenTip, as shown in Figure 8-13. If the ScreenTip contains a help icon, you can click the icon to open a Help window containing specific information related to that formula. You can also click Insert Function at the bottom of the menu, or you can click the Insert Function button in the Function Library group to open a dialog box that helps you choose and apply a function.

FIGURE 8-13
Choosing an option from the Function Library

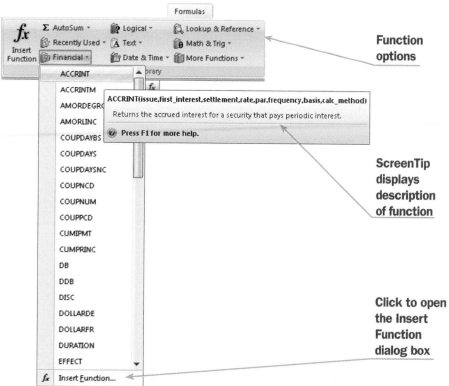

Like any formula, you can modify an applied function by editing the cell references or other formula parts in the Formula bar.

STEP-BY-STEP 8.5

1. Click cell **E6**. On the **Formulas** tab, in the **Function Library** group, click the **Math & Trig** button, then click **CEILING**. The Function Arguments dialog box opens.

2. Type **D6** in the Number text box, type **10** in the Significance text box, as shown in Figure 8-14, then click **OK**. The value in cell D6 is rounded up.

FIGURE 8-14
Function Arguments dialog box

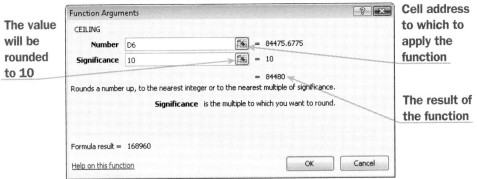

3. Copy the formula to **E7:E11**, then format and add a header, as shown in Figure 8-15.

FIGURE 8-15
The CEILING function applied

	A	B	C	D	E
1	Sales Commissons				
2					
3	Commission Rate	4.25%			
4					
5	Rep Name	Sales Zone	2009 Sales	Commission	Pay
6	Marina Delacort	Northeast	$ 1,987,663	$ 84,475.68	$ 84,480.00
7	Francine Maxwell	Southeast	$ 2,431,108	$ 103,322.09	$ 103,330.00
8	Esteban Blanco	Inside Sales	$ 1,877,121	$ 79,777.64	$ 79,780.00
9	Ping Warburton	Midwest	$ 1,522,431	$ 64,703.32	$ 64,710.00
10	Jesse Fields	Northwest	$ 1,208,341	$ 51,354.49	$ 51,360.00
11	Malcolm Goldberg	Southwest	$ 1,890,236	$ 80,335.03	$ 80,340.00
12					

Values are rounded to the nearest 10

4. Click cell **E12**. In the **Function Library** group, click the **Math & Trig** button, click **SUM**, then click **OK** in the Function Arguments dialog box.

5. Click cell **C12**. In the **Function Library** group, click the **More Functions** button, point to **Statistical**, scroll if necessary, click **MEDIAN**, then click **OK** in the Function Arguments dialog box. The median function shows the number that half of the sales reps earned more than and the other half of the sales reps earned less than.

6. Save the workbook, then leave the workbook and Excel open for the next Step-by-Step.

Create a Chart

Charts are objects that display worksheet data visually using graphics such as lines, bars, or pie pieces. You can distinguish series or categories of data by applying colors and labels and by adding a legend. Charts are used to show relationships between data, such as the growth or decline of sales numbers, or to analyze large quantities of data.

Many charts contain common elements. Line, pie, and bar charts have at least a horizontal line (also called category, or X) and a vertical line (also called value, or Y), also known as an axis. A three-dimensional (3D) chart will have a depth axis (also called series, or Z). Labels are used to define data series, axes, a chart title, or other chart elements. A legend is a type of label that lists the data series and color codes. You can also choose to show the datasheet as a part of the chart. The datasheet is the range of cells used to create the chart.

The first step in creating a chart is to determine the type of chart you should use to best display your data. Table 8-2 outlines different chart options. After you determine the chart type, you select the data to use in the chart, add or remove chart elements, then make style and formatting changes.

TABLE 8-2
Common chart types

CATEGORY	USED FOR
Column or Bar	Compare two or more values in proportion to each other
Line	Changes over time
Pie	Percentages
Area	Trends over time or by category
Scatter (XY)	Displaying data as a collection of points, each having one coordinate on the horizontal axis and one on the vertical axis

When you modify the worksheet data used to create your chart, the chart updates automatically. You can change the numbers, sort data, and make other modifications that will change the results and the appearance of your chart.

 Because a chart is a graphic object, it can be resized, formatted, moved, copied to another worksheet or program, or saved as a graphic file. The handles that you used when inserting objects in Word are used to drag the object to another location in the worksheet or resize to make the chart bigger or smaller.

2-3.2.10
2-3.2.12

S TEP-BY-STEP 8.6

1. Click the **Insert** tab, then in the **Charts** group, click the **Column** button, then click the first **2-D** column chart option. A chart area appears, and the Chart Tools tabs (Design, Layout, and Format) become active.

2. Click the **Chart Tools Design** tab, if necessary, then in the **Data** group, click the **Select Data** button.

3. In the worksheet, select cells **C6:C11**.

STEP-BY-STEP 8.6 Continued

4. In the Select Data Source dialog box, in the Horizontal (Category) Axis Labels section, click the **Edit** button, then in the worksheet, select cells **A6:A11**.

5. Click **OK** in the Axis Labels dialog box. The columns in the chart will be labeled by the sales reps' names, as shown in Figure 8-16.

FIGURE 8-16
Select Data Source dialog box

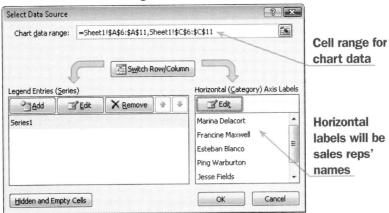

Cell range for chart data

Horizontal labels will be sales reps' names

6. Click **OK** to close the Select Data Source dialog box, click outside the chart, then drag it to position the top-left corner in cell **A14**, as shown in Figure 8-17.

FIGURE 8-17
Chart inserted and moved

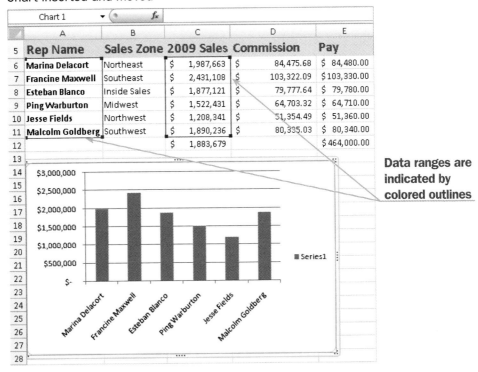

Data ranges are indicated by colored outlines

STEP-BY-STEP 8.6 Continued

7. Click cell **C8**, press **Delete**, type **3269008**, then press **Enter**. The chart resizes to fit the data, as shown in Figure 8-18.

8. Save the workbook, then leave Excel and the workbook open for the next Step-by-Step.

FIGURE 8-18
Modified chart

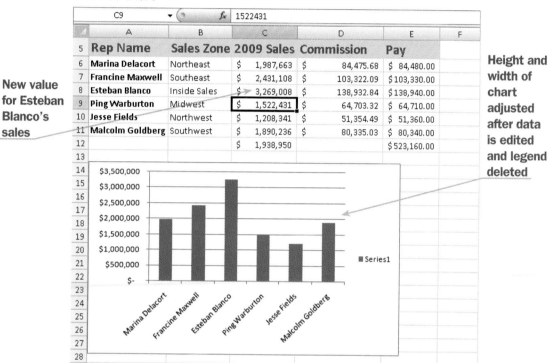

New value for Esteban Blanco's sales

Height and width of chart adjusted after data is edited and legend deleted

Format and Use Charts

2-3.2.9
2-3.2.11

Excel has many layouts and Chart Styles that can be applied to give your chart a different look, change the colors, or add labels that identify an axis or categories. You can also change the font of all labels at once or select a label type and format it separately.

Once you have formatted your chart, you are ready to use it to analyze the chart data. The chart you started creating in the last Step-by-Step compares the sales data for several people side by side. This chart can be used to determine which salesperson had the highest sales for the year 2009. You could also use a bar chart to show this data. If you used a pie chart, it would show the sales figures as percentages of the total sales.

STEP-BY-STEP 8.7

1. Click the **chart**, click the **Chart Tools Design** tab, then in the **Chart Layouts** group, click the **More** button, if necessary, then click **Layout 4**. The chart appears as shown in Figure 8-19.

FIGURE 8-19
Modifying the chart layout

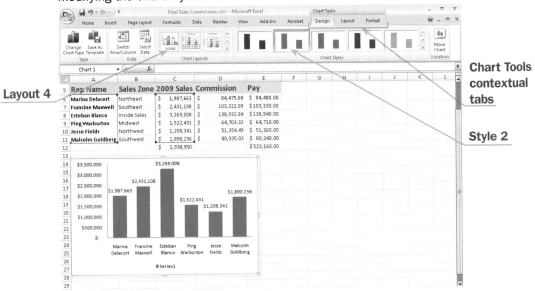

2. In the Chart Styles group, click the **More** button, then click **Style 31**. The chart has a 3D appearance, as shown in Figure 8-20.

FIGURE 8-20
Chart Style applied

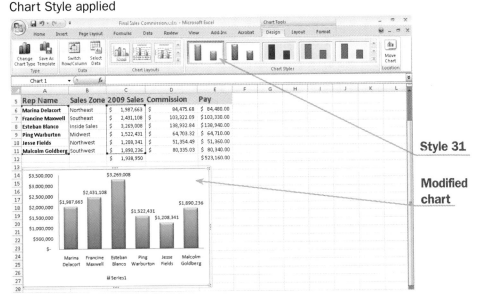

STEP-BY-STEP 8.7 Continued

3. Click the **Home** tab, then use the buttons in the **Font** group to format the chart text as **Arial** and **Dark Blue** (under Standard Colors). All of the text in your chart updates.

4. Click the **horizontal axis element** (sales reps' names), then change the font to **9 point**, **Bold**. The chart appears as shown in Figure 8-21.

FIGURE 8-21
Formatted chart

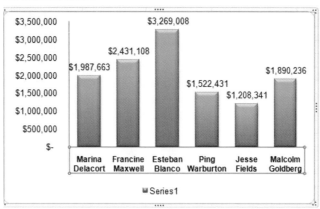

5. Click the **sales numbers**, then change the font to **8 point**, **Bold**.

6. Select cells **A5:E11**, then in the **Editing** group, click the **Sort & Filter** button, click **Custom Sort**, click the **Column Sort by** arrow, click **2009 Sales**, click the **Order** arrow, click **Smallest to Largest**, if necessary, then click **OK**. The columns are reordered. It is now easy to see the largest and smallest numbers in order.

7. Click **Series 1**, which is the legend.

8. Click the **Chart Tools Layout** tab, then in the Labels group, click the **Legend** button, then click **None**. The legend is deleted, as shown in Figure 8-22.

9. Save and close the workbook, then exit Excel.

FIGURE 8-22
Reorganized data

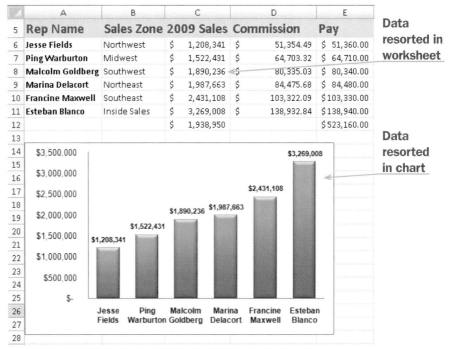

	A	B	C	D	E	
5	**Rep Name**	**Sales Zone**	**2009 Sales**	**Commission**	**Pay**	Data resorted in worksheet
6	Jesse Fields	Northwest	$ 1,208,341	$ 51,354.49	$ 51,360.00	
7	Ping Warburton	Midwest	$ 1,522,431	$ 64,703.32	$ 64,710.00	
8	Malcolm Goldberg	Southwest	$ 1,890,236	$ 80,335.03	$ 80,340.00	
9	Marina Delacort	Northeast	$ 1,987,663	$ 84,475.68	$ 84,480.00	
10	Francine Maxwell	Southeast	$ 2,431,108	$ 103,322.09	$103,330.00	
11	Esteban Blanco	Inside Sales	$ 3,269,008	$ 138,932.84	$138,940.00	
12			$ 1,938,950		$523,160.00	

Data resorted in chart

SUMMARY

- Formulas are the equations used to perform calculations by using worksheet values, constants, and operators.

- To create a formula, you always start with an equal sign. You can type the formula in the cell or use the Formula bar to create or edit a formula. To reference a cell value or cell range in a formula, select the cell(s), or type the cell address or range name.

- Absolute cell references do not change when a formula is copied or moved. Relative cell references change depending on the relationship to the original formula and the copied formula.

- AutoSum is used to access common functions such as SUM or MINIMUM.

- You can fix errors in formulas either by clicking the error list arrow next to the cell that contains the incorrect formula or by using Error Checking, which steps through the worksheet and identifies all potential formula errors.

- Excel has many built-in functions, grouped in the Function Library group on the Formula tab on the Ribbon, by categories such as Math & Trig and Financial.

- A chart displays data visually as a graphic, and it automatically updates when the data is modified. Chart types include pie, bar, and column.

- Charts can have styles applied to the entire chart object, or you can format elements individually.

VOCABULARY *Review*

Define the following terms:

Absolute cell reference	Constant	Mixed cell reference
Arithmetic operator	Datasheet	Reference
AutoSum	Formula	Reference operator
Axis	Function	Relative cell reference
Chart	Label	Syntax
Comparison operator	Legend	

REVIEW *Questions*

SCREEN IDENTIFICATION

Identify the screen elements.

FIGURE 8-23
Screen Identification

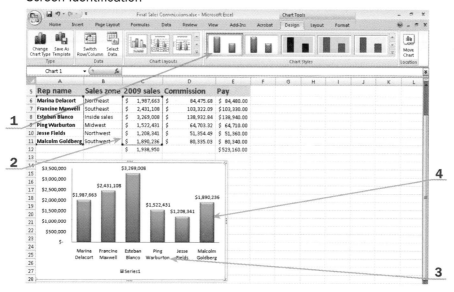

1.

2.

3.

4.

MULTIPLE CHOICE

Circle the correct answer.

1. **A$6** is an example of a(n) _____ cell reference.
    A. Absolute
    B. Relative
    C. Mixed
    D. Constant

2. Which part of the formula **15–(A4/$B$5)*14+3** will be calculated first?
    A. 15–
    B. (A4/$B$5)
    C. *14
    D. +3

3. Which part of the formula **15–(A4/$B$5)*14+3** will be calculated last?
    A. 15–
    B. (A4/$B$5)
    C. *14
    D. +3

4. A _____ chart displays values as percentages.
    A. Pie
    B. Column
    C. Scatter
    D. Line

TRUE/FALSE

Circle T if the statement is true or F if the statement is false.

T   F   1. The Error Checking feature is used to check an individual formula error.

T   F   2. A legend is a type of chart label.

T   F   3. $C$14 is an example of an absolute cell reference.

T   F   4. The vertical axis is also called the X-axis.

T   F   5. % and **+** are examples of mathematical operators.

HANDS-ON REVIEW

1. Open the workbook **Time Card.xlsx**.

2. Create a formula in cell F15 that calculates the sum of the values in cells B10:F10 using AutoSum.

3. Create a formula in cell B11 that multiplies cells B5 and B10, using an absolute reference for cell B5 and a relative reference for cell B10, then copy it to cells C11:F11.

4. Enter a formula in cell F16 that multiplies the values in cells F15 and B5.

5. Use the Error Checking feature to check for formula errors, and fix the errors, if any.

6. Create a pie chart using the values in cells B10:F10.

7. Apply a pie chart style, add a chart title, and change the data labels for the pie wedges to reference cells B7:F7.

8. Save the workbook as **My Time Card.xlsx**, then close the workbook.

PROJECTS

PROJECT 8-1

Open the workbook **Household Budget.xlsx**. In the space below the table, enter the sum of the categories in the first column. Create a chart to show the relationship between the categories. Save the workbook as **My Household Budget.xlsx**.

PROJECT 8-2

Open the workbook **Sales Chart.xlsx**. Add data labels, then drag to increase the chart size. Edit and format the chart title. Apply a chart style. Save the workbook as **My Sales Chart.xlsx**.

 TEAMWORK

With a partner or in a group, come up with a list of four formulas (or one per person if there are more than four in your group), and determine the order in which the calculations will be performed. Identify all operators, and determine which values are constants, absolute cell references, mixed cell references, or relative cell references.

CRITICAL *Thinking*

ACTIVITY 8-1

Find examples of two charts by researching on the Internet or looking in a magazine or newspaper. In a Word document, write a paragraph about each chart describing the chart type, style and formatting, and chart elements. Make conclusions based on the data in the chart. Add whether or not you think the chart is a good representation of the data, and make any suggestions for improvement.

PRESENTATION BASICS

Microsoft Office PowerPoint 2007 is a presentation program that organizes and formats information in slides and outlines. The information can be viewed on a screen as a slide show or printed as handouts.

PowerPoint has many elements and tasks that are the same as other Office programs such as the Ribbon, Quick Access Toolbar, dialog boxes, and other common features.

There are several different views in PowerPoint that can help you edit, preview, navigate through, and organize your presentation. Normal view has three separate panes where you can work and edit. The left pane has tabs that display presentation contents as slide thumbnails (Slides tab) or an outline (Outline tab); the current slide is on the upper-right (Slides pane); the Notes pane at the bottom of the Slides pane is for speaker notes. You can also view your presentation as a slide show.

If you are already working in PowerPoint and you want to start a new presentation, you can use the New Presentation dialog box to choose a blank presentation or select from a number of templates. Templates are preformatted presentations that are organized by theme or by content. When you click a category in the New Presentation dialog box, thumbnails, or small icons, of the available templates appear in the middle pane. Templates include sample text and graphics called placeholders, which you need to replace with your own content.

When editing an existing presentation or working from a template, you can apply text formatting, design themes, and layouts, and you can change the background of slides. You can also insert a new slide and move and copy slides.

View the PowerPoint Window

PowerPoint shares elements of the user interface with Word and other Office programs including the Ribbon, dialog boxes, and scroll bars. Many of the basic program tasks are the same for all Office programs such as starting a program and saving, opening, and closing a file. Figure 9-1 shows the PowerPoint 2007 program window in Normal view.

FIGURE 9-1
PowerPoint window in Normal view

The main work view for PowerPoint is Normal view, where you can enter, format, and edit slides in the Slide pane on the right of the window. You can also display the Slides tab or Outline tab on the left of the window to help organize your slides and data. At the bottom of the windows is the Notes pane, an area for adding speaker notes that can be printed to accompany a presentation but are not visible in a slide presentation.

2-1.2.1
2-1.2.7

Everything on a slide is an object that can be moved, resized, grouped, and formatted. You can delete and add objects on a slide to customize it. Text that you enter or replace from placeholder text is placed in text boxes. Table 9-1 shows different ways to select slides or slide objects.

TABLE 9-1
Selecting portions of presentations or slides

TO SELECT	DO THIS
A slide	Click the slide in the Slides tab
Slide contents	Click the slide, then click the slide object or press Ctrl + A to select all objects on the slide
All of the slides in a presentation	Click the Slides tab, then press Ctrl + A
Adjacent slides	Click the Slides tab, press and hold Shift, then click the top and bottom slide in the desired selection
Nonadjacent slides	Click the Slides tab, press and hold Ctrl, then click each slide individually

Each slide layout type has different default elements on it. Title Slides, Section Headers, and Title Only slide layouts contain only text boxes and are meant to introduce a slide show or a section of a presentation.

Title and Content, Two Content, and other layouts contain text boxes as well as a placeholder in which you can insert text and/or a graphic. If a slide contains a graphic placeholder, it appears as shown in Figure 9-2. Clicking one of the icons on the slide will allow you to insert clip art, a picture from a file, a SmartArt object, a media clip, a chart, or a table. SmartArt objects are charts that show a hierarchy or series such as an organizational chart or a cycle of steps.

FIGURE 9-2
Title and Content slide layout

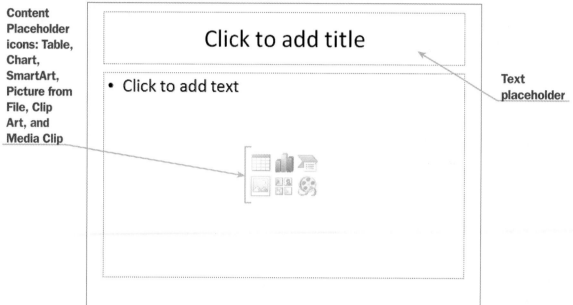

Content Placeholder icons: Table, Chart, SmartArt, Picture from File, Clip Art, and Media Clip

Click to add title

• Click to add text

Text placeholder

S TEP-BY-STEP 9.1

1. Start PowerPoint using the **Start** button or a desktop shortcut. A new, blank presentation, called Presentation1, opens.

2. Click the **Office Button**, then click **Open**.

3. In the Open dialog box, locate the Data Files, then open the file **Employee Orientation.pptx**. The presentation opens to Slide 1, which is a Title Slide.

4. Click the tabs on the Ribbon to see the groups and buttons available. Note that many of the buttons on the Home tab are the same as in Word and Excel, but the other tabs contain PowerPoint-specific tasks.

5. Click **Slide 2** in the Slides pane. Slide 2 is an example of a Title and Content slide, as shown in Figure 9-3.

STEP-BY-STEP 9.1 Continued

FIGURE 9-3
Slide 2

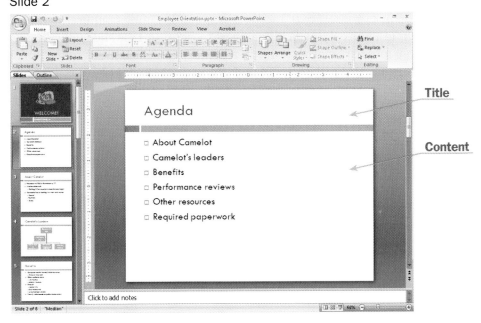

6. Press **Page Down** twice to display Slide 4. The object in Slide 4 is an example of a SmartArt graphic (in this case, a chart).

7. Click the **Outline** tab. The hierarchy of the presentation appears in outline form, as shown in Figure 9-4.

FIGURE 9-4
Outline tab

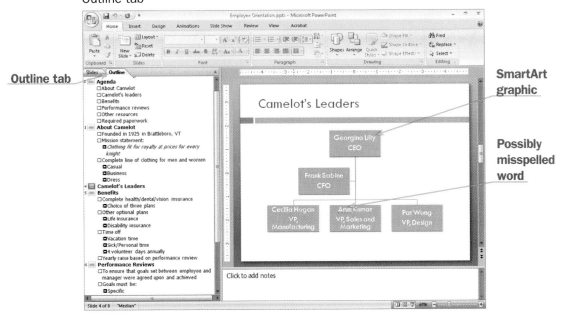

8. Leave the presentation and PowerPoint open for the next Step-by-Step.

Navigate Through a Presentation

Depending on whether the Slide pane or the Slides tab is active, you can navigate through slide elements or between slides in a presentation. You can change between them by clicking the pane or tab in which you want to navigate.

You can move the insertion point by clicking the mouse on a slide object to make it active. There are also many keyboard shortcuts that quickly move the insertion point to a new slide, as shown in Table 9-2. Being familiar with these positioning tools can help you make edits to your presentation efficiently.

When you click on a slide object, it is selected. When dotted lines appear around an object's border, you can edit the text. To be able to move or format the object, click the dotted border. The border becomes a solid line, and you can resize, move, or apply an effect to the object. In select mode, you can press Tab to move between objects on a slide.

You can use the scroll bars to move up and down in the Slide pane or to the next slide in your presentation in the slide window.

2-1.3.1

TABLE 9-2
Navigating through a presentation

KEYBOARD SHORTCUT	MOVES THE INSERTION POINT TO THE
Home	Beginning of the presentation
End	End of the presentation
Page Down, Enter, Spacebar, right arrow, or down arrow	Next slide
Page Up, Backspace, left arrow, or up arrow	Previous slide

STEP-BY-STEP 9.2

1. Click the **Slides** tab, then press the **up arrow** to move to Slide 3.

2. Press **End**. Slide 8, the last slide in the presentation, is active.

3. Press **Home**. Slide 1, the first slide in the presentation, is active.

4. Press the **down arrow**. Slide 2, the next slide in the presentation, is active.

5. In the Slide pane, click anywhere in the bulleted list to select it. The bulleted list has a dotted border, indicating that you can edit the text, as shown in Figure 9-5.

STEP-BY-STEP 9.2 Continued

FIGURE 9-5
Editing a text box

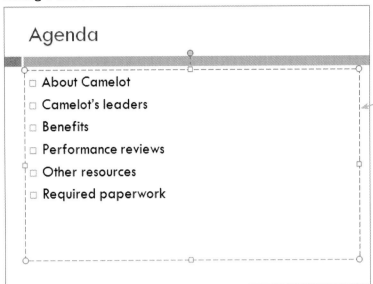

Dotted border
means text
can be edited

6. Press the **down arrow** and the **up arrow** to move up and down in the bulleted list.

7. Click the **dotted border** of the text box. The border becomes a solid line.

8. Press **Tab**. The *Agenda* title text box is selected.

9. Press **Page Down** until you get to Slide 4.

> **Did You Know?**
>
> To select multiple objects, press and hold **Shift**, then select each object, or press and hold the **left mouse** button, then drag the pointer around all objects you want to select.

10. Click the **SmartArt** object to select it, then click the **Frank Sabine** text box. Handles surround the text box, indicating that you can move or edit just the text box.

11. Click **Slide 1** in the Slides tab, then leave the presentation and PowerPoint open for the next Step-by-Step.

Change the Slide View

PowerPoint has many different ways to view your presentation. You can click one of the View buttons on the status bar to change the view, or you can increase or decrease the zoom to see more or less of the presentation on the screen at one time.

PowerPoint has three layout View buttons on the status bar. You have been working in Normal view, which is the main editing window. Slide Sorter view

> **Did You Know?**
>
> Other presentation view options include **Notes Page view**, which shows each slide with a pane below it for speaker notes. Notes Page view is available on the View tab in the Presentation Views group, along with different master page views. A **master page** controls the design, layout, and objects of all slides, handouts, or notes pages in a presentation. You will learn more about notes and master pages in Lesson 10.

shows all of the slides as thumbnails. Slide Sorter view is helpful to quickly move slides to a new position or to delete slides. **Slide Show view** displays the slides as an on-screen presentation. Slide Show view is useful when previewing your presentation as your audience will see it and making sure that the slides and any slide or object transitions appear as you intended. **Transitions** are animation effects that occur when a new slide or slide object appears on the screen.

Changing the zoom in Slide Sorter or Normal view is an easy way to view more or less of your presentation. You can change the zoom by using the Zoom slider or using the Zoom In and Zoom Out buttons on the status bar. To see more of a slide, choose a lower zoom. To magnify your view of a slide, use a higher zoom.

2-4.1.4

STEP-BY-STEP 9.3

1. Click the **Slide Sorter** button on the status bar. The slide show appears as thumbnails, as shown in Figure 9-6.

FIGURE 9-6
Slide Sorter view

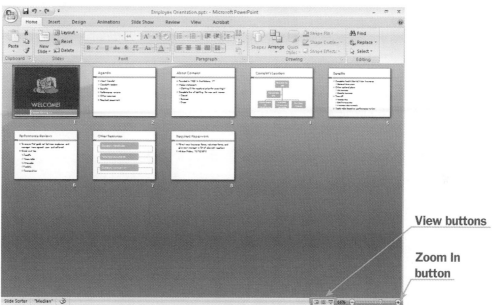

View buttons

Zoom In button

2. Click the **Zoom In** button as many times as necessary to change the zoom level to 100%, as shown in Figure 9-7.

3. Click the **Slide Show** button on the status bar. The slide fills the screen, as shown in Figure 9-8.

STEP-BY-STEP 9.3 Continued

FIGURE 9-7
Increasing the zoom level

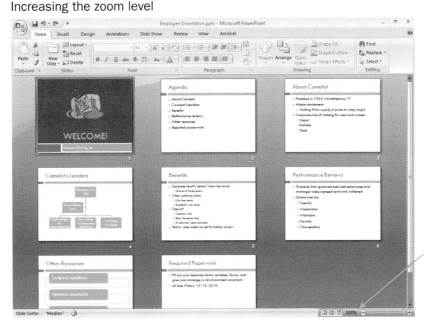

Zoom is now
100%

FIGURE 9-8
Slide Show view

4. Press **Esc** to end the slide show.

5. Click the **Normal** button on the status bar.

6. Close the presentation, do not save changes if prompted, then leave PowerPoint open for the next Step-by-Step.

Create a New Presentation

When you start PowerPoint, a new, blank presentation opens automatically. By default, this presentation is called Presentation1, and the next presentation you create during the PowerPoint session is called Presentation2, and so on. You should save a presentation in order to keep any changes you make.

If you are already working in PowerPoint and you want to start a new presentation, you can use the New Presentation dialog box to choose a blank presentation, choose a slide design, or select a content template. Templates have placeholder text and are preformatted. When you open a new, blank presentation or a slide design template, you can add more slides and choose the slide layout that fits your subject. A content template includes structure and sample text, such as a sales presentation to give to a customer.

PowerPoint comes installed with several default templates, and you can download many more from Microsoft Office Online. Note that you must be connected to the Internet in order to access online templates. You can view these templates through the New Presentation dialog box by clicking a category in the left pane, as shown in Figure 9-9. In the middle pane, click a category if necessary, then click a thumbnail in the middle pane. Click Download in the right pane. Microsoft will verify that your software copy is properly registered, then PowerPoint will download and open the template.

FIGURE 9-9
Downloading a template

To enter text on a slide, you must first click in a text box. By default, **AutoFit** is applied to PowerPoint presentations. When you edit the text, increase the font size, or resize the text box, the font size automatically adjusts.

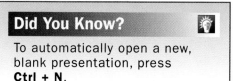

Did You Know?

To automatically open a new, blank presentation, press **Ctrl + N**.

IC³

2-4.1.3

S TEP-BY-STEP 9.4

1. Click the **Office Button**, then click **New**. The New Presentation dialog box opens.

2. Click **Blank Presentation** in the middle pane, if necessary, then click **Create** at the bottom of the right pane. A blank presentation called Presentation2 opens, as shown in Figure 9-10. The presentation is called Presentation2 because it is the second blank presentation you opened in the current PowerPoint session.

FIGURE 9-10
Creating a blank presentation

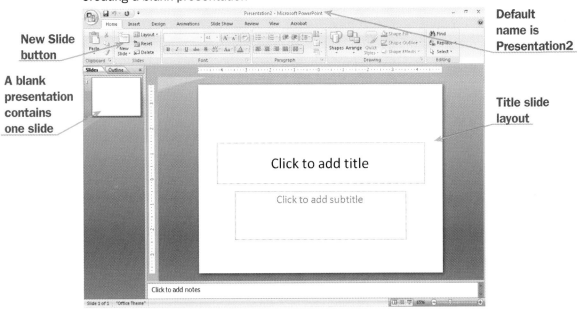

3. Click the Title placeholder, then type **Marketing Presentation**.

4. Click the Subtitle placeholder, then type **Your Name, Marketing Manager**.

5. On the Home tab in the Slides group, click the **New Slide** button arrow, then click **Title and Content**.

6. Type the content on Slide 2 as shown in Figure 9-11, pressing **Enter** after each bullet.

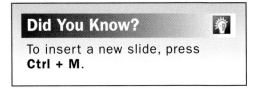

Did You Know?

To insert a new slide, press **Ctrl + M**.

STEP-BY-STEP 9.4 Continued

FIGURE 9-11
Slide 2 content

Spring Mailings

- Print catalog of fall clothing
- DVD with catalog slide show
- In-store promotion sign-ups
- New customer introductory letter

7. In the Slides group, click the **New Slide** button. A new slide is inserted. The Title and Content slide layout, the last layout that was chosen from the New Slide menu, is applied.

8. On the new slide, type **Spring Events** in the title placeholder, then click the **Insert Table** icon in the content placeholder. In the Insert Table dialog box, type **3** in the Number of columns text box, select the number in the Number of rows text box, type **5**, then click **OK**. A table appears with three columns and five rows.

9. Type the table content on Slide 3 shown in Figure 9-12, then drag the column dividers to fit the text.

FIGURE 9-12
Slide 3 content

Spring Events

Drag to adjust column widths to match figure

Month	Location	Event
March	Denver, CO	New retail store opening
April	Brattleboro, VT	Factory tour for preferred customers
May	New York, NY	National Garment Retailers Association (NGRA) meeting
June	San Francisco, CA	New retail store opening

STEP-BY-STEP 9.4 Continued

10. Save the presentation as **Marketing Presentation.pptx**, then leave the presentation and PowerPoint open for the next Step-by-Step.

Did You Know?

By default, PowerPoint uses the title text from Slide 1 as the suggested name for the presentation.

Change the Slide Design

Design Themes are used to apply background, coordinated colors and fonts, and effects to an entire presentation.

You can apply the same font formatting options and text effects to PowerPoint text as you learned to do for Word text. Text can be enhanced by increasing the font size, adding color, or applying formatting such as bolding text. The AutoFit feature is helpful when formatting the font or resizing a text box, because it will automatically adjust the font size of your text to fit the text box.

Theme Colors, Theme Fonts, and Theme Effects are coordinated color palettes, fonts, and graphic effects that update all of your formatting at once.

Just as in any Office program, you can use the Undo and Redo buttons on the Quick Access Toolbar to reverse or reapply an action.

2-3.1.6
2-3.1.8
2-4.1.1

STEP-BY-STEP 9.5

1. Click **Slide 1** in the Slides tab, click the **Design** tab on the Ribbon, then in the Themes group, click the **More** button, then click **Metro**, as shown in Figure 9-13.

FIGURE 9-13
Applying a design theme

STEP-BY-STEP 9.5 Continued

2. In the Themes group, click the **Theme Fonts** button, then click **Apex**. The fonts in the presentation change to Lucida Sans and Book Antiqua.

3. In the Background group, click the **Background Styles** button, click **Style 11**, then click the **Undo** button on the Quick Access Toolbar.

4. In the Themes group, click the **Theme Colors** button, then click **Oriel**.

5. Click **Slide 2** in the Slides tab, select the title text, click the **Home** tab, change the font to **bold**, then change the font color to **Red, Accent 3**.

6. In the Clipboard group, double-click the **Format Painter** button, click **Slide 3** in the Slides tab, apply the formatting to the title text, then press **Esc**.

7. Click the **table** on Slide 3 to select it, click the **Table Tools Design** tab, then in the Table Styles group, click the **Medium Style 2 – Accent 3** style. The slide appears as shown in Figure 9-14.

FIGURE 9-14
Formatted presentation

8. Save the presentation, then leave the presentation and PowerPoint open for the next Step-by-Step.

Careers in Technology

Creating and delivering effective presentations is something you will do in many business situations. You could be asked to present sales data, a marketing plan, new product information, or an employee orientation to colleagues or potential clients. Some important considerations follow:

- **Designing** a presentation and applying animations and text effects that enhance and provide structure to your slides but that do not distract from your message. Too many "bells and whistles" can make your presentation look unprofessional and disorganized. In general, you should never use a font smaller than 18 point.
- **Writing** text on your slides that is organized and clear. Use a maximum of four to five bullets per slide, and use headings appropriately to introduce your presentation, sections of a presentation, and each slide. Your slide text does not always need to be complete sentences, but it should provide a structure for your oral presentation.
- **Delivering** your presentation involves speaking loudly and clearly, expanding on the text that is on your slides (not just reading it), making eye contact with your audience, and pausing for questions. You should always practice the delivery of your presentation, paying attention to the timing of the presentation and making sure that your slides are in order.
- **Handouts** are support materials that contain your slides (possibly additional notes) and leave room for your audience to take notes. PowerPoint allows you to create handouts for your presentation. You will learn to do so in Lesson 10.

Modify a Presentation

You can move, copy, paste, and delete slides in the Slides tab or in Slide Sorter view. Copying and pasting a slide is helpful when the information or layout for the new slide is similar. Slides can be moved by cutting and pasting, or by dragging and dropping. To position the new or pasted slide, click to place the insertion point after the slide that should appear before the new slide in the Slides tab.

Did You Know?

You can change the layout of a previously created slide by clicking the **Layout** button in the Home tab in the Slides group.

When you insert a new slide as you did in a previous Step-by-Step, you can choose a layout that fits the content you will be adding to your slide. Any design, font, or color themes you have applied to your presentation are added automatically to the new slide.

2-4.1.2
2-4.1.5
2-4.1.8

STEP-BY-STEP 9.6

1. Click **Slide 2** in the Slides tab, then on the Home tab in the Clipboard group, click the **Copy** button.

2. In the Slides tab, click beneath Slide 3, then in the Clipboard group, click the **Paste** button.

3. In the Slides tab, click **Slide 3** to select it, then drag it above Slide 2.

STEP-BY-STEP 9.6 Continued

4. In the Slides tab, click **Slide 4**, then press **Delete**.

5. In the Slides group, click the **New Slide** button arrow, then click **Two Content**.

6. Type **Products to Promote** in the title placeholder, then format the title as **bold**, **Red, Accent 3**.

7. In the content placeholder on the left, click the **Insert Picture from File** icon. The Insert Picture dialog box opens.

8. Navigate to your Data Files, click the **T-shirt1.bmp** file, then click **Insert**. The picture is inserted in the left content placeholder.

9. In the content placeholder on the right, click the **Insert Picture from File** icon, click the **T-shirt2.bmp** file, then click **Insert**. The picture is inserted in the content placeholder, and the slide appears as shown in Figure 9-15.

10. Save your work, then leave the presentation and PowerPoint open for the next Step-by-Step.

FIGURE 9-15
Inserting a new slide

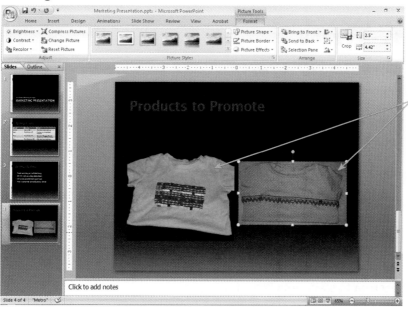

Two Content slide layout places graphics side by side

Preview a Presentation

Y ou already clicked the Slide Show view button on the status bar to view a slide show as it would appear when you are giving a presentation. Now you will navigate through an entire presentation.

In Slide Show view, you can advance and go back to slides using a variety of keystrokes. To advance forward one slide, click the slide, or press the down arrow, Enter, or Tab. To move back one slide, press the up arrow, or Page Up. If you know what the slide number is and want to move to a specific slide, press the slide number, then press Enter.

You cannot edit slide contents in Slide Show view. However, you should always preview the slides in Slide Show view to make sure that no content or objects are cut off and that all of your slides appear in the order that you want. To exit a slide show at any time, press Esc to return to Normal view.

2-4.1.10
2-4.1.11

The Slide Show toolbar is a hidden toolbar that you can use to navigate forward and backward in the slide show, open a menu of slide show options, or activate the pen feature, which allows you to annotate your slides. To access the Slide Show toolbar, position the pointer over the lower-left corner of the slide to make the toolbar appear.

> **Did You Know?**
>
> You can record slide timings when rehearsing your presentation to determine the delivery length of your presentation or to create a self-running slide show.

S TEP-BY-STEP 9.7

1. Click **Slide 1** in the Slides tab, then click the **Slide Show** button on the status bar.

2. Press the **down arrow** to move to Slide 2, then press the **up arrow** to move to Slide 1.

3. Press **Enter** to move to Slide 2.

4. Position the pointer over the bottom-left corner of a slide until the Slide Show toolbar appears, as shown in Figure 9-16.

5. Press the **Next** button on the toolbar. The slide show advances to Slide 3.

6. Click the **screen** to advance to Slide 4.

7. Press **Page Down**, then press **Esc** to end the slide show and return to Normal view. By default, a slide show ends with a black screen.

8. Save and close the presentation, then exit PowerPoint.

> **Did You Know?**
>
> Press **F5** to start a presentation from Slide 1 in Slide Show view, or press **Shift + F5** to view the presentation from the current slide.

FIGURE 9-16
Slide Show toolbar

Click to advance
to the next slide

SUMMARY

In this lesson, you learned:

- A PowerPoint file is called a presentation, and it can be viewed as slides or as an outline.

- PowerPoint shares many of the same features as other Office programs including the Ribbon, dialog boxes, and scroll bars.

- PowerPoint has several unique elements, such as the Slide and Outline tabs, which are used to edit and navigate in your presentation.

- Using the mouse and keyboard shortcuts, you can select and navigate through slides and slide objects.

- You can create a presentation in one of three ways: open a new, blank presentation, use a template installed on your computer, or download a template from Microsoft Office Online.

- To enter information in a presentation, create a text box, select text in a placeholder text box, or enter text directly on a slide.

- You can use the same formatting tools as in Word and Excel to format the font or apply borders and shading.

- Applying a Design Theme can quickly enhance your presentation.

- You can cut, copy, and paste slides and slide objects to modify your presentation.

- You can use many keyboard shortcuts to quickly move to a new location in your presentation.

VOCABULARY *Review*

Define the following terms:

AutoFit	Placeholder	SmartArt
Design Themes	Presentation	Template
Master page	Slide layout	Text box
Normal view	Slide Show view	Thumbnail
Notes Page view	Slide Sorter view	Transition

REVIEW *Questions*

SCREEN IDENTIFICATION

Identify the screen elements.

FIGURE 9-17
Screen identification

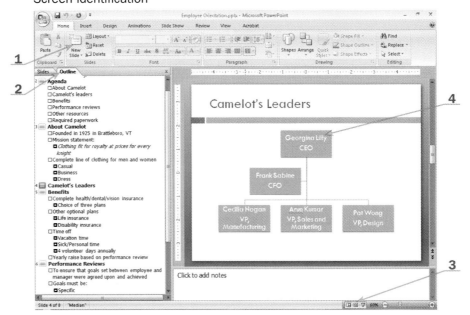

1. _____

2. _____

3. _____

4. _____

MULTIPLE CHOICE

Circle the correct answer.

1. The _____ feature adjusts the font size of a text box as it is modified.
   A. AutoInsert
   B. AutoFill
   C. AutoFit
   D. AutoComplete

2. An organizational chart is an example of a _____ graphic.
   A. Chart
   B. SmartArt
   C. Shape
   D. Text box

3. The main editing view of PowerPoint is _____ view.
   A. Normal
   B. Notes Page
   C. Slide Sorter
   D. Slide Show

4. Which of the following can you do to advance to the next slide in a slide show?
   A. Click the slide.
   B. Press the down arrow.
   C. Press Enter.
   D. All of the above.

TRUE/FALSE

Circle T if the statement is true or F if the statement is false.

T   F   1. Pressing F5 starts a slide show.

T   F   2. Pressing Ctrl + N opens the New Presentation dialog box.

T   F   3. The hierarchy of a presentation is displayed on the Outline tab.

T   F   4. Pressing Ctrl + A selects all of the slides in a presentation.

T   F   5. When a dotted line appears around a text box, you can move or resize it.

T   F   6. Title and Content is a type of Slide Theme.

T   F   7. Press End to move to the end of the presentation.

HANDS-ON REVIEW

1. Open PowerPoint, open the presentation **Orchard House.pptx**, practice navigating through the tabs on the Ribbon, click in the Outline tab, then click the Slides tab.

2. Navigate to Slide 2, click in the content text box, click the outside border to select the text box, then press Tab to select the Alcott Family text box.

3. Use the button on the status bar to change to Slide Sorter view, change the zoom level, then return to Normal view. Close the Orchard House presentation without saving changes.

4. Create a new, blank presentation using the New Presentation dialog box.

5. Type **About Me** as the title and **Your Name** as the subtitle on the slide.

6. Add three additional Title and Content slides, and add information about yourself. Give the slides appropriate titles.

7. Apply any Design Theme, change the background style, and apply a Theme Font.

8. Reorder the slides using the Slides tab by cutting and pasting and using drag-and-drop. Insert a new slide, then delete it.

9. View the presentation in Slide Show view and practice navigating forward and backward in the presentation.

10. Save the presentation as **About Me.pptx**, then close the presentation.

PROJECTS

PROJECT 9-1

Note: If you are not connected to the Internet, choose a template from the Installed Templates category in the New Presentation dialog box. Verify in the right pane that the template was generated by Microsoft.

1. Create a new presentation by downloading one of the Presentation templates from Microsoft Office Online. (*Note:* If you do not have online access, use an installed template.)

2. Replace the placeholder text on three of the slides with your own information.

3. Delete the rest of the slides.

4. Change the Design Theme.

5. Insert a new slide as Slide 3, and insert at least one clip-art image on the slide.

6. Save the presentation as **Template Presentation.pptx**, then close the presentation.

PROJECT 9–2

1. Open the presentation **Youth Theatre.pptx** from your Data Files.

2. View the presentation in Slide Sorter view.

3. Select Slide 5, then press **Delete**.

4. Switch to Normal view.

5. Navigate to Slide 1, then format the slide title as bold, 54-point.

6. On Slide 3, click the **Insert** tab, in the Illustrations group click the **Clip Art** button, then insert a clip-art image.

7. Save the presentation as **Practice.pptx**, then close the presentation.

 TEAMWORK

Open the presentation **Training Presentation.pptx**. As a group, try to create an outline of the slide content on a piece of paper. Display the Outline tab and check your work.

CRITICAL *Thinking*

ACTIVITY 9-1

Using the skills you learned in this lesson, create a blank presentation. Change the title to **Using Presentations,** and change the subtitle to **Your Name.** Add the following information to Slides 2–4.

Slide 2: Considerations when adding text to your slides.

Slide 3: Planning the design and formatting of your presentation.

Slide 4: How to preview and deliver an effective presentation.

Format and add a Design Theme to the presentation. Save the presentation as **Using Presentations.pptx,** then close it.

CUSTOMIZING PRESENTATIONS

OBJECTIVES

Upon completion of this lesson, you should be able to:

- Use slide masters
- Add graphics and media
- Create a SmartArt object
- Format slide objects
- Use animations
- Create a custom slide show
- Print speaker notes and handouts

Estimated Time: 2 hours

VOCABULARY

Alignment

Animated GIF

Animations

Design Themes

Fill

Handout

Layout

Media clip

Order

Slide master

SmartArt

Speaker notes

Transition

Slide masters are used to make changes that affect all slides in your presentation such as adding text or a graphic that appears on each slide. In Slide Master view, you specify the design, layout, and content of common elements such as a slide footer. The Slide Master is also where the Design, Color, and Font Schemes are saved and customized.

After you have entered and formatted text, customized the slide master, and applied a slide design, you are ready to enhance your presentation by adding graphics, formatting, media clips, and animations. Graphics, media, and animation should be used to complement and clarify your text, not to overwhelm your audience, so be careful not to overuse them. Media clips include sound and video. When you add a media clip to a slide, you specify whether or not to have the media play automatically or only when you click it.

You can add graphics from a file, insert clip art, or use shapes. Applying effects to objects, such as adding a Picture Style, or changing the rotation angle, can make your graphic stand out. You can also choose to overlap multiple objects and specify the order in which they appear.

Transitions and animations affect the way objects, text, and slides appear during a slide show. They can include entrance and exit effects, such as having each bullet in a text box fly in from the left of the slide upon entrance and then exit by flying to the right. You can apply animations to each object on a slide or in a presentation, or to specific objects or slides.

Within a presentation, you can choose to save specific slides in a custom slide show that can be run independently or by clicking a hyperlink from within a slide show.

Distributing your slides as a **handout** to your audience allows them to take notes during the presentation and retain a copy of your presentation. **Speaker notes** are reminders that you can associate with a slide and print as a visual guide during your presentation.

Use Slide Masters

Slide Master view contains the slide background and text placeholders that affect the font size, style, color, and position in your entire presentation. If you use a template, you can customize the slide master to modify the template. When you create a slide show using a blank presentation, changes you make to the slide master add a consistent, professional look to all slides.

Style changes include **Design Themes**, changing the background, applying a color scheme, or adding a graphic that appears on all slides. You can also specify the fonts that will be used in the slides in your presentation.

Changing the **layout** of a slide master includes specifying the size and location of text placeholders including the slide footer. Like a footer in a Word document, slide footers can include standard information such as the presenter's name, date of presentation, or a slide number for each slide. Later in this lesson, you will use other master views to create handouts and speaker notes. Any new objects you place on the slide master will appear on all slides in the presentation.

Within Slide Master view, you can choose different formatting for slides that have a different layout (such as Title Slides and Two Content slides). To make changes that affect all slides, click the top slide in the thumbnail pane (labeled 1), which is the slide master. Each slide layout type is shown in the left pane in Slide Master view. Position the pointer over a slide thumbnail to view a ScreenTip with the slide layout title, as well as the numbers of any slides that use that layout.

> **Did You Know?**
>
> A slide master or modified presentation can be saved as a template to be used in future presentations. A template will be saved with the file extension .potx. It is recommended that you save templates in the My templates folder so that they will be available from the New Presentation dialog box.

To create slides with different effects for a new section of your presentation, you need to create a new slide master. When you have multiple slide masters in a presentation, the second slide master is labeled 2, and it includes specifications for all slide layout types.

2-4.1.6

S TEP-BY-STEP 10.1

1. Open the presentation **Party Planning.pptx** from your Data Files. The presentation opens in Normal view.

2. On the Ribbon, click the **View** tab, then in the Presentation Views group, click the **Slide Master** button. The presentation opens in Slide Master view, and the Slide Master tab is active, as shown in Figure 10-1.

FIGURE 10-1
Slide Master view

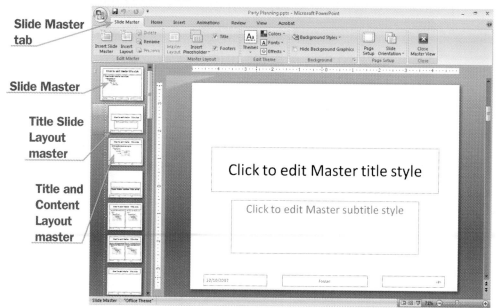

Slide Master tab

Slide Master

Title Slide Layout master

Title and Content Layout master

Click to edit Master title style

Click to edit Master subtitle style

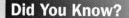

3. Click the **Office Theme Slide Master** thumbnail in the thumbnail pane. The current theme's slide master is the top slide in the thumbnail pane, and it is labeled 1. The changes that you make to the Slide Master slide will affect the entire presentation.

> **Did You Know?**
>
> You can also apply a theme to a presentation in Normal view. Click the Design tab, then click a theme in the Themes group

STEP-BY-STEP 10.1 Continued

4. In the Edit Theme group, click the **Themes** button, then click the **Flow** theme from the gallery. All of the slide layouts update to the Flow theme, as shown in Figure 10-2.

FIGURE 10-2
Flow theme applied to slide master

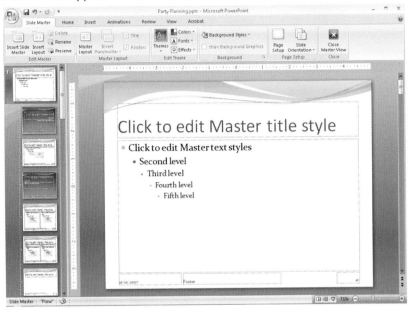

5. Click the **Title and Content Layout** slide master in the thumbnail pane. The changes you make here will only affect slides with the Title and Content layout.

6. Click the **Background Styles** button in the Backgrounds group, then click **Style 2**, as shown in Figure 10-3. The background changes to a light blue.

STEP-BY-STEP 10.1 Continued

FIGURE 10-3
Applying a background style

Background will be applied to all Title and Content slides

Background Styles button

Live preview of background style

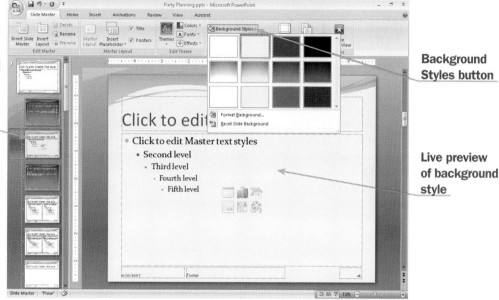

7. Click the **Normal** button on the status bar. Scroll through the presentation and note the changes.

8. Save the presentation as **Event Planning.pptx**, then leave the presentation and PowerPoint open for the next Step-by-Step.

Add Graphics and Media

In Lesson 9, you added graphics from a file using the Insert Picture icon in the content placeholder. Just as you did in Word, you can also insert clip art and use shapes to enhance your presentation. If a slide does not include a content placeholder, you can use the Insert tab to access many types of illustrations and other media.

You can add media clips, such as sound and video, to your presentation. Sound clips can be used to set a mood for a self-running presentation. A video clip can demonstrate a product or service, or it can be used to provide customer testimonials. In order to hear sound clips, you must have speakers and a sound card installed on your computer.

There are a few sound and video clips installed with Microsoft Office. You can also choose to download clips if you are connected to the Internet, choose sound and video stored on your computer, or choose to play a sound from a CD. If you choose the CD option, you must have the CD present when delivering your presentation.

STEP-BY-STEP 10.2

1. Click **Slide 5** in the Slides tab, click the **Insert** tab, then in the Illustrations group, click the **Clip Art** button. The Clip Art task pane opens.

2. Click the **Search in** list arrow, click **Everywhere** if necessary, click the **Results should be** list arrow, then click **All media types** if necessary.

3. Type **bride** in the Search for text box, then click **Go**. Results display in the task pane. (*Hint*: Your results may differ.)

4. Click the image shown in Figure 10-4, drag to position the graphic as shown in Figure 10-4, then click the **slide** to deselect the image.

FIGURE 10-4
Inserting clip art

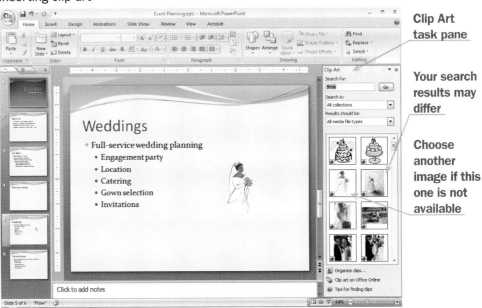

STEP-BY-STEP 10.2 Continued

5. Click the **Insert** tab if necessary, then in the Media Clips group, click the **Sound** button arrow, then click **Sound from Clip Organizer**.

6. Click **Claps Cheers**, click **Automatically** in the alert box, then drag the sound icon to the lower-right corner of the slide.

7. Click the **Slide Show** button on the status bar to preview the slide. The sound plays when Slide 5 displays.

8. Press **Esc** to end the slide show, then click the **Close** button on the Clip Art task pane.

9. Save your presentation, then leave the presentation and PowerPoint open for the next Step-by-Step.

> **Did You Know?**
>
> In addition to video and sound clips, you can add an **animated GIF** to a slide. An animated GIF is a graphic that has a sequence of repeating sound or movement.

> **Did You Know?**
>
> To hide the sound icon from appearing in a presentation, on the Sound Tools Options tab, in the Sound Options group, click the Hide During Show check box to select it.

 Working in a Connected World

Graphics and media can enhance your business presentation. When inserting graphics and media into a presentation, there are three important concerns:

1. Make sure that you have permission to use the art, likeness, sound, or video. Using copyrighted media without permission, unless you are using the material under fair use, an exception to copyright protection, may infringe on the copyright owner's rights. Even if you have permission, give credit to the source, and make sure that you are using it according to the agreement. If you use media that include a person, it is essential that he or she signs a release form allowing you to use his or her image or voice in your presentation.

2. Check the file size of your graphic or media clip. A large file can slow down your presentation, display poorly, and make the file size of the presentation too large to display on the Web or to send over e-mail.

3. Only use media and artwork in a way that complements but does not distract from your presentation. Sound that does not match the mood or contains inappropriate lyrics can turn off your audience. Rehearsing your presentation helps to identify potential issues.

Create a SmartArt Object

SmartArt objects display text graphically and can be used to show a process, hierarchy, cycle, or relationship between objects. There are seven categories of SmartArt objects, described in Table 10-1.

TABLE 10-1
SmartArt categories

CATEGORY	USED TO
List	Add emphasis to a bulleted list.
Process	Demonstrate the order of sequential steps in a workflow, timeline, or process.
Cycle	Display sequential steps in a workflow or a process that repeats when the last step is reached.
Hierarchy	Show information in different levels such as an organization chart or decision tree.
Matrix	Show relationships of parts to a whole.
Relationship	Illustrate conceptual relationships between multiple ideas or sets of data, where there is no process or hierarchy.
Pyramid	Display relationships that show proportions or a hierarchy building upward or downward.

A hierarchy can be used to show a company or department's organizational chart to display who works for whom, as shown in Figure 10-5. A cycle can show steps that repeat in an order, such as the phases of the moon, as shown in Figure 10-6.

FIGURE 10-5
Organization chart SmartArt

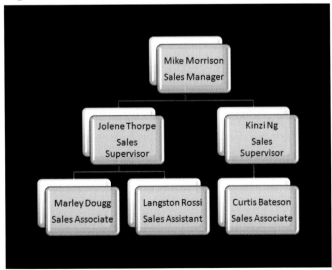

FIGURE 10-6
Cycle SmartArt

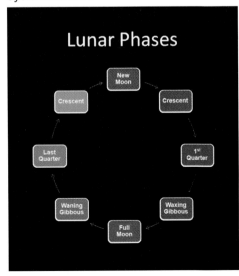

You can create a SmartArt object and then enter text, or convert existing text to a SmartArt object. The text you add to or use to create a SmartArt object can help you to determine the type of object and which layout to use. You can modify a SmartArt layout as necessary if the information changes.

S TEP-BY-STEP 10.3

1. Click **Slide 3** in the Slides tab, then select the bulleted text in the slide.

2. On the **Home** tab in the Paragraph group, click the **Convert to SmartArt Graphic** button, then click **More SmartArt Graphics**. The Choose a SmartArt Graphic dialog box opens.

3. Click the **Hierarchy** category, then click the **Hierarchy** layout. The Choose a SmartArt Graphic dialog box shows previews and descriptions for the Hierarchy category, as shown in Figure 10-7.

> **Computer Concepts**
>
> A chart illustrates relationships between numeric data. Choose to create a chart when you want to show the change in sales numbers or the relationship between production numbers. Choose a SmartArt object to show relationships between information.

FIGURE 10-7
Choose a SmartArt graphic dialog box

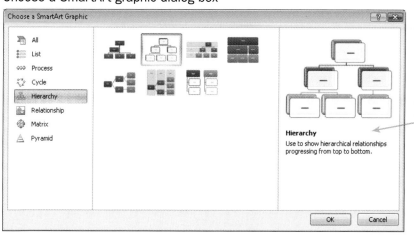

STEP-BY-STEP 10.3 Continued

4. Click **OK**. The organizational chart appears, as shown in Figure 10-8.

FIGURE 10-8
Hierarchy SmartArt

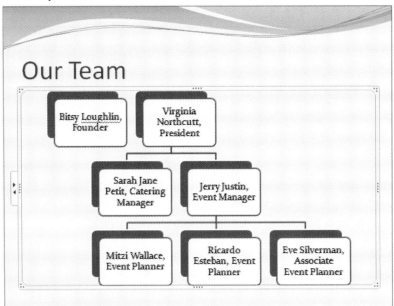

5. Click **Slide 4** in the Slides tab, then click the **Insert SmartArt Graphic** icon in the content placeholder.

6. Click the **Process** category in the dialog box, click the **Basic Chevron Process** layout, then click **OK**.

7. Click the **left** text box, type **Meet Client**, click the **middle** text box, type **Choose Date**, click the **right** text box, then type **Choose Location**. The text font size adjusts to fit in the text box.

8. On the SmartArt Tools Design tab, in the Create Graphic group, click the **Add Shape** button, then type **Select Theme** on the new shape. The SmartArt object appears, as shown in Figure 10-9.

STEP-BY-STEP 10.3 Continued

FIGURE 10-9
Basic chevron process SmartArt

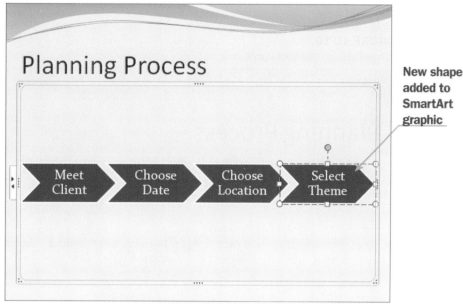

9. Save your presentation, then leave the presentation and PowerPoint open for the next Step-by-Step.

Format Slide Objects

Styles are formats that you can apply to a selected object that enhance the object by adding a border, shadow, gradient, or three-dimensional effect to an image. You can also change a table by using bands of colors to distinguish rows. Styles are available on the *Object* Tools Design tab, where *Object* indicates the element to which you are applying a style (picture, SmartArt, chart, and so on).

When you select the outside border of an object such as a SmartArt object or a chart that has multiple parts, any formatting or styles you apply will be made to the entire object. You can also make changes to just one or to multiple selected parts of an object by clicking the part(s) of the object.

Other formatting choices include adding a fill, or background color or texture, to an object or changing the brightness or contrast to make it dimmer or stand out more.

The alignment of an object refers to its relationship to a slide border (center, left, right, top, or bottom). You can also change the order of a layered object to make it appear in front of or behind another object.

STEP-BY-STEP 10.4

1. In Slide 4, click the outside border of the SmartArt object, then on the **SmartArt Tools Design** tab, in the SmartArt Styles group, click the **Subtle Effect** style. The SmartArt object appears as shown in Figure 10-10.

FIGURE 10-10
Formatted SmartArt object

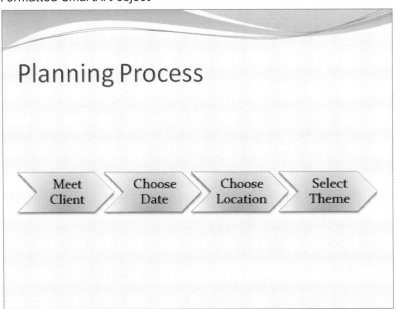

2. Select the text in the **Meet Client** text box, click the **Home** tab if necessary, apply **bold**, then change the font color to **Dark Teal, Text 2**.

3. Click **Slide 5** in the Slides tab, click the **clip art image**, on the Picture Tools Format tab, in the Picture Styles group, click the **More** button, then click the **Beveled Oval, Black** style.

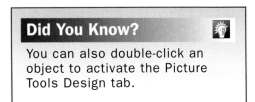

Did You Know?

You can also double-click an object to activate the Picture Tools Design tab.

4. In the Picture Styles group, click the **Picture Effects** button, point to **Glow**, then click **Accent color 4, 18 pt glow** style, as shown in Figure 10-11.

STEP-BY-STEP 10.4 Continued

FIGURE 10-11
Picture Effect added

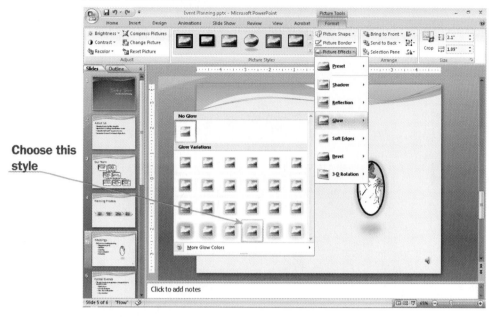

Choose this
style

5. Click **Slide 1** in the Slides tab, click the **Insert** tab, then in the Illustrations group, click the **Shapes** button, then in the Basic Shapes section, click **Oval**.

6. Use the pointer to draw an oval that covers all of the text on the slide. (*Hint:* Reposition the oval if necessary.)

7. Click the **Drawing Tools Format** tab, then in the Arrange group, click the **Send to Back** button. The oval appears behind the text.

8. With the oval still selected, in the Shape Styles group, click the **Shape Fill** button arrow, then click **Blue, Accent 1, Lighter 40%**. The oval is now a light blue.

STEP-BY-STEP 10.4 Continued

9. In the Shape Styles group, click the **Shape Outline** button arrow, click **No Outline**, then deselect the oval. The oval appears as shown in Figure 10-12.

10. Save your presentation, then leave the presentation and PowerPoint open for the next Step-by-Step.

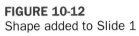
FIGURE 10-12
Shape added to Slide 1

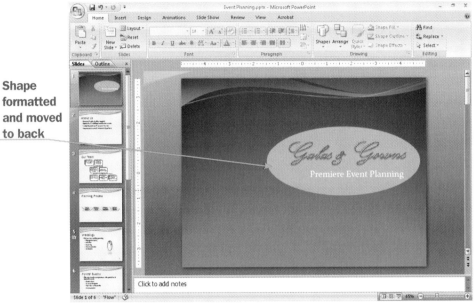

Shape formatted and moved to back

Use Animations

Animations are visual or movement effects, sometimes accompanied by sound, that you can add to an object such as a text box or graphic. You can also apply animations to chart or SmartArt objects as a whole, by part, or by level. Animation effects include entrance and exit effects that can be executed when you click the slide, occur simultaneously with another animation, or occur sequentially.

Slide transitions are animations applied to individual slides or to the slide master, and they affect how slides appear or disappear during a slide show.

To apply an animation or transition, select an object or slide, then use the tools on the Animations tab and in the Custom Animation task pane, as shown in Figure 10-13. To animate an object, click its outside border. To animate an individual element of an object, such as a text box or chart axis, use the Effect Options dialog box, or click the individual part to apply an animation to that section or level. Use Slide Master view to select transition effects for all slides or for slides of a certain type.

FIGURE 10-13
Applying animations

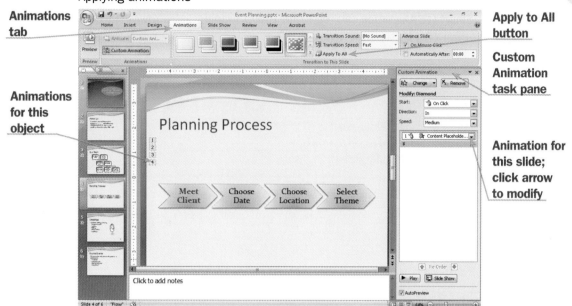

Animations
tab

Animations
for this
object

Apply to All
button

Custom
Animation
task pane

Animation for
this slide;
click arrow
to modify

2-4.1.7

STEP-BY-STEP 10.5

1. With Slide 1 selected, click the **Animations** tab, click the outside border of the Galas & Gowns text box to select it, then in the Animations group, click the **Custom Animation** button. The Custom Animation task pane opens.

2. In the task pane, click the **Add Effect** button, point to **Emphasis**, then click **Spin**. A preview of the spinning text box appears.

3. Click **Slide 4** in the Slides tab, click the outside border of the **SmartArt** object to select it, then in the Custom Animation task pane, click the **Add Effect** button, point to **Entrance**, click **More Effects**, then click **Diamond**. The diamond effect previews.

4. In the Custom Animation task pane, click the arrow next to the Content Placeholder animation, then click **Effect Options**. The Effect Options dialog box opens with the effect in the title bar, in this case, Diamond.

STEP-BY-STEP 10.5 Continued

5. Click the **SmartArt Animation** tab, click the **Group graphic** list arrow, then click **One by one**, as shown in Figure 10-14.

FIGURE 10-14
Diamond effect options dialog box

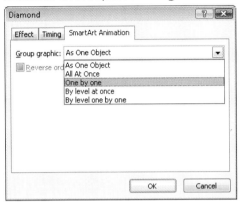

6. Click **OK** to close the dialog box, preview the animation, then click **Slide 1** in the Slides tab. The numbers in the slide and in the effects list indicate the number of clicks required to initiate the animation.

7. In the Transition to This Slide group, click the **Dissolve** transition, then click the **Apply to All** button. All slides in the presentation have the Dissolve transition effect applied to them.

8. Click the **Close** button in the Custom Animation task pane, click the **Slide Show** button in the task bar, then preview the presentation to view the effects you have applied.

9. Save your presentation, then leave the presentation and PowerPoint open for the next Step-by-Step.

Create a Custom Slide Show

A custom slide show is a presentation with a different order or number of slides in a presentation, which allows you to customize a presentation for different audiences.

You can save custom slide shows within a presentation and either run a basic custom show or create a hyperlink to a custom show within your presentation. Hyperlinked custom shows are useful to navigate from a table of contents slide or to jump to slides about a product or service, depending on the audience's interest.

To create or run a custom slide show, use the Slide Show tab, as shown in Figure 10-15. In a presentation, to click a hyperlink, position the pointer over the underlined text, then click. The custom show will start.

FIGURE 10-15
Slide Show tab

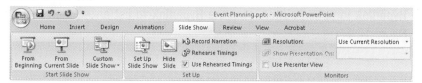

STEP-BY-STEP 10.6

1. Click the **Slide Show** tab, then in the Start Slide Show group, click the **Custom Slide Show** button, then click **Custom Shows**. The Custom Shows dialog box opens.

2. Click **New**, then in the **Define Custom Show** dialog box, type **Weddings** in the Slide show name text box.

3. In the Slides in presentation box, press and hold **Ctrl**, click Slides 4 and 5, then click **Add**. The selected slides appear in the Slides in custom show box.

4. In the Slides in custom show box, click **Weddings**, then click the **up** arrow to move it to the top. The dialog box appears as shown in Figure 10-16.

FIGURE 10-16
Define Custom Show dialog box

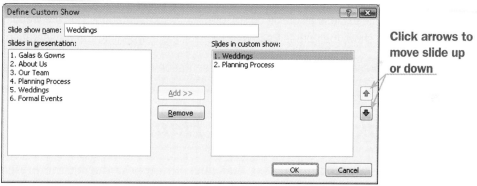

5. Click **OK**, then click **Close** to close all open dialog boxes.

6. Click **Slide 2** in the Slides tab, select the text **weddings** in the second bullet, click the **Insert** tab, then in the **Links** group, click **Action**. The Action Settings dialog box opens.

STEP-BY-STEP 10.6 Continued

7. Click the **Hyperlink to** option button, click the **Hyperlink to** list arrow, then click **Custom Show**, as shown in Figure 10-17.

FIGURE 10-17
Action Settings dialog box

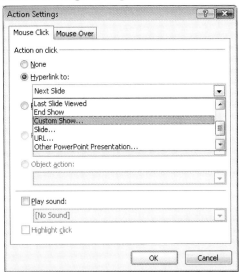

8. Click **OK** twice to close all dialog boxes, preview the presentation, click the **weddings** hyperlink to start the custom show, then press **Esc**. When you click the hyperlink, the presentation moves to Slide 5.

9. Save your presentation, then leave the presentation and PowerPoint open for the next Step-by-Step.

Print Speaker Notes and Handouts

Speaker notes are additional text that does not appear during the presentation but which contains reminders or additional information that will help you when delivering the presentation. To enter speaker notes, click the Notes pane, located under the Slide pane in Normal view, then type the relevant information. You can drag the top border of the Notes pane up or down to show more or less of the speaker notes pane.

Handouts are printouts of your slides. You can specify the number of slides per page or leave room for the audience to write notes during a presentation.

You can choose the number of slides to appear on either handouts or speaker notes (as well as choose other formatting options) or add a header or footer, using the Handouts Master or Notes Master. In either Master view, you have access to tools that create a professional look for your printouts, and you can preview the document.

You can print speaker notes and handouts using the Print dialog box. Click the Print what list arrow, then choose the item to print, specify other options, see a preview, then print.

S TEP-BY-STEP 10.7

1. Move to Slide 1, then drag the top border of the Notes pane up in the slide, if necessary.

2. Click in the Notes pane, then type **Welcome! I am Your Name, Vice President of Galas & Gowns**.

3. Move to Slide 2, click in the Notes pane, type **We do over 50 events per year**, move to Slide 4, then type **We work with you to create the event that you want** in the Notes pane.

4. Click the **Office Button**, point to **Print**, then click **Print**. The Print dialog box opens.

5. Click the **Print what** list arrow, click **Notes Pages**, then click **OK**. Your notes pages print one slide per page, as shown in Figure 10-18.

FIGURE 10-18
Speaker notes

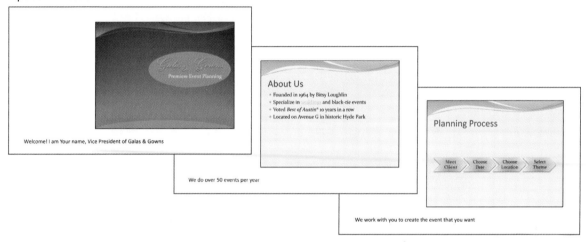

6. Click the **View** tab, then in the **Presentation Views** group, click the **Handout Master** button. The presentation appears in Handout Master view.

7. In the Page Setup group, click the **Handout Orientation** button arrow, then click **Landscape**. The page will print wider than it is long.

8. In the Placeholders group, deselect the **Header** and **Date** check boxes, then type **Galas & Gowns** in the footer placeholder. The placeholder with **<#>** will display the page number.

9. In the Background group, click the **Background Styles** button, click **Style 5**, then close master view.

STEP-BY-STEP 10.7 Continued

10. Open the Print dialog box, click the **Print what** list arrow, click **Handouts**, then click **Preview**. The handouts will appear as shown in Figure 10-19 when printed.

11. Close Print Preview, save and close the presentation, then exit PowerPoint.

FIGURE 10-19
Preview of handouts

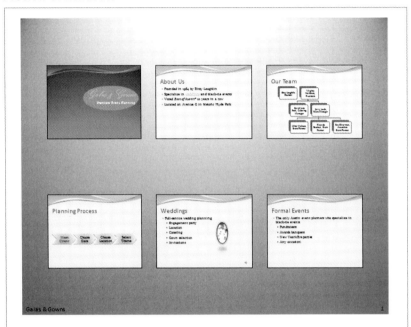

SUMMARY

- PowerPoint has three master views: Slide, Handout, and Notes. In each view, you can set up the layout of your slides for printing or presenting. You can add backgrounds, footers, or other formatting and layout options. In Slide Master view, you can edit slide layouts or create multiple slide masters.

- You can add graphics such as shapes, Clip Art, or graphic files. You can add media clips to add sound and video to the presentation, which run automatically or when clicked during a presentation.

- SmartArt objects are visual representations of information, shown by level or in a sequential order. Examples include organization charts, timelines, and cycles.

- Slide objects can be formatted in many ways using the contextual tabs that appear when the object is clicked. You can apply various styles to an object to enhance the border, add a reflection, or make other changes. You can also change the alignment or order of an object to create layering or stacking effects.

■ Animations and transitions are used to apply entrance, exit, movement, or sound effects to objects and slides.

■ Graphics, media, formatting, animations, and transitions should all be used in a way that enhances your audience's experience or understanding but which does not detract from the message of your presentation.

■ Creating a custom slide show allows you to tailor the slides or slide order of a presentation for different audiences. You can run or create a basic custom show that displays only the slides you have selected, or create a hyperlink in a presentation to a custom show that you can use to create a table of contents slide.

■ Speaker notes and handouts are printouts of your presentation that show an image of each slide. Speaker notes contain reminders to the presenter about questions to ask or additional information. Handouts are distributed to your audience to take notes on or as a copy of the information from the presentation.

VOCABULARY *Review*

Define the following terms:		
Alignment	Handout	SmartArt
Animated GIF	Layout	Speaker notes
Animations	Media clip	Transition
Design Themes	Order	
Fill	Slide master	

REVIEW *Questions*

SCREEN IDENTIFICATION

FIGURE 10-20
Screen identification

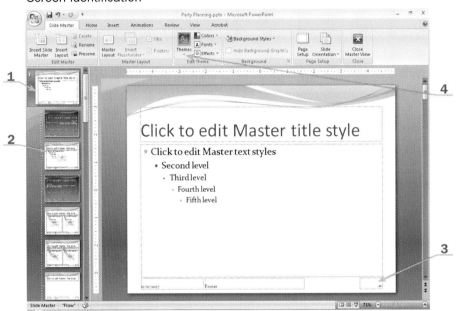

Identify the screen elements.

1.

2.

3.

4.

MULTIPLE CHOICE

Circle the correct answer.

1. All of the following are types of masters except _____.
   A. Slide
   B. Handout
   C. Notes
   D. Layout

2. Changing the _____ moves objects in front of or behind other objects.
   A. Orientation
   B. Alignment
   C. Order
   D. Layout

3. To insert a link to a custom show, click the _____ button.
   A. Actions
   B. Hyperlink
   C. Insert Custom Show
   D. Slide Show

4. All of the following are types of media except _____.
   A. Transitions
   B. Sound
   C. Video
   D. Animated GIFs

TRUE/FALSE

Circle T if the statement is true or F if the statement is false.

T F 1. Notes pages are usually distributed to your audience.

T F 2. Each presentation can have only one slide master.

T F 3. You can save a slide master as a template.

T F 4. A timeline is an example of a SmartArt object.

T F 5. Charts and SmartArt objects refer to the same types of objects.

T F 6. Transitions and animations affect how objects appear and disappear during a presentation.

HANDS-ON REVIEW

1. Open the presentation Coronado Theatre.pptx, then switch to Slide Master view.

2. Apply a design theme to the slide master, modify the fonts on the Title master, then switch to Normal view.

3. On Slide 3, add an appropriate clip art image and sound effect. Have the sound effect play only when clicked.

4. Create a SmartArt chart using the bullets on Slide 4. Choose an appropriate SmartArt category and layout.

5. Format the SmartArt object by changing the font and fill of one of the shapes. Apply a picture style to the clip art image on Slide 3.

6. Apply an animation to the SmartArt graphic on Slide 4, and modify the animation so that the effect is applied one object at a time. Apply slide transitions to the entire presentation.

7. Create a custom slide show using Slides 1, 5, and 6. Save it as Classes.

8. Add speaker notes to at least three slides. Use Notes Page master view to set up the notes pages. Use Handout master view to set up the handouts by changing the background and orientation.

9. Preview your presentation, and make any necessary changes. *Note:* If you are not connected to a color printer, your preview will display in black and white.

10. Save the presentation as Final Coronado Theatre.pptx, then close it.

PROJECTS

PROJECT 10-1

Open the presentation Juice.pptx. Use the master views to format the slides, handouts, and notes pages. Apply slide transitions in slide master view. Add footers to the handouts and notes pages. Use the bullets to add a new SmartArt graphic to Slide 3. Apply an animation to each part of the SmartArt graphic. Preview your presentation, and make any necessary changes. Save the presentation as Product Presentation.pptx.

PROJECT 10-2

Note: You must have a CD and CD drive available to complete this project.

Open the presentation Fitness Trainer.pptx. Insert a CD into your CD drive. On Slide 1, click the Insert tab, and in the Media Clips group, click the Sound button arrow, then click Play CD Audio Track. In the Insert CD Audio dialog box, enter the tracks, start time, and end time, then click OK. Choose to have the sound play automatically. Preview your presentation, and make any necessary changes. Save the presentation as Fitness Presentation.pptx.

 TEAMWORK

Open the presentation Nicholas Farms.pptx. View the presentation as a slide show. Individually, make a list of the things you find distracting or would change about the presentation. Compare your list with the group, and decide which changes should be made. As a group, modify the presentation, and make a list of the changes that you made. Preview your presentation, and make any necessary changes. Save the list of changes in a Word document called Improvements.docx, and save the modified presentation as Improved Farm Presentation.pptx.

CRITICAL*Thinking*

ACTIVITY 10–1

Create a new presentation called My Speaker Notes.pptx. Think about the information that you want to appear on the slide, as well as the information that you should include in speaker notes. Add four slides, and insert information about yourself or a topic that interests you. Apply formatting and transitions if you like. Add speaker notes as appropriate, and print them. Practice running your presentation using your speaker notes, then make any necessary changes. Save and close the presentation.

DATABASE ESSENTIALS

Microsoft Office Access is a **database management system** (DBMS). Like a filing cabinet, a DBMS is used to organize information so that it can be entered, searched, and analyzed. Files in Access are called databases.

You may not realize it, but you come across databases many times a day. Stores use databases to record sales and inventory; the catalog at your library uses a database to keep track of books and other media; and your digital audio or video player uses databases to organize music and other media.

A **database** organizes information in records. A record contains the complete information on one entity in the database, such as an employee. Within each record are several **fields** that contain one item of data, such as the employee's ID number, last name, or hourly wage. A database can contain thousands of records that can be easily sorted and analyzed.

Each record in a database should contain at least one distinct field, called a **primary key**. A primary key is used to make sure that each employee, product, or other entity is unique.

Computer Concepts

Why use a database? Tables in Word and Excel can also be used to organize and analyze data. Access can be used to perform a more complex analysis of data, demonstrate relationships between data, and ensure that no redundant information is entered.

Records are organized, stored, compared, and analyzed using a variety of tools, outlined in Table 11-1.

TABLE 11-1
Database objects

DATABASE OBJECT	ICON	USED TO
Table		Store data in columns and rows, similar to an Excel table
Query		Retrieve information based on search criteria, similar to a filter in Excel
Form		View, add, and update data in tables and records
Report		Display the contents of a table or the results of a query
Macro		Perform tasks related to a database object, such as adding a command button, without using programming language
Module		Perform tasks related to a database object; similar to a module but uses Visual Basic for Applications (VBA), a program language

A database can contain multiple objects of each type, each object showing different **relationships** between data. Objects can reference the same record, but each object displays a different result. For instance, an employee record for Jessica Maxwell, a new sales associate, can appear in a table showing all female employees, in a table showing all employees in the sales department, and a report showing all employees who make less than $40,000. Jessica Maxwell's record only appears once in the database, however. You can edit and delete relationships in the database.

Understand Databases

Databases can be very complex and are usually meant to be used by many people who update and search for information. In order to accurately track employees, inventory, and other areas for a company, government agency, or your own project, you must make sure that your database is accurate by adding new data, editing current data, and deleting outdated data.

Once your database is up to date, you can reorganize it or add new objects in order to analyze or display the data so that you can share it with others. Data can be printed in a report, sent as an attachment to e-mail, converted to another application such as Excel, or used to populate specific databases such as product inventory for an online store.

You can create a database from scratch or by importing data from a spreadsheet or other source. Before you begin creating a database, you need to answer the following questions:

1. What is the purpose of the database?

2. What information will be included in the database? What information do I want to be able to track in the future? What information do I want in reports?

3. How will the data be organized in tables? Convert data into columns and rows if necessary. Each row will be a record, and each cell is a field.

4. How will I ensure uniqueness? Determine what the primary key will be such as a product ID number or Social Security number.

After you have determined the basic questions, you will also want to decide what relationships between tables are necessary to analyze or clarify data, and design your database so that it is easy to enter, edit, and create reports based on the data.

Identify Access Screen Elements

When you first start Access, the Getting Started with Microsoft Office Access window appears. This window allows you to create a new, blank database, choose a database template, learn about Access, or open a recently used database.

ETHICS IN TECHNOLOGY

Because a database is used to store a variety of information, it can be used for many purposes. A doctor's office might store patient medical records in a database. Entering inaccurate information can have serious consequences for the patient. The information in a medical record is also confidential, so keeping it private is another important consideration.

Database users should follow certain guidelines in order to keep the information in a database accurate and confidential information secure.

- **Accuracy:** Data should be entered correctly and kept up to date to avoid complications or miscalculations.

- **Authorization:** Confidential data can be restricted in order to preserve a person's privacy or so that sensitive material is not revealed.

- **Responsibility:** When you come across personal data, do not share that data with those who do not need to know. Follow your company's guidelines for sensitive data that pertains to a person, a product, or finances.

Access shares some elements of the user interface with Word and other Office programs such as the Ribbon, dialog boxes, and scroll bars. Many of the basic program tasks are the same for all Office programs such as starting a program and saving, opening, and closing a file. The Microsoft Office Access 2007 program window is shown in Figure 11-1.

FIGURE 11-1
Access window

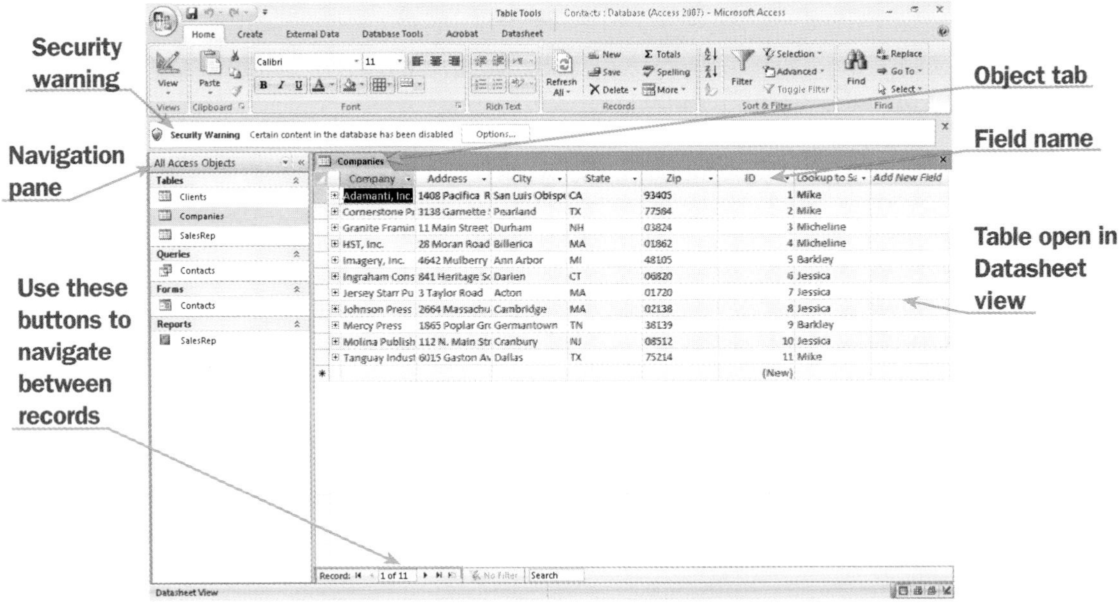

To add, edit, and manage database objects, use the **Navigation Pane**. The Navigation Pane can be organized by object type, category, date, and other views. When you have multiple database objects open, you can click the object's tab to activate it.

S TEP-BY-STEP 11.1

1. Start Access using the **Start** button or a desktop shortcut. The Getting Started with Microsoft Office Access window opens.

2. Click the **Office Button**, then click **Open**.

3. In the Open dialog box, locate the Data Files, then open the file **Contacts.accdb**.

4. Click the tabs on the Ribbon to see the groups and buttons available. Note that some of the buttons on the Home tab are features you used in other applications, but most of the tabs and buttons are different.

Computer Concepts

A database is a dynamic tool, meaning that it is designed to be adaptable. Forms provide a user-friendly interface to enter information. You can also easily add, delete, and modify fields and objects as the requirements of your database change. In Datasheet view, there is always an option available to add a new field or record to make sure that your database fits your changing needs.

STEP-BY-STEP 11.1 Continued

5. If the Navigation Pane title bar does not say All Access Objects, click the list arrow, click **Object Type**, then in the Tables section of the Navigation Pane, double-click the **Companies** table. The object opens in Datasheet view, and the cursor is positioned over the first record in the Company field.

6. In the first cell of the table, click the first click the **plus sign** (+) next to Adamanti, Inc. to display the records associated with that company. The datasheet appears as shown in Figure 11-2.

FIGURE 11-2
Table with expanded records

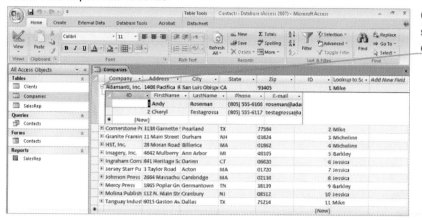

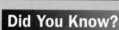
Click minus sign to collapse

7. Click the **Close** button at the top right of the table to close it.

8. In the Navigation Pane, double-click the **Contacts** query, then double-click the **Contacts** form. The Contacts query lists all the contacts; the Contacts form displays them individually.

9. Click the **Contacts query** tab, close the object, then close the Contacts form.

Did You Know?

Access assumes that every database can possibly contain information that could be harmful to your computer. All of the files used in this book are safe to use, and the screenshots in this book (except Figure 11-1) show the content enabled. You can ignore the Security warning, or click the Options button to open the Microsoft Office Security Options dialog box, click the Enable this content option button, then click OK.

STEP-BY-STEP 11.1 Continued

10. In the Navigation Pane, double-click the **SalesRep** report. The report opens, as shown in Figure 11-3.

FIGURE 11-3
SalesRep report

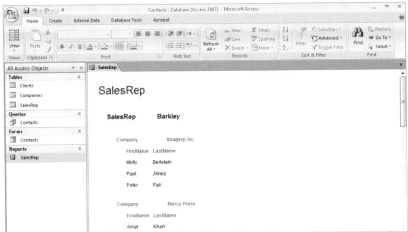

11. In the Navigation Pane, click the **All Access Objects** button arrow, then click **Tables and Related Views**. The database objects are regrouped, as shown in Figure 11-4.

FIGURE 11-4
Navigation Pane sorted by Tables and Related Views

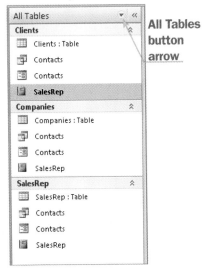

12. Close the database, then leave Access open for the next Step-by-Step.

Create a New Table

All database information is stored in one or more tables. You should define and populate the tables in your database before creating other objects.

You can create tables in three ways: from scratch, by using a table template, or by importing data from another program or file. If you import data, it must be organized in columns and rows or in another format that clearly determines fields and records. A new table should include the primary key, all field names, and the associated field values.

Defining the types and characteristics of data for each field helps ensure the integrity of your database. A table uses a **property sheet**, available in Design view, which allows you to set **field properties**, which define the attributes and appearance of your table and data.

Did You Know?

As with other Office files, when you create a database, you save it with a new name. Access 2007 databases use the file extension **.accdb**. Data in an Access file is automatically saved to the database as it is updated, although you may be prompted to save a database if you had added objects or restructured data. You cannot save a database with a new filename unless you rename it using an Explorer window.

Field properties include setting a character limit, applying formatting, setting decimal places, determining a default value, and using an input mask. An **input mask** provides clues to the data to be inserted, such as YYYY-MM-DD to indicate that the date November 4, 2010 should be entered as 2010-11-04. **Data types**, listed in Table 11-2, determine the data that can be entered in a field. Other data types available include OLE objects, attachments, hyperlinks, and Lookup Wizards.

TABLE 11-2
Commonly used data types

FORMAT	USED FOR
Text	Numbers and letters that are not used in calculations; up to 255 characters
Memo	Text longer than 255 characters or that uses Rich Text Formatting
Number	Any number (fraction or integer) used in calculations except monetary numbers
Currency	Monetary values
Date/Time	Date and time values (each entry stores both)
AutoNumber	Generating unique numbers as a record is entered into the database
Yes/No	Values that have only two options such as Yes/No, True/False, or On/Off

Fields should contain the smallest possible unit of data. For instance, instead of one field for CityStateZIP, make City, State, and ZIP three separate fields. Field names should define the data that will be included. Field names can contain spaces, but with some database uses, such as exporting information to a Web site, spaces can be problematic.

You can enter table information in a datasheet using columns and rows in Datasheet view, which is similar to working in an Excel spreadsheet. A row of data, also

Did You Know?

There are reserved words in Access that should not be used as field or object names. Words such as Date, Function, and Index should be avoided, because they are also used in queries and calculations. If you try to enter a reserved word, you will get a warning. You should choose another name for your field or object to avoid errors.

called an **instance**, contains all of the information about one record. A column of data, also called an **attribute**, contains related data such as all employees' last names.

S TEP-BY-STEP 11.2

1. Click the **Office Button**, then click **New**.

2. In the Getting Started window, in the New Blank Database section, click the **Blank Database** icon.

3. In the right pane, select the text in the File Name text box, type **Products**, click the folder icon, navigate to your Data Files, click **OK** in the File New Database dialog box, click **Create** in the right pane of the Getting Started window, then click in the first column in the table. A new, blank database opens with a table called Table1 in Datasheet view. The first field in the ID column is selected. On the Ribbon, in the Data Type & Formatting group, the Data Type is listed as AutoNumber, as shown in Figure 11-5.

FIGURE 11-5
New, blank database

ID field is an
AutoNumber

ID field is
automatically
added to
Table 1

4. Double-click **Add New Field** at the top of column 2, type **ProductName**, then press **Enter**. Access assigns the Text as the data type, then moves to a new blank field.

5. In the **Add New Field** column, type **Price**, click outside of the column, click the column head, then on the Table Tools Datasheet tab, in the Data Type & Formatting group, click the **Data Type** list arrow, then click **Currency**.

6. In the **Add New Field** column, type **Quantity**, click outside of the column, then click the column head, click the **Data Type** list arrow, then click **Number**.

7. Position the pointer on the right **column** border of the ProductName field, click the left mouse button, then drag to the right to widen the column until the field name is visible.

8. On the Table Tools Datasheet tab, in the Views group, click the **View** button arrow, then click **Design View**. The Save As dialog box appears, where you are prompted to save the table.

9. Type **Products** in the Table Name text box, then click **OK**. The table appears in Design view, with the Field Properties pane open, as shown in Figure 11-6.

STEP-BY-STEP 11.2 Continued

FIGURE 11-6
Table in Design view

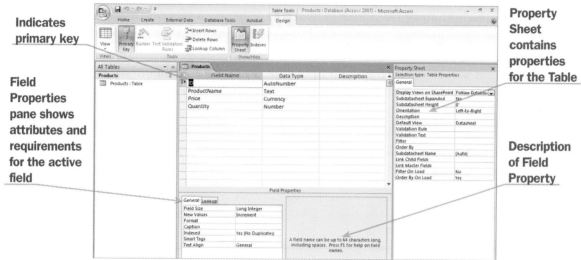

Indicates primary key

Field Properties pane shows attributes and requirements for the active field

Property Sheet contains properties for the Table

Description of Field Property

10. Click **ProductName** in the Field Name column, then in the Field Properties pane, on the General tab, click in the **Required** box, click the **arrow**, then click **Yes**, as shown in Figure 11-7.

FIGURE 11-7
Making a field required

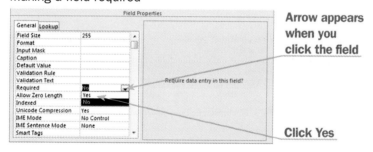

Arrow appears when you click the field

Click Yes

11. In the Views group, click the **View** button arrow, click **Datasheet View**, click **Yes** to save the table, then leave the database and Access open for the next Step-by-Step.

Enter Records in a Database

Once you have set up your table by defining the primary key, fields, and data types, you are ready to enter records.

You can enter information directly in Datasheet view, pressing Tab to move between fields. When you press Tab after entering data in the last field of the record, a new record becomes active. Until you move to a new record, the AutoNumber field does not update.

If you enter invalid field data that does not match the specified data type, you will get an error message and be prompted to convert the data to the proper format, get help, or reenter the data.

You can also use a form to enter records. A **form** is a window that contains all of the information about a specific record. Forms are useful for data entry or editing. Use the database navigation tools at the bottom of Datasheet view to move between records. You can add a form to your database using tools on the Create tab. Forms can be modified or formatted.

Using data from another source such as an Excel worksheet, rather than retyping data, is another important way to ensure that your data is accurate. Before you import data, you must set up the data to include the correct fields. If your table includes an AutoNumber field, this will be added to the table as you import.

Access uses wizards to guide you through importing data and other tasks. A **wizard** is a series of dialog boxes that ask questions and verify information in order to correctly complete the task. Wizards are helpful because they can point out potential errors as well as help with an unfamiliar process.

STEP-BY-STEP 11.3

1. If necessary, click in the ID field for row 1. This will be the entry for the first record in your table.

2. Press **Tab**, type **Hammock**, press **Tab**, type **65**, press **Tab**, type **15**, then press **Tab**. The number 65 is formatted as **$65.00** and the number 1 appears in the ID field, as shown in Figure 11-8.

FIGURE 11-8
Record 1 added

AutoNumber is updated

Currency formatting applied

New record is active

3. In record 2, indicated by (New) in the ID column, press **Tab** to move to the ProductName field, type **Lawn chair**, press **Tab**, type **23.5**, press **Tab**, then type **32**. Repeat the sequence for record 3, typing **Picnic table**, **399**, and **14** in the three fields.

4. In record 4, type **Porch swing** in the ProductName field, type **Porch swing** again in the Price field, then press **Tab**. A warning icon and menu open, as shown in Figure 11-9.

FIGURE 11-9
Invalid data type

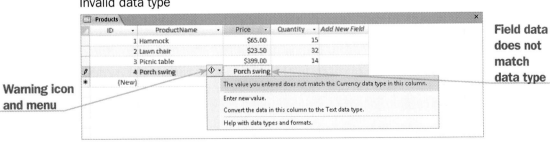

Warning icon and menu

Field data does not match data type

STEP-BY-STEP 11.3 Continued

5. Click **Enter new value** on the menu, type **199**, press **Tab**, type **10**, press **Tab**, then press **Ctrl + S** to save the table data.

6. On the Ribbon, click the **Create** tab, then in the Forms group, click the **Form** button, click the **Home** tab, in the Views group click the **View** button arrow, then click **Form View**. A new form opens on its own tab.

7. Click the **New (blank) record** button on the Navigation bar, click the **ProductName** text box, then use Figure 11-10 as a reference to enter the data for record 5. Close the Products form, click **OK** when prompted to save the form, then click **OK** to save the form as **Products**.

FIGURE 11-10
Form view

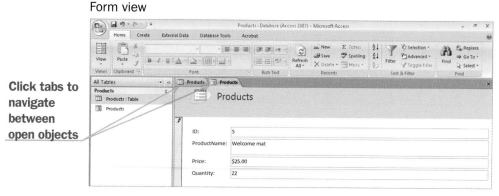

8. Click the **External Data** tab, then in the Import group click the **Excel** button. The Get External Data dialog box opens.

9. Click the **Browse** button, navigate to your Data Files, click the **Import Products.xlsx** file, then click **Open**.

10. Click the **Append a copy of the records to the table** option button, click **OK**, then click **Yes** to close the table.

11. Navigate through the Import wizard, selecting all defaults, click **Finish**, then click **Close**.

STEP-BY-STEP 11.3 Continued

12. In the Navigation Pane, double-click **Products: Table**. The new records are imported. Adjust the width of the ProductName column until all the product names are visible, as shown in Figure 11-11.

13. Leave the database and Access open for the next Step-by-Step.

FIGURE 11-11
Records imported

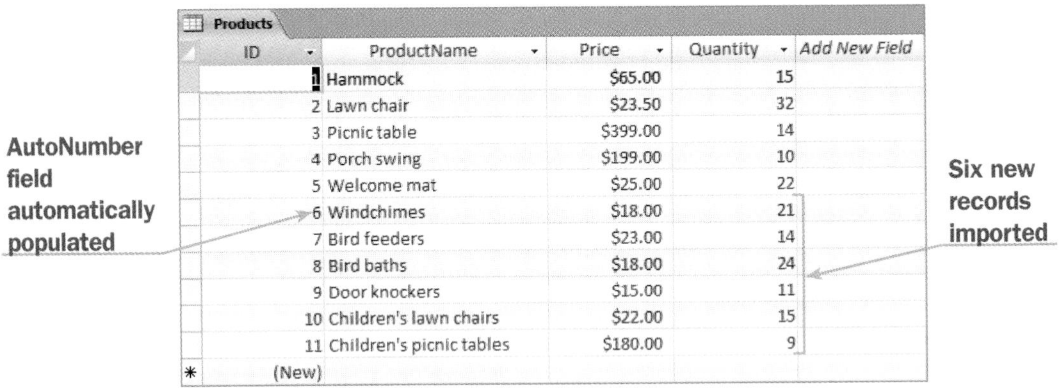

	ID	ProductName	Price	Quantity	Add New Field
	1	Hammock	$65.00	15	
	2	Lawn chair	$23.50	32	
	3	Picnic table	$399.00	14	
	4	Porch swing	$199.00	10	
	5	Welcome mat	$25.00	22	
	6	Windchimes	$18.00	21	
	7	Bird feeders	$23.00	14	
	8	Bird baths	$18.00	24	
	9	Door knockers	$15.00	11	
	10	Children's lawn chairs	$22.00	15	
	11	Children's picnic tables	$180.00	9	
*	(New)				

AutoNumber field automatically populated

Six new records imported

Add and Delete Fields

In Datasheet view, the column to the right of the last defined field contains the header Add New Field. In order to add a field to the table, simply click on the column header, then type the field name. To insert a new field in between other fields, select the field to the right of where you want the new field to appear, then click the Insert button on the Table Tools Datasheet tab in the Field & Columns group. You can also drag a column header to a new location.

Unless you define the data type, Access will assign an appropriate data type based on the information entered into a field. If you type a date, Access will apply the Date/Time format. When a data type is not easily recognized, Access assigns the Text data type.

When you delete a field in a database, you lose all information in that field for all records. Deleting a field cannot be undone, so you should not do it unless you are certain that you do not need to save the information. Deleting a primary key field can cause serious consequences to your database, such as no longer being able to identify records.

You can delete a field in Datasheet view by deleting the column. In Design View, use the Delete Rows button on the Design tab, in the Tools group.

STEP-BY-STEP 11.4

1. Double-click the **Add New Field** column header, then type **Discount**.

2. Click away from the column, select the **Discount** column head, click the **Table Tools Datasheet** tab, then in the Data Type & Formatting group, click the **Data Type** list arrow, then click **Number**.

STEP-BY-STEP 11.4 Continued

3. Type **10** in all fields in the Discount column.

4. Select the Price column head, then on the Table Tools Datasheet tab in the Field & Columns group, click the **Insert** button. A new column called Field1 appears.

5. In the Field & Columns group, click the **Rename** button, then type **Color**.

6. Using Figure 11-12 as a reference, type the data in the Color field.

FIGURE 11-12
New field inserted

ID	ProductName	Color	Price	Quantity	Discount	Add New Field
1	Hammock	White	$65.00	15	10	
2	Lawn chair	Brown	$23.50	32	10	
3	Picnic table	Brown	$399.00	14	10	
4	Porch swing	Brown	$199.00	10	10	
5	Welcome mat	Multiple	$25.00	22	10	
6	Windchimes	Copper	$18.00	21	10	
7	Bird feeders	Gray	$23.00	14	10	
8	Bird baths	Copper	$18.00	24	10	
9	Door knockers	Brass	$15.00	11	10	
10	Children's lawn chairs	White	$22.00	15	10	
11	Children's picnic tables	White	$180.00	9	10	
*	(New)					

Enter Color data

7. Double-click the **Add New Field** column header, type **Manufacturer**, then enter data in at least two of the fields.

8. Select the Manufacturer column head, then on the Table Tools Datasheet tab in the Fields & Columns group, click the **Delete** button. A warning box opens, asking if you want to remove all data from this field.

9. Click **Yes** in the warning box.

10. Save the database, then leave the database and Access open for the next Step-by-Step.

Modify Records

You can edit records in Datasheet view or Form view. Datasheet view is helpful if you want to see all records in a table while updating data. Form view is useful when you want to see all information about one record at a time. In both views, you can navigate between fields by pressing the Tab key or by clicking in a field.

When you delete a record, you lose all information in that record permanently. When you delete a field, you will be prompted to confirm the deletion, just as you will when deleting a record.

You can navigate between records using the Record Selector buttons that appear at the bottom of the Access window. These buttons are shown in Table 11-3.

TABLE 11-3
Record selector buttons

ICON	BUTTON NAME
⏮	First Record
◀	Previous Record
▶	Next Record
⏭	Last Record
▶⁎	New (blank) Record

STEP-BY-STEP 11.5

1. Click in the **Price** field for the Hammock record, select the data if necessary, type **85**, then press **Tab**.

2. In the Quantity field for the Hammock record, type **14**.

3. On the Navigation Pane, double-click the **Products form** to open it.

4. Click the **Next record** button twice to move to record 3.

5. Press **Tab** three times, then type **12** in the Quantity field.

6. Click the **Last record** button, then type **19** in the Quantity field.

7. Click the **New (blank) record** button, then enter the new record information, as shown in Figure 11-13.

FIGURE 11-13
Data entered in record 12

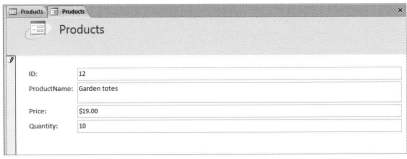

8. Click the **Products Table** object tab, select the entire row for record **7**, then on the Home tab, in the Records group, click the **Delete** button. A warning box opens.

9. Click **Yes** to permanently delete record 7.

10. Close the database, saving changes to the Products table, then exit Access.

SUMMARY

- Access is a database management system (DBMS) that is used to organize and analyze data.

- Databases store information about entities in records and fields. A record contains all of the information about one instance in the database, and fields show different attributes of data.

- Access objects include tables, reports, queries, forms, macros, and modules.

- The Navigation Pane can be used to open and switch between database objects.

- A database can contain multiple objects of each type, each object showing different relationships between data. Objects can reference the same record, but each object displays a different result.

- It is important to keep databases current and to provide security measures to protect confidential information.

- A database should include a field that is unique to all records. It can be a Social Security number or an AutoNumber that Access assigns to your database as new records are added.

- Tables are used to store data. You can define the types of data and use the property sheet to set data entry restrictions such as required fields or maximum field length.

- You can enter records in a database using datasheet view or Form view, or you can import data from another file using a wizard.

- When you delete fields or records, they are permanently removed from the database.

VOCABULARY *Review*

Define the following terms:

Attribute	Form	Property sheet
Data type	Input mask	Query
Database	Instance	Record
Database management system (DBMS)	Macro	Relationship
	Module	Report
Field	Navigation Pane	Table
Field properties	Primary key	Wizard

REVIEW *Questions*

SCREEN IDENTIFICATION

Identify the screen elements.

FIGURE 11-14
Screen identification

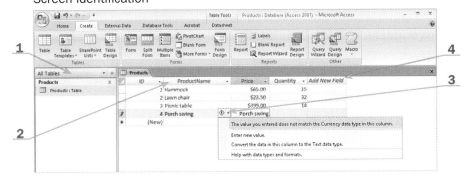

1. _____

2. _____

3. _____

4. _____

MULTIPLE CHOICE

Circle the correct answer.

1. In a database program, the smallest amount of information is a _____.
    A. Field
    B. Cell
    C. Instance
    D. Record

2. A column in an Access table is also called a(n) _____.
    A. Field
    B. Record
    C. Instance
    D. Attribute

3. A(n) _____ is used to guide data entry by providing clues as to what to enter.
    A. Macro
    B. Attribute
    C. Input mask
    D. Form

4. A(n) _____ is a field that is unique for all records.
   A. Module
   B. Primary key
   C. Macro
   D. Attribute

5. Text, memo, and AutoNumber are all examples of _____.
   A. Field properties
   B. Attributes
   C. Forms
   D. Data Types

TRUE/FALSE

Circle T if the statement is true or F if the statement is false.

T   F   1. A report retrieves information based on search criteria.

T   F   2. Objects can reference the same record.

T   F   3. A row of data is called an instance.

T   F   4. If you see a security warning when you open a database, close it and contact your
           technical support person.

T   F   5. You cannot save a database with a new filename unless you rename it using
           Windows Explorer.

HANDS-ON REVIEW

1. Open Access and create a new, blank database called **Frisbee Club.accdb**.

2. Identify as many Access screen elements as you can.

3. Change the name of Table 1 to Members. Use the ID AutoNumber field as the primary key.
   Add four fields:

FIELD NAME	DATA TYPE
FirstName	Text
LastName	Text
JoinDate	Date/Time
Dues	Currency

4. Using information of your choice, enter two records in the database using Datasheet view.
   Create a Form using the default layout, save it as Members, then enter two records in
   Form view.

5. Import the Excel file Members.xlsx into the table.

6. Add a field called Level in Datasheet view. Insert 1, 2, or 3 for all records.

7. Delete record 4, then change the data in Form view for record 6.

8. Save any changes to the database objects, then close Access.

PROJECTS

PROJECT 11-1

Open the database Inventory.accdb. Enter a new record using information of your choice in the Inventory table in Datasheet view. Use the Navigation Pane to open the Inventory form, then enter a new record. Enter another record in Form view, but this time, type text in the Quantity field. Click OK in the warning box, then enter a number. Complete the information in the new record. Save and close all open database objects, then close the database.

PROJECT 11-2

Note: You must be connected to the Internet in order to complete this project.

Start your browser, then visit three sites that use databases to populate product data or information. Suggested sites include online stores or reference sites such as www.imdb.com or www.wikipedia.org. Search for information on each site, and think about how the results of your search might be stored in the database. Consider what data types are set up, and, if possible, determine what the primary key might be.

 TEAMWORK

Divide the terms in the vocabulary list evenly among the members of your team. Each team member should create flash cards for his or her terms that have the definition on one side and the term on the other side. Practices quizzing each other until you are familiar with all of the terms in the lesson.

CRITICAL*Thinking*

ACTIVITY 11–3

Make a list during the day of all of the databases you interact with or observe at your school or business and how they are used. Keep track of them on a piece of paper, then create a Word document called **My Databases.docx**. Add a three-column table to the document that lists the database, where you encountered it, and how it was used.

MODIFYING AND ANALYZING DATABASE INFORMATION

OBJECTIVES

Upon completion of this lesson, you should be able to:

- Create a new form
- Enter and edit form data
- Sort data
- Filter data
- Create a query
- Create and print a report

Estimated Time: 2.5 hours

VOCABULARY

Filter

Filter By Form

Find

Form

Label

Layout

Query

Replace

Reports

Selection

Style

Businesses and institutions rely on databases to supply many kinds of information. For example, hospitals have enormous databases with thousands of fields and records. Patient information may include fields that record personal information, medical fields, insurance information, physician and medical providers, as well as fields containing emergency contacts. Medications, medical supplies, and staff members may also be included in the database. Different professionals who use those databases may only need to see a small number of fields or look for some key information, so they use forms created for their specific uses.

Queries are used to easily access information. Reports also are important for displaying information in a readable and organized format. You may want to create meaningful reports that will allow others to use the information you have gathered from your data.

Wizards are useful when creating database objects. Each object has requirements such as tables or queries to reference, relationships, and layout options. Using wizards will help to ensure that your queries, forms, and reports will meet your needs.

Create a New Form

To start a new form, use the tools on the Create tab. Notice in Figure 12-1 that the Create tab offers options for Tables, Forms, Reports, and Other. Within the Forms group, selecting any of the tools will allow you to create a specific type of form. If you wish to see all the fields in your database, you may want to use the Form button. The Form button is an easy way to access all the information, but it is not useful if you wish to isolate certain fields, create forms that are specific for different groups of users, or edit fields.

FIGURE 12-1
The Create tab

If you need a form that is specific for different users or purposes, in the Forms group, click the More Forms button arrow, then click Form Wizard. The Form Wizard allows you to choose the specific table or query for your data as well as the fields you wish to select. The Form Wizard will also allow you to choose the layout in which the data will be displayed—columnar, tabular, datasheet, or justified. You can preview styles by clicking the appropriate option button. You can apply styles to forms, which aids in usability for multiple users. For example, if you plan on creating a number of forms, you may want to use the same styles for related forms. Finally, the Form Wizard will prompt you to choose a name for your form. If you create forms that will be available to multiple users, you should carefully consider the naming convention.

S TEP-BY-STEP 12.1

1. Start Access using the **Start** button or a desktop shortcut.

2. In the Getting Started with Microsoft Office Access window, click **Blank Database**.

3. In the File Name text box, type **Personnel**, use the **Folder** button to navigate to and select your Data Files folder if necessary, then click **Create**.

4. On the Ribbon, click the **External Data** tab, then in the Import group, click the **Excel** button. The Get External Data—Excel Spreadsheet dialog box opens, prompting you to select the data source.

5. Locate and open the file Personnel.xls from your Data Files, click the **Import the source data into a new table in the current database** option button if necessary, then click **OK**. The Import Spreadsheet Wizard opens.

6. Click **Next**, click the **First Row Contains Column Headings** check box, click **Next** twice, click the **Let Access add primary key** option button if necessary, click **Next**, accept all other default choices in the wizard, then click **Finish**. If the Save import steps check box is selected, deselect it, then click **Close**.

STEP-BY-STEP 12.1 Continued

7. In the Navigation Pane, double-click the **Personnel** table to open it, click the **Create** tab, then in the Forms group, click the **More Forms** button, then click **Form Wizard**. The Form Wizard opens, as shown in Figure 12-2.

FIGURE 12-2
Form wizard

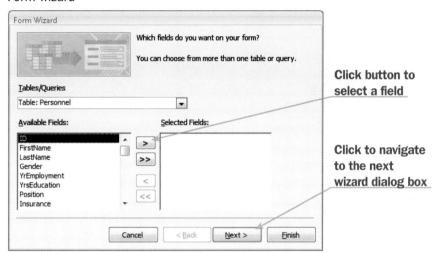

8. In the Available Fields list, click **FirstName**, then click the **Add Field** button. FirstName 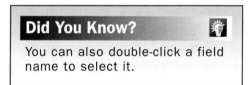 appears in the Selected Fields pane.

9. Repeat Step 8 for the **LastName**, **Address**, **City**, **State**, and **Zip** fields, then click **Next**.

10. Click the **Tabular** option button, click **Next**, click the **Module** style, then click **Next**.

> **Did You Know?**
>
> You can also double-click a field name to select it.

STEP-BY-STEP 12.1 Continued

11. Select the text in the What title do you want for your form? text box, type **Addresses**, click the **Open the form to view or enter information** option button if necessary, then click **Finish**. Close the Field List if necessary. The form appears as shown in Figure 12-3.

12. Save the database and form, then leave the database and Access for the next Step-by-Step.

FIGURE 12-3
New form

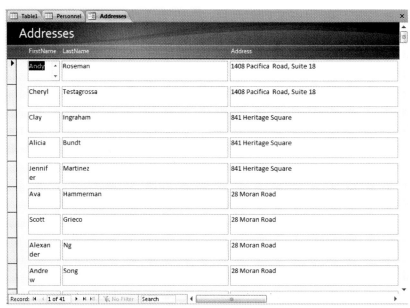

Enter and Edit Form Data

When a form is open, users can enter and edit any of the field data and add new records if desired. However, only the fields on the form can be filled with this form. Any new fields must be added into the table or query that was used as the source to create the form.

Using the navigation buttons at the bottom of the form, you can move through the database one record at a time, go directly to the beginning or the end, or add a new record. Selecting the New (blank) record button adds a new record to the end of the data table. Each field that you have chosen for the form appears, and you can press Tab to move from field to field. You may enter as many new records as you wish.

You can easily update a record by moving to the desired record and typing in new information. If the database contains many records, you can use the Find feature, located on the Home tab in the Find group. If

> **Computer Concepts**
>
> **Right-clicking**
> Many shortcuts can be accessed by right-clicking an object. When you right-click a database object tab, you can save, close, rename, and perform other relevant commands. Right-clicking can provide quick access to task- or object-specific commands, all of which are also available on the Ribbon.

the first record found is not the one you want, you can use more specific search criteria, or press Find Next to move through the database. You can also use the Replace tool to make changes. For example, you could update a business address for multiple contacts for the same company.

You must first save the form before you can update the table on which the form is built. Access will prompt you to save changes if you try to close an object. After saving changes in any form or table that a form is using, the changes will appear in both objects.

STEP-BY-STEP 12.2

1. Click the **Home** tab, then in the Views group, click the **View** button arrow, click **Layout View**, then position the pointer over the column borders and drag to adjust the column widths so that all data is visible.

2. In the first record, switch to Form view, then change Andy's first name to **Andrew**.

3. Right-click the **Addresses** tab, then click **Save**.

4. Click the **Personnel** tab, confirm that Andy is now Andrew, as shown in Figure 12-4, click the **Addresses** tab.

FIGURE 12-4
Form View

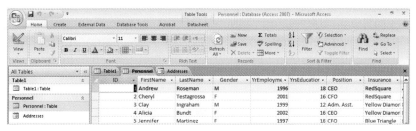

5. Click the **New (blank) record** button, then enter the following information: **John Dolan, 3 Taylor Rd., Acton, MA 01720**.

6. On the Home tab, in the Find group, click the **Replace** button. The Find and Replace dialog box opens.

7. Scroll to the last record, type **93405** in the Find What text box, type **93406** in the Replace With text box, specify to search in the Zip field, click **Replace All**, click **Yes** in the warning box, then close the Find and Replace dialog box.

8. Save and close the **Addresses** form.

9. Save and close the Personnel table, then reopen it. The changes you made are now visible.

10. Scroll to the bottom of the table, select the record for **John Dolan**, then on the Home tab and in the Records group, click the **Delete** button, then click **Yes** in the warning box.

11. Save the Personnel table, then leave the table, database, and Access open for the next Step-by-Step.

DATABASE INFORMATION MANAGERS

Database information managers design, create, and manage databases that fit a company or institution's specific needs. Database professionals are increasingly in demand as information is stored and retrieved electronically and over the Internet. What qualifications would you need?

- You need to understand the business or institution in order to design a database that is robust enough to handle its needs. You need to be aware of how goods, services, personnel, and customers interact and design the objects in the database so that all their needs are met.
- Knowing different database software packages, such as Access, SQL, and other programs, is essential. Many databases are used for internal monitoring, such as inventory and planning, and externally by customers, such as with an online store. Knowing which database program is best for the project and how to use it will make the database creation and programming run smoothly.
- An eye for design is also helpful, if not crucial. The elements in forms, queries, and reports need to be presented in a manner that is attractive, readable, and organized. Businesses operate more efficiently and customers are happier when they have databases that are easy to interact with.
- Finally, database management is much more involved than just creating forms and entering data. Large databases require constant monitoring and care. Incorrect types of entries into fields can corrupt a database. It is important to maintain data integrity, back up data, provide security, and protect sensitive information.

Sort Data

As you probably noticed when you entered in new records in the Form, the new records appear at the end of the list. This may be fine for data entry, but there are times when you need to sort data by a particular field. For instance, you may want the list to be arranged alphabetically by last name or perhaps arranged chronologically by a date field.

As in Excel, to sort data by rows, you need to select all the fields in the row. You can easily sort databases by field (column) and the accompanying data. To perform a sort, open the table that contains the data, then click a field name to select the field. On the Home tab, in the Sort & Filter group, you can sort using the Ascending button (A to Z or 1, 2, 3) or the Descending button (Z to A or 3, 2, 1).

You can also sort data using a form. Although you cannot click the field name, you can click the data in a field and then choose the correct sorting tool—ascending or descending. To clear all the sorts you have made, click the Clear All Sorts button. When you close your table, you can preserve the order of the last sort if you save it before closing.

STEP-BY-STEP 12.3

1. In the Personnel table, click the field name **YrEmployment**, then on the Home tab in the Sort & Filter group, click the **Ascending** button. The data has been arranged, as shown in Figure 12-5.

FIGURE 12-5
Table sorted in ascending order

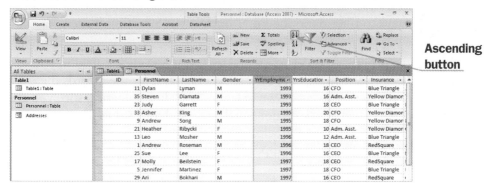

2. Click the **ID** field name, then click the **Descending** button.

3. Click the **LastName** field name, then click the **Ascending** button.

4. Save your changes to the Personnel table.

5. Open the **Addresses** form, click the **zip code** in the first record, then click the **Descending** button, as shown in Figure 12-6.

FIGURE 12-6
Form sorted in Descending order

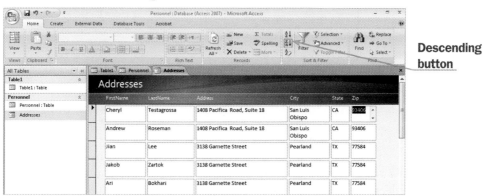

6. Save and close the Addresses form, then leave the database and Access open for the next Step-by-Step.

Filter Data

Sometimes you may want to use only specific records in your database. For example, you might want to view records of a certain zip code or employees from a specific company. Using the filter feature, you can choose only the records that meet the criteria you set. You can then copy or print those records and toggle back to the entire database. The database is never actually modified, just your view of it. The filter tools are located on the Home tab in the Sort & Filter group. There are three ways to filter data: the Filter button, the Selection button, or the Advanced Filter Options button.

The easiest tool is Filter. In order to use the tool, you first click a field in your database, click the Filter button in the Sort & Filter group, then select criteria. Only the records that meet the criteria are displayed in the AutoFilter menu, as shown in Figure 12-7. In a numerical sort, you also have an option to choose number filters that equal, do not equal, are less than a value, are greater than a value, or are between two values. By deselecting the Select All check box, you can pick the value(s) you want to use for your filter. Once your filtered data appears, you can print it, copy and paste, or use it as you wish. You will also notice that in the field name you have used as your filter, you will see a filter sign with a down arrow indicating that the data is filtered and sorted in an ascending order. After you click OK, the records you have filtered will appear in the window, and the field column contains a filter icon. The Toggle Filter button is now active, so to display the entire table, simply click the Toggle Filter button.

FIGURE 12-7
AutoFilter menu

YrsEducatior ▾	Position ▾	Insurance ▾	Company ▾	Address ▾

(AutoFilter menu shown overlaying the datasheet with the following options)

- A↓ Sort Smallest to Largest
- Z↓ Sort Largest to Smallest
- ✖ Clear filter from YrsEducation
- Number Filters ▸
  - Equals...
  - Does Not Equal...
  - Less Than...
  - Greater Than...
  - Between...
- ☑ (Select All)
- ☑ (Blanks)
- ☑ 10
- ☑ 12
- ☑ 13
- ☑ 15
- ☑ 16
- ☑ 18
- ☑ 20

OK   Cancel

(Partial visible column data: son Press 2664 Massachu; ery, Inc. 4642 Mulberry; son Press 2664 Massachu; Inc. 28 Moran Road; Inc. 28 Moran Road; ite Framin 11 Main Street; ham Cons 841 Heritage Sc; y Press 1865 Poplar Gr; ery, Inc. 4642 Mulberry; y Press 1865 Poplar Gr)

Another way of filtering data is to select certain criteria and use that selection as a filter. For example, to show records for a specific company or zip code, you can select one item in a database, click the Selection button on the Home tab in the Sort & Filter group, then select additional specifications.

The Filter By Form filter option is helpful if you need to use two or more criteria. In the Sort & Filter group, click the Advanced Filter Options button, then click Filter By Form. A form, similar to the datasheet, appears with all the field names in the top row. In the row under the field names, you will see an arrow if you click a cell. Click the arrow to see a menu with filtering options.

Did You Know?

Sorting and filtering data does not create a new object in the Navigation Pane; they are a temporary means of analyzing data.

S TEP-BY-STEP 12.4

1. With the Personnel table open, click the **YrEmployment** field.

2. On the Home tab, in the Sort & Filter group, click the **Filter** button. The AutoFilter menu appears.

3. Deselect the **Select All** check box, click **1996**, **2001**, and **2006**, make sure that **Sort Smallest to Largest** is selected, then click **OK**. The data is filtered, as shown in Figure 12-8.

FIGURE 12-8
Smallest to largest sort

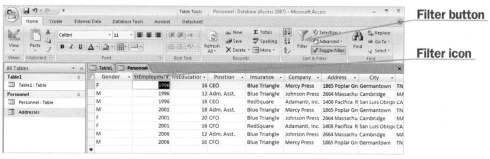

4. In the Sort & Filter group, click the **Toggle Filter** button.

5. Find a record that has **11 Main Street** in the Address field, then select the number **11**.

6. In the Sort & Filter group, click the **Selection** button, then click **Contains "11"**. The addresses of 11 Main Street, 112 N. Main Street, and 6015 Gaston Avenue, Suite 211 appear, as shown in Figure 12-9. If you cannot see all of the Gaston Avenue address, widen the address column.

FIGURE 12-9
Results of selected sort

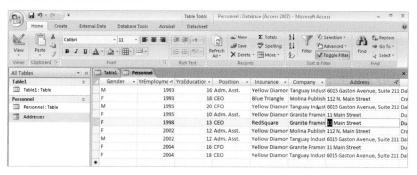

7. Click the **Toggle Filter** button, click the **Advanced Filter Options** button, then click **Clear All Filters**.

8. Click the **Advanced Filter Options** button, then click **Filter By Form**.

9. Click the **cell** beneath the Gender field, click the **arrow**, click **F**, click the **cell** beneath the YrsEducation field, click the arrow, click **16**, click the **cell** beneath the Position field, click the **arrow**, then click **CEO**.

STEP-BY-STEP 12.4 Continued

10. Click the **Toggle Filter** button. Two records appear: Sue Lee and Alicia Bundt, as shown in Figure 12-10.

11. Click the **Toggle Filter** button, close the table without saving changes, then leave the database and Access open for the next Step-by-Step.

FIGURE 12-10
Filter By Form sort

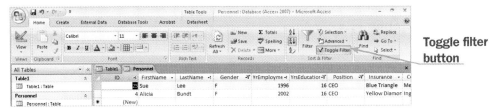

Create a Query

In order to reuse frequently searched-for criteria or to create a search object that other users can apply, you can save it as a **query**. Once a query is created, it can be used over and over again and will reflect any new data added to the table. A query can be a simple request for fields, or it can include more powerful actions such as calculations.

To begin a simple query that will return information on all the records in your database, click the Create tab, and in the Other group, click the Query Wizard button. A New Query dialog box opens with four query types in the right pane. When you click a query type, its description appears in the left pane. The Simple Query Wizard may meet most of your needs. After you select a query type, you choose the tables or previously created queries to include in your new query. Next, you choose the fields to use in the query, then name the query. The information appears in table format and can be printed, saved as an Access object, or exported to another Microsoft application.

To create a query that limits the records to ones that meet the criteria you wish to select, click the Query Design button in the Other group on the Create tab. The first window prompts you to select the tables or queries you wish to use. Once you add at least one table or query, you can close the Show Table dialog box, and a box for each table or query will appear in the top part of the pane, as shown in Figure 12-11. The bottom part contains a design grid. Using the labels on the left, you can indicate the fields, table, filters, and sorts for the query. You can enter a field name by clicking the list arrow and clicking a field or by dragging the field name from the field list to the Field box.

FIGURE 12-11
New Query

Fields
included
in query

Labels in
the design
grid

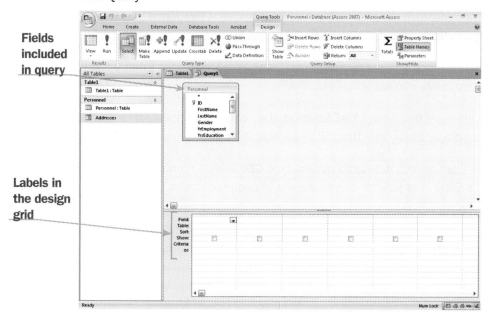

You do not need to select sort criteria, but you may wish to for at least one field such as last name. If you want to set criteria, enter that information in the Criteria box. You can enter additional criteria in the or box to expand your search. To view the query results, switch to Datasheet View. To refine the query, return to Design View. When you are finished, you can save it and then can open it again using the Navigation Pane.

Did You Know?

You can specify the following five **labels** in the design grid: *Field, Table, Sort, a Show check box* for displaying the information, *Criteria,* and *or* (which gives you another opportunity to limit a search).

STEP-BY-STEP 12.5

1. Click the **Create** tab, then in the Other group, click the **Query Wizard** button. The New Query dialog box opens.

2. Click **Simple Query Wizard**, if necessary, click **OK**, click the **Tables/Queries** list arrow, then click the **Personnel** table in the first Simple Query Wizard dialog box.

3. Add the **FirstName**, **LastName**, **Address**, **City**, **State**, and **Zip** fields to the Selected Fields pane, then click **Next**.

4. Type **Addresses2** as the title, select the **Open the query to view information** option button if necessary, then click **Finish**. All the records are included in the query.

5. Close the Addresses2 query, then on the **Create** tab, in the Other group, click the **Query Design** button.

6. In the Show Table dialog box, on the Tables tab, click **Personnel**, if necessary, click **Add**, then click **Close**. The Personnel table appears in the top pane.

STEP-BY-STEP 12.5 Continued

7. In the design grid, click the **arrow** in the first Field box, click **FirstName**, add **LastName** to the second Field box, click the **arrow** in the Sort box, then click **Ascending**.

8. In the third Field box, select **YrEmployment**, then type **>1996** in the Criteria text box. The query will show all employees who started after 1996.

9. In the fourth Field box, select **YrsEducation**, then type **>16** in the Criteria text box. The query will show all employees with more than 16 years of schooling.

10. In the fifth Field name box, select **Position**, type **CEO** in the Criteria text box, type **CFO** in the or box, then press **Enter**. The position names appear in quotation marks. The query setup is complete, as shown in Figure 12-12.

FIGURE 12-12
Completed query

Field:	FirstName	LastName	YrEmployment	YrsEducation	Position	
Table:	Personnel	Personnel	Personnel	Personnel	Personnel	
Sort:		Ascending				
Show:	☑	☐	☑	☑	☑	☐
Criteria:			>1996	>16	"CEO"	
or:					"CFO"	

11. On the Query Tools Design tab, in the Results group, click the **View** button arrow, then click **Datasheet View**. The query appears as shown in Figure 12-13.

12. Right-click the **Query1** tab, click **Save**, type **Employment History** in the Query Name text box, then click **OK**.

13. Leave the database and Access open for the next Step-by-Step.

FIGURE 12-13
Viewing query in datasheet view

Table1 | Employment History

FirstName	LastName	YrEmployme	YrsEducatior	Position
Molly	Beilstein	1997	18	CEO
Bob	Bistri	1999	18	CEO
Paul	Jones	2002	18	CFO
Amar	Khan	2006	16	CFO
Asher	King	1995	20	CFO
Dylan	Lyman	1993	16	CFO
Jennifer	Martinez	1997	18	CFO
Monica	Pappalardo	2001	20	CFO
Patricia	Ramirez	2004	16	CFO
Andrew	Song	1995	18	CFO
Cheryl	Testagrossa	2001	16	CFO
Lindsay	Thompson	2004	18	CEO
Jakob	Zartok	2003	18	CFO
*				

Create and Print a Report

Query data is displayed in a datasheet. You can save query results in a more polished format using reports. You can customize reports by adding objects such as company logos and text boxes. Reports are saved as objects and are updated as the database is modified.

To create a simple report that includes all of the data and fields in a selected table or query, select the object in the Navigation Pane. Click the Create tab, then in the Reports Group, click the Report button. The report will appear with the exact data that was in the query or table. You cannot modify data, but you can add graphics, change field names, modify the layout, or change the fonts and apply a style to the report.

The Report Wizard provides many formatting options and is especially useful if you do not need all the fields in a table or query. When you click the Report Wizard, the first dialog box that appears asks you to choose the table or query you will be working with and then select the fields you need. You can also pick a grouping level, which allows you to sort your data by a certain criterion (such as a company or particular address) and pick a sort order for the data within that group label. You can pick a **layout** (stepped, block, or columnar, for example) as well as an orientation of the paper (landscape or portrait). You can also select a **style** for the report and get a preview by selecting a style. Finally, you can enter a title for your report and save it.

S TEP-BY-STEP 12.6

1. On the Ribbon, click the **Create** tab, click **Employment History** in the Navigation Pane, then in the Reports group, click the **Report** button. The report appears, as shown in Figure 12-14.

FIGURE 12-14
Report Layout Tools Format tab

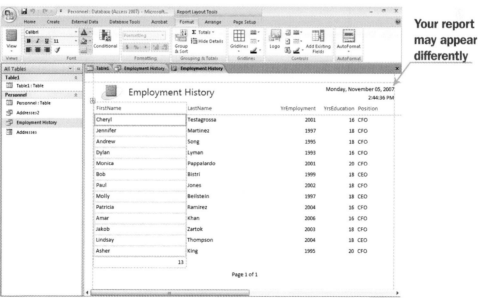

2. Select the text **Employment History** in the text box, then type **Employment and Education History**. The text box automatically widens to fit the text, and the Report Layout Tools Format tab becomes active.

STEP-BY-STEP 12.6 Continued

3. If necessary, click the **date** text box, press **Delete**, click the **time** text box, then press **Delete**.

4. Change the field names as follows:

FIELD NAME	CHANGE TO
FirstName	First Name
LastName	Last Name
YrEmployment	Year of Entry
YrsEducation	Years Education

5. Select the first cell under Year of Entry, then in the Font group, click the **Center** button. Repeat for **Years Education**.

6. Save the report as **EmpEducation**, then close the report and all open objects.

7. Click the **Create** tab, then in the Reports group, click the **Report Wizard** button. The Report Wizard opens.

8. Click the **Tables/Queries** list arrow, click the **Personnel** table if necessary, select the following fields: **FirstName**, **LastName**, **Company**, **Position**, **Phone**, **E-mail**, then click **Next**.

9. Double-click **Company**, click **Next**, click the first text box list arrow, click **LastName**, click **Ascending**, then click **Next** twice.

10. Click the **Module** style, click **Next**, type **Contacts** as the report title, then click **Finish**. The report opens in Print Preview.

11. Click the **Close Print Preview** button, switch to **Layout** view, then resize the text boxes to fit the data.

12. Click the **Office Button**, point to **Print**, then click **Print Preview**. The report appears as shown in Figure 12-15.

13. Save and close all database objects, close the database, then exit Access.

STEP-BY-STEP 12.6 Continued

FIGURE 12-15
Previewing a report

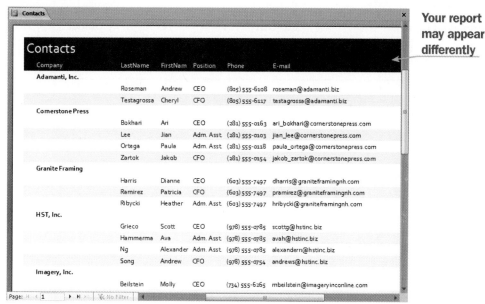

Your report
may appear
differently

SUMMARY

■ Access allows you to modify and analyze data through a number of means and to create new objects such as forms, reports, and queries that can be used often and tailored to individual users' needs.

■ Forms are objects created to allow users to access only the information they need to see or modify in a database. Forms also allow users to enter new records.

■ Records can be found by either moving through them one at a time or by using the Find tool on the Home tab. The Replace tool allows users to change the same information on a number of records.

■ To Sort data in a table, click the field name, and use the Sort Ascending or Sort Descending tool found on the Sort & Filter group on the Home tab. The data can be rearranged by that field.

■ Filtering is a tool for finding records that contain specific information. The search can be done simply by using the Filter tool; by selection if you choose a text string or numerical entry; or by using Filter By Form if you need to filter by more than one field. To return to the entire datasheet, press the Toggle Filter button.

■ Queries are created to allow users to search for information and to save the search criteria so that the information can be used repeatedly. Queries can be simple and based on one field or more complex, using more than one field and also allowing users to enter certain criteria on data within fields.

■ Reports are created and saved in order to display information in an attractive and useful format. Individual items within reports can be formatted, and items such as text blocks or logos can be added.

VOCABULARY *Review*

Define the following terms:

Filter	Label	Reports
Filter By Form	Layout	Select
Find	Query	Style
Form	Replace	

REVIEW *Questions*

SCREEN IDENTIFICATION

Identify the screen elements in Figure 12-16.

FIGURE 12-16
Screen identification

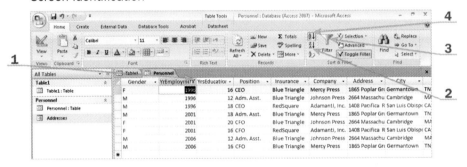

1. _____

2. _____

3. _____

4. _____

MULTIPLE CHOICE

Circle the correct answer.

1. All of the following appear as objects in the Navigation Pane except _____.
    A. Tables
    B. Filters
    C. Forms
    D. Reports

2. Unless data is sorted, all new records appear _____ .
   A. At the top of the database
   B. In a different color
   C. In the appropriate alphabetical order
   D. As the last record

3. To return to the full datasheet after applying a filter, _____ .
   A. Press Esc
   B. Click the Filter Toggle button
   C. Click Filter again
   D. Right-click the tab

4. To make changes to the format of a report, you need to be in _____ view.
   A. Layout
   B. Print Preview
   C. Datasheet
   D. Report

TRUE/FALSE

Circle T if the statement is true or F if the statement is false.

T   F   1. Forms must contain all the fields in the table associated with it.

T   F   2. In an Ascending Sort, records with blank information in the sort field will appear at the bottom of the datasheet.

T   F   3. Filters can only be performed with one set of criteria.

T   F   4. Data in queries will be updated when the database is modified.

T   F   5. Once Reports are created, the format cannot be modified.

T   F   6. Queries appear as objects in the Navigation Pane.

HANDS-ON REVIEW

1. Open the database Inventory.accdb from your Data Files. Create a new form from the Inventory table using the Form Wizard. Include all fields, choose the Columnar layout and the Civic style, and accept all other defaults.

2. Add a new entry in the form for a pair of socks using information of your choosing. Replace all instances of Clothing with Clothes in the Category field.

3. Switch to the Inventory table, sort ascending by Price, then sort descending by Color.

4. Apply a filter that shows all Accessories, then remove the filter. Apply a filter that shows all items with a Price less than $10.00, then close the table without saving changes.

5. Create a query in Design view based on the Inventory table. Add the Category field, and set the criteria to Clothes. Add the Quantity field, and set the criteria to less than 14. Add the Color, Price, and Product fields without criteria. View the query in Datasheet view, then save the query as Reorder.

6. Use the Report Wizard to create a report based on the Reorder query. Choose all fields but category, select the Civic style, accept all other defaults, then title the report Reorder. View the report, then save it and close the database.

PROJECTS

PROJECT 12-1

Open the Frisbee Club database. In the Members table, add a new field called Team. Assign the members evenly to two different teams with names of your choice. Sort the field in a descending sort. Create a Query that will list the first and last names of all members who joined after 6/1/09. Save the query as New Members.

PROJECT 12-2

Open the Products database. Create a report using the Products table that will list, by Manufacturer, the highest- to lowest-priced products. The report should include all fields. Set up the report in landscape orientation, and select an attractive style. Title the report Manufacturers. If any fields do not fully appear, be sure to check the layout, and make sure the report is readable.

 TEAMWORK

Have your team design a database that would serve the needs of a library. The library needs to have patron demographic information (address, phone numbers, work information, and e-mail). It needs information about the books and other holdings in its collection so that patrons can search in different ways. It also needs a way to record which items are on loan, when they are due, and which patrons want to reserve them. Create a form that would gather patron information, a query that would allow the librarian to find out which books a patron has, and a report that lists overdue books.

CRITICAL *Thinking*

ACTIVITY 12–1

Internet search engines are actually databases. They use keywords in fields. Go to several search engines and use the Advanced Search feature. Examine the layout of the search forms. Which ones are most helpful? Perform a search for databases and Access. Which search engine's results were most helpful?

INTEGRATION

VOCABULARY

Address block

Destination file

Embed

Export

Field

HTML

Import

Integrate

Link

Mail merge

Paste Special

Source file

Information for business, school, or personal uses can be repurposed. The same facts and figures can be used in an Access report to distribute to a board of directors, in an Excel spreadsheet that tracks sales, and in a PowerPoint presentation for potential investors. Using data from one application in a file created in another application is called integration.

The process of adding data from another file or program into another document is called importing. Taking information and saving it with a new file type is called exporting. You can import and export information of many types between Office applications as long as the format is consistent. For instance, a Word outline is set up in a hierarchy and can be used to add information to a PowerPoint presentation.

You can also save files in a format that makes them viewable on the Internet. HTML (HyperText Markup Language) is a format that can be published as a part of a Web site and viewed using a browser.

Microsoft Office applications have many shortcuts and ways that you can integrate data. Reusing data can save you time and ensure accuracy by not introducing errors when retyping data. Using wizards is a good way to ensure that your data will import and export properly.

In this lesson, you are the president of Natural Office Consulting, an environmental consulting company. Natural Office Consulting analyzes its clients' business practices, and it provides them with suggestions for making their business more environmentally friendly. You have two employees: Julia Susskind, the office manager, and Raul Ernesto, the consultant. You have 32 clients in the New England area, and you are looking for investors so that you can expand the business. You will use the skills you have learned in this book and apply new skills to create a mailing and other business documents by importing and exporting data.

Perform a Mail Merge

Credit card companies, charities, and other large organizations use **mail merges** to create personalized and customized mailings. To customize a letter that will be sent to each person on a mailing list, companies create a **destination file** such as a letter. The destination document contains fields that correspond with fields or columns in a contact list, as shown in Figure FP-1. The contact list, which is usually an e-mail contact list, database, or spreadsheet, is called the source file.

FIGURE FP-1
Sample mail merge

When the merge is performed, the source document is used to populate the fields and create separate letters for each record or contact. An **Address block** is a merge option that selects fields such as title, name, address, city, state, and zip to insert a mailing address for each record, as shown in Figure FP-2. You can also use mail merge to create envelopes, a client directory, or e-mail.

FIGURE FP-2
Address block

To perform the mail merge, you will open a business letter in Word (the destination document), then use the Mail Merge wizard to locate the source document, assign fields, and merge the information.

S TEP-BY-STEP FP.1

1. Start Word using the **Start** button or a desktop shortcut, then open the document **Merge Letter.docx** from your Data Files.

2. If necessary, on the **Home** tab in the Paragraph group, click the **Show/Hide** button to view nonprinting characters, then position the insertion point in the second blank line ¶ after the date.

3. Click the **Mailings** tab, then in the Start Mail Merge group, click the **Start Mail Merge** button, then click **Step by Step Mail Merge Wizard**. The Mail Merge task pane opens.

4. At the bottom of the Mail Merge task pane, click **Next: Starting document**, click **Next: Select recipients**, then click **Browse** in the Use an existing list section. The Select Data Source dialog box opens.

5. Navigate to your Data Files, click the file **Merge Contacts.xlsx**, click **Open**, then in the Select Table dialog box, click **OK**. The Mail Merge Recipients dialog box opens.

6. Click the **check box** at the top of the list next to Data Source to deselect all records, click the **four check boxes**, as shown in Figure FP-3, then click **OK**.

FIGURE FP-3
Mail Merge Recipients dialog box

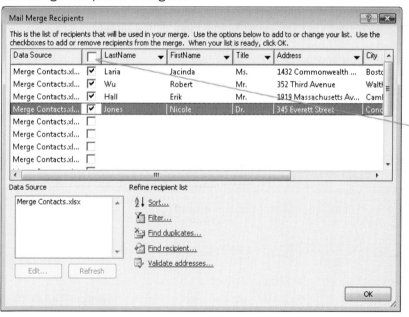

7. Click **Next: Write your letter**.

STEP-BY-STEP FP.1 Continued

8. Click **Address block** in the Write your letter section. The Insert Address Block dialog box appears, as shown in Figure FP-4.

FIGURE FP-4
Insert Address Block dialog box

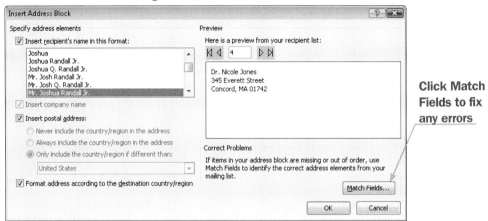

Click Match Fields to fix any errors

9. Click **OK**, then position the insert point before the colon after the word *Dear*.

10. On the Mailings tab in the Write & Insert Fields group, click the **Insert Merge Field** button arrow, click **Title**, press **Spacebar**, click the **Insert Merge Field** button arrow, then click **LastName**.

11. Click **Next: Preview your letters**. The letters appear, as shown in Figure FP-5.

FIGURE FP-5
Merged document

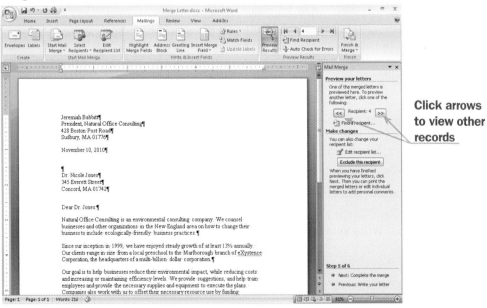

Click arrows to view other records

STEP-BY-STEP FP.1 Continued

12. Click the **Previous** arrow to scroll through the letters for Recipients 1–3, click **Next: Complete the merge**, use the Save As command on the Office Button menu to save the merged letters as **Completed Merge Letters.docx**, then close the document.

13. Leave Word open for the next Step-by-Step.

Link an Excel Chart in Word

Y̶ou already know that data you copy to the Clipboard can be pasted into a file. When you paste data or objects, the information remains in the source and is embedded in the destination file. Any updates you make to the source file will not be reflected in the embedded location.

You can use the Paste Special feature to link data or an object between two files. When a link occurs, the source and destination data are connected, and changes you make in one are reflected in both. If you rename, move, or delete one of the files, the link is broken.

> **Note** ☑
>
> In order to maintain a link between the two files, you are not asked to rename the workbook or document. If you need to reuse the original file at a later date, copy both the workbook and document to a new folder within your Data Files before starting this Step-by-Step.

S̶TEP-BY-STEP FP.2

1. Start Excel using the **Start** button or a desktop shortcut, then open the workbook **Profit 1999-2009** from your Data Files.

2. Select the chart, then on the Home tab in the Clipboard group, click the **Copy** button. The chart is copied to the clipboard.

3. Switch to Word, open the file **Investor Letter.docx** from your Data Files, then position the insertion point in the blank line before *We hope that*.

4. On the **Home** tab in the Clipboard group, click the **Paste** button arrow, then click **Paste Special**. The Paste Special dialog box opens.

> **Did You Know?**
>
> Linking files can be helpful to ensure that you have the most current data. However, it also increases the file size of the destination file, so you should use it only when necessary.

STEP-BY-STEP FP.2 Continued

5. Click the **Paste link** option button, in the As section, click **Microsoft Office Excel Chart Object**, then click **OK**. The chart is pasted in the Word document, as shown in Figure FP-6.

FIGURE FP-6
Linked chart

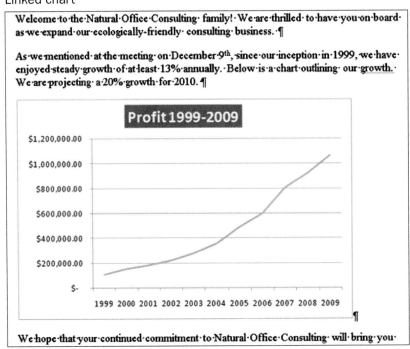

6. Switch to Excel, click cell **B12**, change the value to **1181040**, save and close the workbook, then exit Excel.

7. Switch to Word if necessary, right-click the chart, click **Update Link**, then view the changes in the chart, as shown in Figure FP-7.

8. Save and close the document, then exit Word.

STEP-BY-STEP FP.2 Continued

FIGURE FP-7
Updated chart in Word

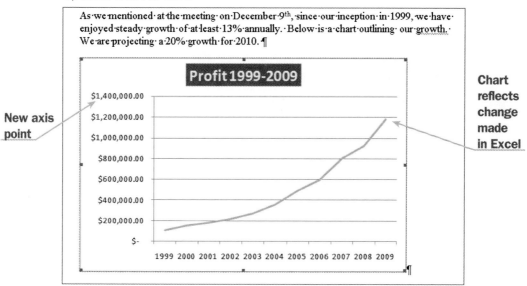

Import a Word Outline into PowerPoint

A Word outline can be used to create a PowerPoint presentation, since they both rely on hierarchical data. When a presentation is created using an outline, PowerPoint assigns heading levels, slide breaks, and bullets depending on the headings in the document. You can use your cutting, pasting, and formatting skills to fix any errors once the outline has been imported by working in Outline view. Applying styles and backgrounds will make the imported slides look professional.

S TEP-BY-STEP FP.3

1. Start PowerPoint using the **Start** button or a desktop shortcut.

2. On the Home tab in the Slides group, click the **New Slide** button arrow, then click **Slides from Outline**. The Insert Outline dialog box opens.

3. Navigate to your Data Files, click the file **Presentation Outline.docx**, then click **Insert**.

STEP-BY-STEP FP.3 Continued

4. In the Slides pane, click the **Outline tab**, then click **Slide 2** in the outline, if necessary. The outline appears as shown in Figure FP-8. The slide breaks are accurate, but all of the text appears in the Title text box of the slides.

FIGURE FP-8
Imported outline

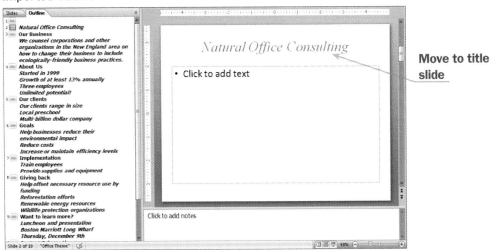

5. In Slide 2, move the company name to be the master title in Slide 1, then delete the now-blank Slide 2.

6. For the remaining slides, assume that the first line of text in each slide is the slide title, then move the remaining text to the content placeholder. Use cut and paste, centering, and bullets to reorganize the slide information. To add a hyperlink for the e-mail address on the last slide, select the text, then press Ctrl + K to open the Insert Hyperlink dialog box.

7. Apply the **Concourse** theme, then click **Slide 9**, if necessary. Your presentation should appear similar to the one shown in Figure FP-9.

FIGURE FP-9
Finished presentation

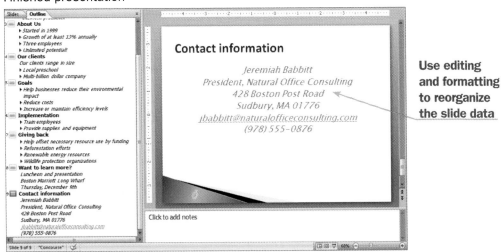

8. Save the presentation as **Investor Presentation.pptx**, then save and close PowerPoint.

Export an Access Report to the Web

Saving a file as HTML prepares it for publication on the Web. Any Office file can be saved in HTML and then used as a page on a Web site.

STEP-BY-STEP FP.4

1. Start Access using the **Start** button or a desktop shortcut.

2. Open the database **Sales.accdb** from your Data Files, then open the **Sales Growth** report.

3. Click the **External Data** tab, then in the Export group, click the **More** button, then click **HTML Document**. Enable content, if necessary.

4. In the Export—HTML dialog box, click the **Browse** button, then in the File Save dialog box, navigate to your Data Files, then click **Save**.

5. Click the **Open the destination file after the export operation is complete** check box to select it, then click **OK**.

6. Click **OK** in the HTML Output Options dialog box. The report opens as an HTML page in your browser, as shown in Figure FP-10.

7. If prompted, do not save Export steps.

8. Close the HTML report document, click **Close** in the Export - HTML Document dialog box, then exit Access.

FIGURE FP-10
HTML file in Internet Explorer

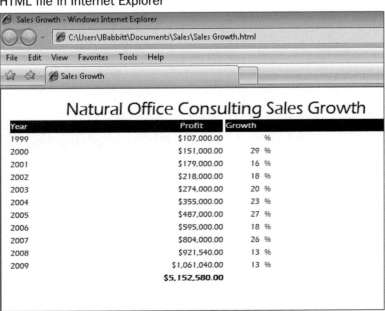

GLOSSARY

A

Absolute cell reference A cell reference that does not change no matter where you paste the formula.

Address block A mail merge option that selects fields such as title, name, address, city, state, and zip to insert a mailing address for each record.

Alignment The relationship of data to the border of a page, slide, cell, or text box.

Ampersand A nonprinting character (&) used in headers and footers to differentiate elements.

Animated GIF A graphic that has a sequence of repeating movement that can be accompanied by sound.

Animations Visual or movement effects, sometimes accompanied by sound, that you can add to an object such as a text box or graphic, or to a level of a SmartArt object.

Application A software program, such as Microsoft Word or Excel, used to perform a specific task.

Arithmetic operator Percentages (%), plus signs (+), asterisks (*), and other characters used in mathematical calculations.

Ascending A sort order that arranges data alphabetically (A–Z) or numerically (1, 2, 3).

Attribute A column of data that contains related data in a database, such as employees' last names.

AutoComplete A feature that finishes words as you type them.

AutoCorrect A feature that fixes common typing mistakes automatically as you type.

AutoFill A feature used to continue text or numbers in a sequence or pattern such as 1, 2, 3, or 10, 15, 20.

AutoFilter A feature that selects data using the criteria of the current table.

AutoFit A feature that adjusts the formatting of text or data to fit in a certain space.

AutoSum A function used to quickly perform a calculation on a range of cells.

Axis A horizontal or vertical line in a chart.

B

Border Graphic lines that can be used to separate headers, footers, or columns, or to outline a text box or other object.

Building Block Frequently used text and other content that you can insert in Word documents.

Bulleted list A list of items of equal importance. Each item is preceded by a dot or other small graphic.

C

Cell The intersection of a row and column.

Cell address The column letter and row number of the cell.

Chart An object that displays data visually using graphics such as lines, bars, or pie pieces.

Clip art A searchable collection of drawn graphics, artwork, and photography stored on your computer or available for download.

Clipboard A feature that stores items that you cut or copy from one file, to be placed in another location or file in the same program or in another application.

Close To terminate the use of an open file but leave the program window open.

Column Text separated vertically on a page or in an article into two or more parallel paths. In a table, a collection of vertical cells.

Comment   A balloon attached to specific text, used to pose questions to the author, or to make notes.

Comparison operator   Used in a formula to indicate criteria such as greater than (>), equal to (=), or less than or equal to (<=).

Conditional formatting   Formatting that changes depending on the value, such as the color of numbers that are positive or negative.

Constant   In a formula, a number that does not change.

Contextual tab   A tab available on the Ribbon only when certain actions or selections are made, which provides context- and task-specific tools and buttons.

Copy   To save an item to the Clipboard without removing the selection from its current location.

Copyright   The legal protections afforded a creative work, such as a book, song, computer program, or piece of art.

Crop   To remove portions of a graphic.

Cut   To save an item to the Clipboard by removing the selection from its current location.

D

Data type   A specification that determines the data that can be entered in a field.

Database   A program, such as Microsoft Access, that organizes information in records.

Database management system (DBMS)   A system or program, such as Microsoft Access, that organizes information like a filing cabinet, so that it can be entered, searched, and analyzed.

Datasheet   The range of cells used to create a chart.

Descending   A sort order that arranges data alphabetically (Z–A) or numerically (3, 2, 1).

Deselect   To click outside of selected text or items.

Design Theme   In PowerPoint, used to apply background, coordinated colors and fonts, and effects to an entire presentation.

Desktop publishing (DTP)   A program, such as Microsoft Publisher, that provides sophisticated tools to create newsletters, flyers, and other publications.

Destination   When merging or integrating data, the location where the data or object will be inserted.

Dialog box   A window that opens when more information is needed before an action can be performed.

Dialog box launcher   A small arrow in the corner of a group on a tab that provides access to a dialog box.

Draft layout   A view that shows page breaks as lines, allowing you to edit while viewing more of the document on the screen.

Drag-and-drop   To move or copy selected text or items to a new location using the mouse.

Draw table   A tool that uses a pointer to choose the position and size of table cells by drawing them.

E

Edit   To change the content of text.

Embed   To paste data or objects into a destination file without any connection to the source.

Endnote   In Word, a list of sequential notes that appears on the last page of a document and provides citations or explanations.

Eraser   A tool used to merge cells in a table.

Exit   To shut down a program, freeing up memory and resources for your computer to perform other tasks.

Export   The process of taking information and saving it with a new file type.

F

Field   One item of data, such as an employee's ID number, last name, or title.

Field properties   The attributes and appearance of tables and data, such as setting a character limit or determining a default value.

File extension A unique suffix added to filenames that indicate the program in which it was created.

Fill A background color or texture that can be applied to an object.

Filter To exclude certain categories of data from view without deleting them from the spreadsheet or database object.

Filter by Form An Access feature used to filter by two or more criteria.

Find To look for all instances of a word or phrase.

Font Type styles, such as Arial and Calibri.

Footer Text that appears along the bottom margins of pages, containing information such as the title of the document, page number, date, and other relevant identifying information.

Footnote In Word, sequential notes that appear at the bottom of the page on which the citation or explanation appears.

Form An Access window that contains all of the information about a specific record, and which is used for data entry or editing.

Form Wizard An Access feature that guides you through the creation of a form.

Format To make enhancements to the text, such as bolding.

Format Painter A tool that copies the formatting of selected text.

Formula A combination of operators, function words, numbers, or cell references used to perform a calculation.

Formula bar A box that displays the contents of the active cell and is used to edit a formula or cell contents.

Full Screen Reading view A view that shows the document without the Ribbon, ruler, or other tools, in order to optimize reading from the screen.

Function Words that Excel recognizes as part of a calculation, such as SUM, to total a range of values or AVG to find the average of a range.

G

Gridline A nonprinting line that separates cells.

H

Handout A printed copy of your presentation that you distribute to your audience so that they can take notes.

Header Text that appears along the top margins of pages, which contain information such as the title of the document, page number, date, and other relevant identifying information. In a table, a row or column that describes the data.

Help A resource that can assist in performing a task.

Help Desk A group of computer professionals who are able to troubleshoot and solve computer issues.

HTML (HyperText Markup Language) A file format that allows data to be viewable on the Internet.

I

Import The process of adding data from another file or program into another document.

Input mask Text that provides clues to the data to be inserted, such as YYYY-MM-DD to indicate that the date November 4, 2010 should be entered as 2010-11-04.

Insertion point A blinking line that indicates where the text you type will appear.

Instance A row of data that contains all of the information about one record.

Integrate To use data from one application in a file created in another application.

Intellectual property Things that people create, manufacture, invent, or design and that are protected by copyright, trademark, or patent laws.

J

Justify To make text evenly spaced between the left and right margins.

L

Label A text box used to define data series, axes, a chart title, or other chart elements.

Landscape A page layout option where the page is wider than it is tall.

Layout   To specify the size and location of text boxes and objects.

Legend   A chart label that lists the data series and color codes.

Link   To connect data or an object between two files so that changes you make in one are reflected in both.

M

Macro   A task related to a database object, such as adding a command button, created without using programming language.

Mail merge   A Word feature used to create customized letters, e-mails, or labels using a source file, such as a workbook or contact list.

Master page   A PowerPoint view where you can specify the design, layout, and objects of all slides, handouts, or notes pages in a presentation.

Media clip   Sound and video that you can add to a slide in a presentation.

Merge   To combine multiple adjacent cells into one.

Mini toolbar   A task-specific toolbar that appears and disappears depending on the action you are performing.

Mixed cell reference   A cell reference where either the column letter or row number is absolute but the other is relative.

Module   A task related to a database object; similar to a module but uses Visual Basic for Applications (VBA), a program language.

N

Name box   A box that displays the name of the active cell or range (or when a range of cells are selected, the upper-left cell in the range).

Navigation Pane   An Access window that can be organized by object type, category, date, and other views.

Non-printing character   Tabs, spaces, paragraph marks, and other characters that are not visible in the printed document.

Normal view   The default view for editing and data entry.

Notes Pages view   A PowerPoint presentation view option that shows each slide with a pane below it for speaker notes.

Number format   A format such as date, currency, or decimal, which specifies how numerical data will appear.

Numbered list   A list of items of ascending importance. Each item is preceded by a number or letter.

O

Office Button   A button at the top of the screen that includes options for common program tasks such as opening, saving, and printing.

Office Clipboard   A feature that stores up to 24 items that you cut or copy from one file, to be placed in another location or file in the same program or in another Office application.

Operating system   The program that controls the basic operation of your computer.

Order   To change the position of overlapping objects to appear in front of or behind each other.

Orientation   To make the text read from top to bottom or another direction.

Outline   A multilevel list that indicates a hierarchy, or structure, of elements.

Outline view   Shows the hierarchy of your document by displaying headings and indented sub-headings or text paragraphs.

Overtype mode   A mode where as you type each character, it replaces the next character.

P

Page Break Preview   An Excel worksheet viewing mode that displays blue lines that indicate where the page breaks will occur.

Page Preview   A view that can help to identify adjustments you want to make to page breaks, column width, row height, and more.

Paragraph formatting   To adjust the line spacing to add or remove space between lines, indenting lines, or inserting space between paragraphs.

Paste   A feature used to insert items copied to the Clipboard into a new location or file.

Paste Special A feature used to link data or an object between two files.

Pixel A dot that makes up the smallest unit of a graphic image.

Placeholder Sample text in templates that you need to replace with your own text.

Point The measurement for font sizes.

Portrait A page layout option where the page is taller than it is wide.

Presentation A program, such as PowerPoint, that organizes and formats information in slides and outlines.

Primary key A distinct field in a database that is used to make sure that each record is unique.

Print To create a hard copy of a document.

Print Layout view A view that displays margins and page breaks to show how the document will appear when printed.

Print Preview A feature used to verify that your page layout does not need any modification.

Program window The main work area, where you will enter, format, and edit information.

Proofread To look through the document as your intended audience will in order to fix things such as using the wrong word.

Property sheet A window in Access Design view that allows you to set the field properties of a table in a database.

Pull quote A quotation from an article displayed in a text box.

Q

Query To retrieve information based on search criteria.

Quick Access Toolbar A toolbar at the top of the program window that contains buttons for saving, undoing, and redoing tasks.

Quick Part A building block of frequently used text that you can insert in Word.

Quick Style A feature that changes all of the attributes of a document based on the style to which text has been assigned.

Quick Tables A preformatted table, such as a calendar, that you can insert in a document.

R

Range A selection of two or more adjacent or non-adjacent cells that can be named in order to reference them in a formula without selecting the cells.

Realign To change the relationship of data to the border of a page, slide, cell, or text box.

Record The complete information on one entity in the database, such as an employee.

Redo To repeat a task you have undone.

Reference A cell address, a range such as A5:G5, or a named range, used in a formula.

Reference operator Used to indicate a range of cells, such as a colon (:) to reference the cell area A5:G6, or a comma (,) to reference multiple cells or ranges.

Relationship A connection between data among different database objects.

Relative cell reference A cell reference that changes based on the location of the formula.

Replace To look for and change all instances of a word or phrase.

Report A database object that displays the contents of a table or of the results of a query in a readable and organized format.

Ribbon A bar with several tabs that group command buttons into related categories.

Row A collection of horizontal cells.

Ruler A tool used to adjust paragraph formatting or tabs, or to assist in placing objects on a page.

S

Sans serif A font with no lines at the end of strokes on a letter.

Save To store the updates you have made to your document and keep the file with its current name and in its current location.

Save As To save a document for the first time, with a new filename or a different location to retain the original file.

Scale To keep the proportions of column width, row height, and font size, while making each smaller or larger to fit to the page size.

Screen resolution The amount of information shown on your screen.

ScreenTip A window that displays when you move the mouse over a button that says the name of the button and any keyboard shortcuts.

Script font A font that looks like calligraphy or handwriting.

Scroll bar A bar used to move up and down in the screen when there is more information that can be viewed at once.

Section break Used in Word to make text appear on a new page or to create sections with different pagination, headers or footers, paragraph formatting, or layout options.

Select To highlight text or items in order to apply editing or formatting.

Serif A line at the end of a stroke on a letter.

Shade To format an area of text with grayed or colored tint.

Show/Hide ¶ A Word button used to display or hide non-printing characters.

Sidebar A text box next to an article that highlights additional information that is related to the text.

Slide layout A PowerPoint layout with default elements and layout.

Slide master Used to make changes that affect all slides in your presentation such as adding text or a graphic that appears on each slide.

Slide Show view A PowerPoint view that displays slides as an on-screen presentation.

Slide Sorter view A PowerPoint view that displays slides as thumbnails. Slide Sorter view is helpful to quickly move slides to a new position or to delete slides.

SmartArt object A diagram that shows a hierarchy, process, or series, such as an organizational chart or a cycle of steps.

Sort To arrange data in sequential order, such as numeric or alphabetical.

Source file When merging or integrating data, the location where the original data or object is stored.

Speaker note A reminder that you can associate with a slide and print to use as a visual guide during your presentation.

Spelling & Grammar A built-in dictionary tool used to identify possible misspellings and grammatical errors.

Split To add a divider and create multiple cells from one.

Spreadsheet A program, such as Microsoft Excel, that organizes data in rows and columns.

Status bar A bar at the bottom of the program window that includes options for changing the view or navigating in your file.

Style A feature used to create consistent formatting among text with similar importance.

Suite A group of programs, such as Microsoft Office, with different functions, which are designed to work together to share information and create a variety of files.

Superscript A raised font set above normal letters.

Synonym A reference tool that displays synonyms, or words with the same meaning.

Syntax A rule used in Excel to perform calculation without errors.

T

Tab A marker on the horizontal ruler that you can adjust to change the paragraph or line indentation.

Table Information organized in horizontal rows and vertical columns. In Excel, an area that can be formatted, sorted, or filtered independently of the rest of the worksheet.

Table of contents A list of a document's section titles and page numbers.

Table Styles A feature used to apply formatting including shading, borders, and fonts to an entire table at once.

Template A preformatted file that contains sample text, layouts, and objects.

Text box An object that contains text but that can be resized, moved, and repositioned like a graphic.

Theme   Colors, fonts, graphics, and layouts applied to a variety of templates in multiple applications.

Thesaurus   A reference tool that displays synonyms, or words with the same meaning.

Thumbnail   A small icon that represents a template or document.

Toggle button   A button that you click once to turn on the feature and click again to turn it off.

Track changes   A Word feature used to keep track of the insertions, deletions, and formatting changes you make while editing.

Transition   PowerPoint animation effects that occur when a new slide or slide object appears on the screen.

U

Undo   To reverse an action, starting with the most recent task.

W

Web Layout view   A view that removes page breaks and shows how a document would appear if saved to the Web.

White space   The term used in desktop publishing and word processing for the blank areas of the page.

Wizard   A series of dialog boxes that ask questions and verifies information needed to correctly complete a task.

Word processing   A program, such as Microsoft Word, used to create documents such as memos or reports.

Workbook   An Excel file that contains three worksheets, by default.

Worksheet   In Excel, a group of cells saved in a workbook.

Worksheet window   In Excel, the main work area where you will enter, format, and edit information.

Wrap   To increase row height automatically without changing the width so that data appears in multiple lines.

Z

Zoom   To change the magnification of a document.

Zoom level   The percentage higher or lower than what will be printed.

INDEX